POLAND

A TRAVELLER'S GAZETTEER

POLAND

A TRAVELLER'S GAZETTEER

by

ADAM ZAMOYSKI

JOHN MURRAY
in association with
Azimuth Editions

First published in 2001
by John Murray (Publishers) Ltd.,
50 Albemarle Street, London w1s 4bd
in association with Azimuth Editions

A catalogue record for this book is available from the British
Library.

ISBN 0-7195-5772-0

Typeset in Minion

Printed and bound in Great Britain by PJ Print

CONTENTS

Introduction   7

Author's note   26

Notes on pronunciation   28

Gazetteer   29

Historical Glossary   287

Polish Kings and Princes   294

Royal family trees   297

Map of Poland   302

INTRODUCTION

WHILE foreigners often joke about Poland's frequent frontier changes, Polish intellectuals traditionally make quips about whether Poland is a place, a concept, or just a state of mind. In effect, Poland's frontiers have changed less than those of most major European countries, and the same quips could be made about other nations. But the fact remains that Poland feels somehow different from its neighbours, and there are reasons for this.

The area it occupies was by-passed by some of the strongest influences that shaped the rest of medieval Europe. The Romans stopped just short in the south, the Celts never quite made it from the west. Even the Vikings, who penetrated every country as far as Sicily in a great westward arc and at the same time moulded the early shape of what was to be Russia in the east, never penetrated significantly into Poland.

And when external influences did penetrate, the Poles showed a truly heroic defiance to universally accepted dictates. One only has to look at how they treated architectural fashion. The first building in the Renaissance style in Poland dates from 1502, and the first Baroque one from 1584 – both of which testify to Polish society's access to the latest ideas and its taste in implementing them. Except for the fact that those who had taken a liking to Renaissance architecture went on erecting it until the 1670s, almost a century after it had been 'superseded' by the Baroque, and that Baroque buildings were being built until 1799, several decades after the neo-Classical style had displaced that. And concurrently with this aesthetic debate people went on building Gothic churches, in stone up to 1600, and in wood until the 1750s – about the time that the 'Gothick' revival was beginning in England. Such independence of mind begs many questions about a people.

The recorded history of Poland begins, to all intents and purposes, in 966. In that year Mieszko I, king of the Polanian Slavs, accepted Christianity for himself and his people. His son Bolesław enlarged the realm and gained acceptance with both the Holy Roman Emperor Otto III and with the Pope. The Pope made Bolesław's capital of Gniezno into an archbishopric in the year 999 with dependent sees at Kraków, Wrocław and Kołobrzeg. The Emperor came to Poland in the following year and presented Bolesław with a crown. At Bolesław's death in 1025, his kingdom prefigured the present Polish state in size and shape.

Poland in 1025

Poland continued to be ruled by Mieszko's successors, the Piast dynasty. But in 1138 it was divided up into five duchies to accommodate the rival ambitions of king Władysław the Wrymouth's five sons. A system of feudal relationships between these duchies was established, but some of them were sub-divided further, and the whole area might easily have become Balkanised, like so much of Germany and central Europe. The burgeoning towns that had become the capitals of the duchies filled up with foreign merchants from east and west who felt allegiance, if at all, only to their prince. In fact, a widely accepted concept of a Polish polity, referred to as *corona Regni Poloniae*, maintained a sense of kinship between the rulers and the knighthood of the individual provinces. It only required a serious external threat to reassert it.

The first threat came from the Tatars, who ravaged southern and eastern Poland. Their defeat at the Battle of Legnica in 1241 gave rise to the image of Poland as the defender of Europe against the hordes of the East, an image that persists to this day. Another threat came from the Teutonic Knights, and this too gave rise to a potent image dominating the Polish political mind. This German order of crusaders had established itself at Chełmno in 1226, ostensibly to defend the area against the pagan tribes of Prussia. Its growing power, in conjunction with the expansion of the German Northern March, threatened to take over all Poland's northern provinces and cut her off from the sea.

In the 1280s, the Piast princes and the Polish Church hierarchy began to work for reunification of the fragmented country. Władysław the Short, Duke of Kujavia, retrieved several other provinces and had himself crowned King of Poland in 1320. The

The Polish Principalities 1138

process of consolidation came to fruition in the reign of his son Kazimierz the Great (1333–70). This remarkable man was, according to the chronicler Jan Długosz writing in 1370, 'set upon the purpose of leaving Poland, which he had found built poorly in clay and wood, magnificently walled and radiant'. He erected over 50 castles, fortified some 30 towns, and built nearly 40 churches. He also, in 1364, founded an academy in Kraków that was to grow into the Jagiellon University.

But, at this moment, just as Poland was developing into a homogeneous European state, she also took a fateful turning. In the 1340s

Kazimierz annexed Ruthenia and later became overlord of Moldavia, initiating the absorption of non-Polish territories and the eastward extension of Polish interests. Kazimierz had no direct heirs, and his crown went to his nephew Louis of Anjou, king of Hungary. Louis had only two daughters. One was to marry a Habsburg and rule Hungary; the other, married to Sigismund of Luxemburg, was to have Poland. But the Polish lords seized on the still unmarried one, the ten year old Jadwiga, and imposed their own choice of husband on her: Iogaila, Duke of Lithuania, who was baptised Władysław.

Lithuania was a small state that had expanded rapidly, provoking fierce attack from the Teutonic Knights in the west and its Russian neighbours in the east. It was this that impelled Iogaila (or Jagiełło as he was known in Polish) to seek Poland's support by marrying Jadwiga in 1386. In the following century the combined state ruled by the dynasty which had taken his name repeatedly defeated the Teutonic Order and recuperated Gdańsk and parts of Prussia. By dynastic arrangements sons and grandsons of Jagiełło ruled not only in Poland and Lithuania, but also in Silesia, Bohemia and Hungary. In the hundred years after that, the remainder of the Teutonic Order's state and that of the German knights in Livonia came under the Polish crown. By the end of the Middle Ages, Poland had become the centre of a huge Jagiellon conglomerate.

These developments were to bring enormous advantages in cultural terms. The first elements of what one might properly call architecture had been brought in with Christianity, and the first artefacts of any degree of sophistication were mainly ritual objects of religious or royal significance. The leaders in the cultural development of the country were the monastic orders. The Benedictines founded their first monastery in Poland in the 990s. After the Benedictines came the Cistercians, one group from the abbey of Morimond in Burgundy, another from Saxony. They were followed by Franciscans, Dominicans, Premonstratensians and others.

The Benedictines introduced the Romanesque style; the Cistercians, followed by the Franciscans and the Dominicans, spread their distinctive forms of Gothic, depending on which country or cultural tradition they came from. They brought the theory and the example, but they relied on local execution, thereby initiating native production. They also had to accept that in a land poor in building stone but rich in timber, all but the greatest buildings had to be made of wood, which imposed its own engineering, and therefore stylistic, imperatives. By the twelfth century the skill of local craftsmen could bear comparison with any contemporary work-

The combined Kingdom of Poland and Lithuania 1466

manship, and sometimes excelled: the bronze doors of Gniezno Cathedral, made in the 1170s, are a great Romanesque work of art on a European scale. The monasteries also fostered education, and the first literary work written in Poland, the Chronicle of Gallus, was the work of a Benedictine monk.

Most of the early art originated in or was filtered through Burgundy, but as time passed, the variety of cultural influences increased. German artistic forms followed the merchant patriciate of cities such as Kraków. Flemish and north-German influences rode on the back of trading links through Gdańsk and other Hanseatic ports. The Teutonic Order, which had turned itself into a state by the early 1300s, set about fortifying and developing its territory in a sophisticated brick-built Gothic, which spilled over into neighbouring Mazovia. French influences trickled into Silesia via southern Germany and Bohemia.

The Polish lands had always attracted Jewish settlers, mainly from the east, but their expulsion from England in 1291 and the waves of persecution in Germany and France following the great plague of 1348–9, the Black Death, brought them flooding into Poland from the west in hundreds of thousands. They were granted special rights and encouraged to settle in towns and cities all over southern Poland. (In the north, where the towns were governed under a German system known as Magdeburg Law, they were excluded from city centres, and could only settle on the periphery.) The southern cities, such as Kraków and particularly Lwów, also had strong communities of Armenian and Italian merchants, and trading links with the east and with southern Europe.

It was these connections - the Italian and the Eastern - that were to prove the most formative influence on Polish life over the next period. From the 1450s onwards a remarkable number of young Poles went to Italian universities to complete their studies. They brought back with them works of art and books, which ensured that the aesthetic message of the Renaissance reached Poland earlier than most of northern Europe. They also brought back humanism, the outlook that underlay the Renaissance and gave it meaning, and this ensured that Polish society took a very different direction from that of most of its neighbours over the next couple of centuries. The eastern connection would curiously complement this.

The first Renaissance building in Poland (1502) coincided with the act of *Nihil Novi* (1505), which crowned a long process of transference of royal prerogatives to the national parliament, the *Sejm*. These two developments only narrowly preceded Martin Luther's act of defiance in 1517, which was to initiate the Reformation and open up the philosophical debate on the purpose of life on earth. In 1526 the death in battle of the last Jagiellon king of Hungary put an end to Polish involvement in Hungary and Bohemia, and entailed the loss of Silesia for the next four hundred years. On the economic plane, the discovery of America and the resulting increase in the availability of precious metals meant that the agricultural and ship-building materials Poland produced in abundance fetched a higher price, and the country prospered as never before.

This combination of political liberty, intellectual emancipation and material wealth assured a high degree of civilized life for the enfranchised class, the large gentry caste or *szlachta*. The extraordinary degree of religious freedom guaranteed in Poland at a time of increasing persecution elsewhere made the country a haven for people of every persuasion. Such religious diversity, added to the already impressive racial and cultural mix, made for a vibrant pluralistic society, as open in matters of politics to proto-communist utopias as to traditional monarchy, as open to Protestantism, Orthodoxy and Judaism as to Catholicism, and as open to eastern style and taste as to those of the European mainstream. Not surprisingly, this period saw the first expressions of what one could truly call a 'Polish' style.

Mainly on account of its new-found wealth, the szlachta now

joined, and even for a time superseded, the Church and the Crown as patrons of the arts. They may have been the nouveaux-riches of Europe, but they were also highly educated. Erasmus himself was moved to 'congratulate the Polish nation [which] can now compete with the foremost and the most cultivated in the world'. As a result, they did not waste their wealth.

They imported architects to redesign their houses or build new ones for them. They went to Italy or employed agents to buy paintings and sculptures with which to fill them. Realising the opportunities on offer, artists and craftsmen travelled to Poland. (Many stayed, founding dynasties which were still building and decorating houses and churches two hundred and fifty years later.)

The first Renaissance architects working in Poland were Florentines or inhabitants of other Tuscan cities. They were soon joined by others from Lombardy and the Ticino, and later by a few Paduans. In the north, Dutch Mannerist architects were active in Gdańsk and other towns of Pomerania and Prussia. But Renaissance architecture in Poland quickly developed its own peculiarities, and within a few decades had evolved into a distinct style, incorporating elements of Gothic architecture alongside new fads such as the fantastically ornate parapets concealing pitched roofs. The Poles' love of ornament and contour made itself strongly felt in all the arts. This disadvantaged local painters steeped in the Gothic tradition in favour of the Italian painting being imported in large quantities, but encouraged the more sophisticated school of Polish sculpture.

This golden age favoured talent in every sphere. As well as being the age of Copernicus and religious debate, it was also one of luxury and courtliness. Music was written and performed increasingly widely in church, at court and in the noble home. Literature flourished, giving rise to some of the most remarkable political and religious literature of this period of conflict in Europe, and also to a whole crop of fine poetry in a vigorous new Polish that was even then being honed.

To Poles and visiting foreigners alike, it seemed that the country was safely launched into the modern world and sailing towards a brilliant future conceived along the principles of Renaissance humanism. But the ideals of the Renaissance were to have a hard time of it over the next centuries. The Jagiellon dynasty, which was the only formal link between Poland and Lithuania, died out in 1572. Three years earlier, in 1569, the Polish and Lithuanian nobility had enacted the Union of Lublin, which created the Commonwealth of Two Nations, a multi-national republic ruled by a sovereign parliament, the Sejm, presided over by an elective monarchy. This ambitious experiment in democracy was to have an unfortunate history.

Although the entire szlachta had a vote, which made Poland's technically the most representative parliamentary system in Europe, other estates did not, which meant that the Sejm did not truly represent the active citizenship. Parliamentary processes were cumbersome and relied on the principle of consensus, which became increasingly difficult to achieve. Projects for doing something about it were discussed throughout the early part of the seventeenth century, but nothing was done until it was too late.

The Polish Commonwealth was the largest state in Europe after Muscovy, and at the height of its power and wealth. But this wealth was poorly managed. It was based on agricultural produce and raw materials, and since these produced such enormous income at the time, there was little investment in industry. The country became caught in an unfavourable trade cycle of paying for finished products with raw materials whose value was steadily falling. Instead of building up a firm economic base, the Poles lived from hand to mouth, losing ground against the increasingly developed countries of western Europe.

Poland's position of international power was also deceptive. Polish armies had grown used to victory on battlefields as distant as Muscovy and Moldavia, keeping at bay Russians, Turks, Austrians and Swedes. But the weakness of state structures and finances were gradually undermining this capability. In 1648 the Cossacks mutinied and, aided by the Tatars, devastated south-eastern Poland. The Swedes seized on this opportunity, followed by Muscovy and Brandenburg, with the result that between 1648 and 1667 the Polish Commonwealth became one huge battlefield. Gradually, the Poles marshalled their forces and repelled all the invaders, but it had been an expensive victory.

The episode ruined the country, destroyed the cities and caused such chaos that the framework of the state never quite recovered. The depredations of the Swedes in particular were so thorough that hardly a building was left intact the length and breadth of the country. Economically, the country drifted on its natural riches, falling behind other European states. Politically it subsided into anarchy. It was still capable of effort - as it demonstrated in 1683, when king Jan III Sobieski led his army to shatter the Turkish advance into Europe at the gates of Vienna. But these were the last spasms of a dying organism. The Polish Commonwealth was by now at the mercy of its enemies.

Russia, of which Peter I had taken the title of Emperor in 1721,

Prussia, of which Frederick I had declared himself king in 1701, and the Habsburg Empire, had all come to realise that a weak and ungovernable Poland was a very convenient thing. They therefore undertook to make sure that it stayed that way. As early as 1717, Russia had sent friendly troops into Poland to help keep order while the Sejm met. Under their 'protection' a treaty was signed in which Russia became guarantor of Poland's territorial integrity and also of its constitution, which meant that nothing could be changed

The Polish Commonwealth 1569

without Russian approval. Poland had, in effect, lost her sovereignty, and she was to drift along in this condition through the first half of the eighteenth century.

Ironically, this period of steady decline punctuated by calamity, a period of intellectual stagnation in which all the joyful empiricism of the Renaissance was overtaken by an uneasy conformism, as religious freedoms were gradually stripped away under the influence of Catholic orthodoxy - happens also to have been the most exuberant and in many ways the most original in artistic terms.

The Renaissance style was superseded by Mannerism and then Baroque, a style that might have been invented to please the Poles. Every feature of the culture of the Polish Commonwealth found buxom and often unruly expression through this idiom, which was to dress the country's decline in glittering splendour and blind the Poles to their fate with its dazzle.

The Baroque style went hand in hand with the counter-Reformation, and Poland was one of the counter-Reformation's greatest triumphs. It began in 1564 with the arrival of the Jesuits in Poland. They set out to win over the hearts and minds of the szlachta, primarily by establishing a network of colleges throughout the Commonwealth providing a free education to all comers - including the sons of Protestants and Orthodox families. Needless to say, most of the young men left as Catholics.

This coincided with a drift back to spirituality and asceticism. The number of religious communities rose from 220 in 1572 to 565 in 1648. Apart from anything else, this meant the building of 345 new churches and monasteries. As the period of the Reformation had seen very little church-building, there was also a need for new parish churches all over the country. The Baroque style, an expansive, self-confident form of expression with direct Roman connexions, a statement of Catholicism if ever there was one, found riotous purpose in this need.

Baroque art allowed for a seemingly limitless display of splendour, which also permitted magnates and less exalted noblemen to create their own apotheoses or those of their families. And this was the age of the grandee in Poland. The couple of dozen richest families lived like Indian maharajahs, a couple of hundred or so more could have outshone any European aristocrat, and the rest led a more humble existence limited by their income. But all of them, from the wealthiest to the poorest, did everything to project an image of themselves that was invariably far grander than their circumstances. The magnates at the top of the pyramid lived in great fortified palaces, such as Wiśnicz or Krzyżtopór, the poorest landowners inhabited often quite small wooden houses, but even these were laid out with palatial presumption.

This presumption was partly born of a curious element in Polish life, more than a fashion and less than a culture, a state of mind and being known as 'Sarmatism'. This derived originally from the myth that the szlachta were not Slavs like the peasants, but descendants of a noble warrior race issuing from the Black Sea steppe known as the Sarmatians. This conveniently differentiated them from everyone else, without, curiously, preventing new arrivals in the ranks of the szlachta, even if they happened to be foreign nobles, from being considered as part of the fold. The attitude that this myth gave rise to was one of total superiority over everyone else, and its principal external manifestations were an extravagant manner, an accent on supposed warrior virtues, and a love of everything to do with the horse, the fight and the East. Jewel-encrusted arms and armour, usually of eastern style, richly embroidered horse-tack and caparisons, oriental carpets and Persian brocades, and all manner of object heavy with gold, silver and precious stones were richly prized.

Baroque architecture was unexpectedly accommodating to Sarmatism and its wilder expressions. Indeed, baroque interiors were positively enhanced by the presence of large numbers of servants dressed as Janissaries. The result was a kind of pseudo-oriental High Baroque, which mixed this predominantly Italian style with Persian and Ottoman elements. The need for ornament and self-glorification gave a welcome boost to painting and sculpture. The art of portraiture revived, both in the form of huge apotheoses and in the humbler, unique form of the semi-primitive coffin portrait.

This effervescence was given added zest by the need to rebuild after the Cossack and Swedish wars, which had devastated the country. New and more splendid churches and palaces replaced the old ones, and the whole of Warsaw, which had suffered particularly badly, was rebuilt at this time. The principal architect active here was neither Italian nor Polish, but a Dutchman who settled in Poland, Tilman van Gameren, alias Gamerski. He popularised a northern classical Baroque style, but neither he nor the early eighteenth-century introduction of French classicism and later of Dresden Rococo disturbed the Sarmatian daydream. In whatever form, Baroque art and architecture continued to proclaim an increasingly hollow substance. With its conceits and its classical or biblical allusions, it was the art of make-believe. For the Polish nobility, it was whistling in the dark.

Darkness had indeed fallen. The country had reached a nadir of anarchy under the rule (1696-1763) of the two Saxon kings, Augustus the Strong and his son Augustus III (who could only be described as the Fat). Political life ground to a virtual halt, the system crippled by a handful of knaves supported by hordes of fools. The level of education among the szlachta had sunk to such depths that political discourse became all but impossible. Nevertheless, a small number of highly-placed Poles began to work for reform, political, social and above all educational. Although influenced and encouraged by the European Enlightenment, they were not initially inspired by it. The movement for reform had roots in the political and social traditions of the Polish Renaissance, whose best values it sought to revive, and only added to these such elements of modern English, French and later American thinking as accorded with them. As a result, it was refreshing and humanistic without being as revolutionary or as irreligious as the mainstream of the western European Enlightenment.

In 1764, after the second Augustus' death, Stanisław Poniatowski was elected king. He belonged to a party which wanted to reform the country, and having been a lover of Catherine the Great of Russia, he could hope for some outside support. He immediately put in train a whole programme of reforms, but Catherine was wary of letting the Poles put their house in order. Even more wary was Frederick of Prussia, who had recently taken Silesia from the

Habsburgs and now dreamed of extending his dominions further, mainly at the expense of Poland. Between them, they stirred up trouble and opposition to the king's programmes, bringing about a civil war which culminated in their armed intervention and the partition of the country in 1772.

Nevertheless, a profound revolution was taking place in Poland, as society awoke to the realities of life. On 3 May 1791 the Polish parliament voted a new constitution, the first written one in Europe, which reformed the state along liberal lines and laid the foundations for prosperity and strength. This was something which Russia and Prussia could not countenance. In 1792 they intervened to abolish it, each taking another slice of Polish territory in the process. After a last military effort by General Tadeusz Kościuszko to wrest independence, Poland's three neighbours divided up the rest of the country between themselves, wiping her name off the map.

Thwarted in his political programme, the king had fostered the revival of the country by other means. Apart from being a great art-lover, Stanisław Augustus was acutely aware of the educational value of the arts and their subliminal power. He brought artists to Poland and sent promising young Poles to study abroad. He built up a collection of paintings, sculpture, drawings, prints and medals, which he intended to turn into a *Museum Polonicum* but in the meantime made available to artists and craftsmen. In addition, he started up a number of manufacturing ventures in the decorative arts. He erected around the throne a panoply of architecture, sculpture and painting designed to enhance the prestige of the monarchy and strengthen the state. Every building that went up during his reign, be it the Royal Castle in Warsaw or a small customs-post, was the fruit of great care.

The king liked the monumentality and the roundness of baroque art, but felt it had become too firmly associated with the period of Poland's decline. On the other hand the virtues of antiquity implicit in neo-Classicism held didactic relevance for Poland. He therefore introduced his own hybrid neo-Classicism, which spread through the country, proclaiming a whole set of values as it went (it is worth noting that opponents of these values and of the Stanislavian court continued to put up aggressively Baroque buildings well into the 1790s). This was art as statement par excellence.

The importance of Stanisław Augustus' reign is that he and a number of like-minded people managed to redefine the collection of peoples inhabiting the territory of the expiring Commonwealth into something that one can recognise as the modern Polish nation. By retrieving from oblivion all that was best in the past and giving it a gloss in line with the times, they gave the Poles a tradition to cling to in the dark days of partition. By marrying some of the contradictions between the exclusive ethos of the szlachta and the vigorous culture of the Polish peasantry, they created a common ground on which these two elements could stand and fight the hopeless fight of the next two hundred years. The small white neo-Classical manor house of this period became a powerful symbol of patriotic virtue with which all classes of society could identify.

Although the Polish state had been wiped from the map in 1795, a Duchy of Warsaw was established by Napoleon, which lasted from 1806 to 1813. The Congress of Vienna in 1815 set up a Kingdom of Poland with the Tsar of Russia as king. This tried to secede from Russia in 1830, but was subjugated in the following year and incorporated into the Russian Empire. From then until 1918, there was no Polish state of any kind.

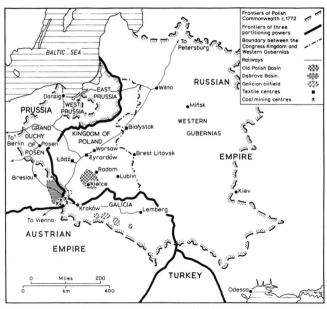

The Lands of Partitioned Poland ca.1860

The three parts of the country, being anchored to three entirely different socio-economic systems, developed at different rates and in different ways. The Austrian-held part of Poland, including Kraków, was treated by its Habsburg masters as an agricultural province, and its industrial development was inhibited. This meant that those with large estates did well, while the peasants, who had no industry to take up the slack and therefore divided their land up between their offspring, remained extremely poor. In the German-occupied west, on the other hand, a low level of industrial development was achieved relatively early. Keen competition with the German minority meant that a kind of Protestant ethic in reverse ruled and even the peasantry did well. A prosperous middle class emerged in Poznań and the other cities, and this shows strongly in their architecture. The Russian-occupied part of Poland contained the only industrialised region of the old Polish Commonwealth, the Kielce basin, and as Russia's industry was in its infancy, the Polish lands became the industrial powerhouse of the Russian Empire. The textile boom-town of Łódź supplied the whole empire with cotton, and the Warsaw railway works produced all the rails and rolling-stock to create the Russian railway network. Economically, some parts of Poland fared very well under foreign rule. And whether there was a state or not, Polish society survived, adhering to its own culture, and Polish art continued to evolve, albeit in curious ways.

The regenerative processes initiated by the last king did not end with his reign, but continued to bear fruit well into the nineteenth century, spurred on by the need to make further statements. Artistic activity reflected the ideological discussions on the subject of where Poland belonged and where it should be going. The desire to underline the country's cultural affiliation to Europe found expression in the magnificent flowering of early nineteenth-century neo-Classical architecture. This was followed by a reaction towards the intimate and personal, as well as to the ancient, which spawned a crop of Romantic, neo-Gothic historicism. On the heels of this came a 'Sarmatian' revival, giving rise to the neo-Baroque and some orientalism.

Sculpture was starved of patronage as the court disappeared and the aristocracy went into retreat, while none of the government and municipal projects that were increasingly keeping it alive in other countries were forthcoming. Even subscriptions were liable to be banned on political grounds. The Thorwaldsen monument to Copernicus was sufficiently neutral to be allowed, but Mickiewicz, Chopin, Poniatowski and other national heroes had to wait for the best part of a century.

Painting also lacked government patronage and, during the first part of the century, public gallery space. It relied on private patronage, and this, as was the case with music and literature, involved it in the great national dialogue on the causes of Poland's downfall and the possibility of national resurgence. The painters of the Romantic movement were dominated by the Napoleonic and post-Napoleonic epos, turning out heroic genre scenes. They were suc-

ceded in the middle of the century by more determinedly national-
ist artists who graphically recalled the glories and sufferings of
Poland's past. They in turn were followed by more subtle genre
painters who created an image of life in the old days. Some dwelt on
peasant life, as it were bringing this class into the national fold,
while others turned landscape into patriotic statement.

A degree of cosmopolitanism manifested itself at the turn of the
century, with the vogue for eclecticism, the Viennese Secession, Art
Nouveau and Modernism. In Poland, these were often mixed in
with elements of folklore. Similarly, the Young Poland movement
in literature, whose message was couched in the most modern and
international artistic language, was nevertheless harnessed to the
cause of national liberation. Not surprisingly, all Polish art suffered
something of a jolt when this finally came, in 1918.

The collapse of the three empires which had partitioned the
country gave Poland her chance, and on 11 November 1918 independence was proclaimed in Warsaw. The new-found freedom had
to be vigorously defended against German claims in the west and
against the Bolshevik invasion, which was defeated at the gates of
Warsaw in 1920.

The necessity of reconstructing the long neglected and devastated
country offered an extraordinary opportunity for architects in particular. The process was vitiated by lack of funds and then the great
depression, but the crop of functional Modernist public and residential architecture that did see the light of day is very impressive.

While society as a whole was fired by a fairly populist enthusiasm as it got on with the job of reconstruction, the artistic and literary elites were suffering from a slight cultural hangover. They had
spent the nineteenth century carrying on an ever more subtle discourse on the problems afflicting the body and soul of the nation.
Once it had fulfilled its role of handmaiden to the national cause, art
could be practised for its own sake. It could therefore rejoin the
European mainstream. Poles enthusiastically embraced the succession of movements that agitated European art in the first half of the
century, some taking their inspiration from France, others from
Germany, others still from Russia, and many of them not only travelled but worked or settled in other countries. This means that
much of their work is scattered abroad, while in Poland it has been
somewhat neglected since the Second World War - in the art-historical world the accent since 1945 has been heavily on the saving
and reconstruction of the older artistic fabric. It is not difficult to
see why.

In 1939 the whole country was overrun by Germany and Soviet

Russia, and one of the most savage programmes of human and cultural destruction in the annals of mankind was initiated. The country lost 6 million people, representing nearly one-fifth of its population. In that number were virtually the entire Jewish population of Poland, which had played such a significant part in the cultural life of the past century.

The country also lost a staggering proportion of its artistic heritage. Everything that could be moved was looted by someone at some stage, and only a fraction found its way back. Many fine buildings and works of art were destroyed, while entire cities were flattened. Warsaw suffered more than any other city in the world, losing over half (800,000) of its inhabitants and an estimated 90 per cent of the cultural heritage contained in it, including many collections sent there for safekeeping.

Territorial Shift 1939-1945

To cap it all from the cultural point of view, the whole country was then subjected to the iron grip of Soviet ideology for the next fifty years. Repression of artists not toeing the party line could be brutal as well as soul-destroying, and it crushed three generations at least, leaving a heritage that is both brutish and monstrously ugly.

The arts were harnessed to the task of ushering in the Soviet dawn through the style known as Socialist Realism, the heroic representation of factory workers forging steel or soldiers marching with determination towards the final victory of socialism. While the results are not without interest to those with a sense of humour, artistically as well as historically the regime effectively blighted all cultural activity. Only poster art and, from the 1960s onwards, films and music avoided the heavy hand of Soviet influence.

Possibly the greatest failure in cultural terms of the half-century of communist rule in Poland is something that started out with the best intentions and should have been one of its signal successes - the whole sphere of conservation and reconstruction of the national heritage. The destruction wrought on this by the military actions of 1939 and 1944–5, as well as specific actions such as the Warsaw Ghetto Uprising and the Warsaw Uprising and the consequent demolition of Warsaw, are impossible to describe adequately. The task facing those who meant to rebuild the country was therefore immense and unprecedented, the resources at their disposal seemingly negligible. The destruction was so complete in many cases, most notably the old city centres of Warsaw and Gdańsk, that fundamental questions of art-historical policy further complicated an argument already fraught with politics. Which stage in the evolution of a building or which of the buildings that had succeeded each other on the same site should be chosen opened up huge scope for discussion.

The achievement of the art historians is there for all to see: the historical centres of Gdańsk and other cities, and above all the total reconstruction of a large part of Warsaw, crowned with the breathtaking recreation of the Royal Castle. But in most cases, and certainly in Warsaw, the overall planning was so defective that the resuscitated centre is essentially cut off from the city proper, and fulfills the role of a show-piece and not the heart of the capital. Worse, the reconstruction followed the taste of the day and not only left out all styles later than neo-Classicism, it actually involved the pulling down of many fine nineteenth-century buildings. In spite of all the effort that went into rebuilding it, Warsaw is still a gigantic mess, the scars of the Second World War defacing the urban landscape and interfering in normal human life.

But it is outside the great cities that the conservation machinery failed spectacularly. Half-a-dozen great country houses that had survived the war relatively unscathed have been adequately maintained. Tens of thousands of others have been allowed to rot, with occasional brutal encouragement. Indeed, were it not for the unique position of the Catholic Church and its ability to get things done, there would be little left to look at except ruins in large areas of the country. For the Church has looked after its buildings with devotion and intelligence, and they now represent the overwhelming majority of things worth looking at in Poland. Were it not for the surviving wooden churches (which many a progressive priest might have felt tempted to replace) we could have no sense of the most common experience of the past - for the great majority of churches, synagogues, mosques, palaces, manor houses and dwellings had always been made of wood. Unfortunately, these remnants often stand in a cultural desert, surrounded by ugliness and aesthetic insensitivity. There are very few places in Poland where an ensemble survives, as they do in so many parts of western Europe.

Yet the very mess that is present-day Poland can yield some unique experiences. And although it is the great cities, even those that have suffered as badly as Warsaw, Gdańsk or Wrocław, that are the cultural treasure-houses, the most delightful surprises are to be found in small market towns or even in the depths of the country. It is only by driving around it that one can capture any of the feel of Poland and derive real rewards from it. No more than a little information is needed to transform a drive through this ostensibly ravaged part of Central Europe into a deeply rewarding ramble down some of the more curious cultural byways and over some of the seminal cross-roads of the shared heritage of the Continent.

AUTHOR'S NOTE

All choice is subjective, and the listing in this book is neither comprehensive nor definitive in any way. I have of course listed those things about the importance of which there is no discussion, even where I cannot muster great enthusiasm myself. I have also listed things which have struck me and which I believe can say something about Poland's history or culture - or which I simply find amusing. Then there are the short entries, usually referring to churches or castle ruins, which I have supplied because I myself have often been maddened when driving around to see something on a hill and not know what it is. I have listed a number of things in private hands which are not accessible to the public, simply because I think it is interesting to know that they are there as one passes through the area.

I have not written in detail about the great cities, as anyone intending to spend more than five days (for which the information here is more than adequate) in one of them ought to acquire a specialised local guide. Nor have I covered museums in any detail, as they supply their own literature.

It would have been pointless to give opening times, since these are as changeable as they are easy to get around. The only thing that should be imprinted on every visitor's brain is that Mondays are no good for anything.

As in England, the parish church in Poland is usually a sort of repository of local history. Most churches in Poland used to be open all day, but as a result of a recent rash of vandalism and burglary this is no longer the case. If closed, the key can usually be obtained from the parish priest without any difficulty (he usually lives next door). Castles and country houses belonging to an institution but not open to the public are usually accessible with a smile and a sincere request. Those that are derelict can usually be investigated by walking through any gap in the fence, though there may be some morose looks from peasant families billetted in outhouses - again, a smile can usually do the trick.

All comments and judgments are entirely my own, and the snippets of information I have provided are there for personal, often random reasons, and should not be taken as a sign of the importance of an object. I make no apologies for style, although I realise that some may find the switches from note form to description surprising.

I should like to take this opportunity to thank Professor Andrzej Rottermund for his support and encouragement with this project, and Dr Robert Kunkel for his help in checking dates and artists. My thanks also to Inez Krupińska-Grabowska for drawing the road maps, and to Anikst Associates for the city plans.

Key to Symbols:

✦   worth stopping if it's on your way

✦✦   worth making a detour

✦✦✦   a must if you're in striking distance

NOTE ON POLISH PRONUNCIATION

Polish words may look complicated, but pronunciation is at least constistent. All vowels are simple and of even length, as in Italian, and their sound is best rendered by the English words 'sum' (a), 'ten' (e), 'ease' (i), 'lot' (o), 'book' (u), 'sit' (y).

Most of the consonants behave the same way as in English, except for 'c', which is pronounced 'ts'; 'j', which is soft, as in 'yes'; and 'w', which is eqivalent to English 'v'. As in German, some consonants are softened when they fall at the end of a word, and 'b', 'd', 'f', 'w', 'z' become 'p', 't', 'k', 'f', 's' respecctively.

There are also a number of accented letters and combinations peculiar to Polish, of which the following is a rough list:

ó = u, hence Kraków is pronounced 'Krakoof'.

ą = nasal a, hence sąd is pronounced 'sont'.

ę = nasal e, hence tęcza is pronounced 'tencha'.

ć = sharp ch as in 'cheese'.

cz = ch as in 'catch'.

ch = guttural h, as in 'loch'.

ł = English w, hence Bolesław becomes 'Boleswaf', Łódź 'wootj'.

ń = soft n, as in Spanish 'manana'.

rz = French j, as in 'je'.

ś = sharp sh, as in 'sheer'.

sz = sh as in 'bush'.

ż = rz.

GAZETTEER

ALWERNIA   MAP 21

Baroque **Bernardine monastery**, 1630–76. Local pilgrimage centre. Named after the sanctuary of St Francis at La Verna in Italy, which it emulates.

ANDRZEJEWO   MAP 25

Characteristic Mazovian late Gothic **parish church**, begun 1526. Interesting vaulting in chancel and sacristy. Chapel 1612.

ANTONIN   MAP 11 ✦✦

Hunting lodge, built for Prince Antoni Radziwiłł in 1824, by *Karl Friedrich Schinkel*. The house, standing in a Romantic park, is one of Schinkel's most original and imaginative buildings. It is built entirely of timber around one great hall which rises through all four storeys, and supported by a central column which also acts as chimney. Antoni Radziwiłł married Louise of Hohenzollern, daughter of Prince Henry of Prussia, brother of Frederick the Great. A widely respected figure, he was named Viceroy of the Duchy of Posen, the main block of Polish lands taken by Prussia during the Partitions of Poland. He was also a patron of the arts and an amateur composer. Among the house-guests in October 1829 was the young Fryderyk Chopin, who called it a 'paradise'.

Radziwiłł **sepulchral chapel**, first half of 19th century, pseudo-Romanesque, richly decorated in theByzantine style, with late Gothic sculptures.

ARKADIA   MAP 17 ✦✦

Romantic park laid out by *Princess Helena Radziwiłł* between 1778 and 1821, to resemble landscapes by *Poussin*, complete with huts of Philemon and Baucis for hospitality, the grotto of Sybil for reflection, a river of Oblivion and an island of Dreams. The centrepiece is the Temple of Diana, originally conceived in 1783 by *Szymon Bogumił Zug* as the Temple of the Night, with a glass cupola blown specially in St Petersburg and painted ceiling by *Jean Pierre Norblin*. On the island is a 'tomb' of Princess Helena herself, with a copy of *Bernini's* St Cecilia and the inscription *"j'ai fait Arcadie, et j'y repose"* (a 'tomb' of Rousseau was thrown out when the French Revolution turned nasty). The numerous other structures progress from classical remains, such as the Roman aqueduct, 1784, and the High Priest's House, ca. 1820, both by *Zug,* with pieces of Renaissance sculpture and ornament from StVictoria's chapel in the collegiate church at Łowicz; to the Gothic Cottage (for Melancholy), and the Keeper's House, both ca. 1800; and numerous stone fragments, some of them antique. The park was more than just a playground. The Princess wrote a guidebook explaining its elaborate thematic programme, but since she kept rebuilding and rearranging, this became increasingly confused. See also NIE-BORÓW

AUSCHWITZ: SEE OŚWIĘCIM

BABICE   MAP 21
Ruined **castle** of the bishops of Kraków, 13/14th and early 15th century.

✦✦ BABORÓW (BAUERWITZ)   MAP 14
Wooden **cemetery church**, 1702. Frescoes and furniture early 18th century.

BABSK MAP 17

Neo-Classical **country house** and farm buildings, first half of 19th century. **Parish church** and vicarage also neo-Classical, 1809.

BACHÓRZEC MAP 29

Church of St Catherine, wooden, built 1760 by Count Antoni Krasicki. Contemporary wall-paintings.

BĄCZAŁ DOLNY MAP 22 ✦

Parish church, wooden, 1667.

BĄKÓW (BANKAU) MAP 12 ✦

Wooden **parish church**, Gothic, early 16th century. Gothic triptych, second half of 14th century.

BARANÓW MAP 20 ✦✦

Renaissance **castle** built for Rafał Leszczyński between 1591 and 1606 by *Santi Gucci*. Stucco work second quarter of 17th century, by *Giovanni Battista Falconi*. West wing with gallery and decoration

remodelled for Prince Stanisław Lubomirski, who acquired the castle in 1677, in Baroque style, 1695–1700, by *Tilman van Gameren*. An important building, with some unusual stonework, but heavily restored and rather arid. **Church** of St John the Baptist, 1607, with 19th century additions.

BARCIANY (BARTEN) MAP 16

Monastic **castle** of Teutonic Knights, by master-builder *Winricus*, begun 1325. An early example of a castle built to withstand attack by cannon. **Parish church**, second half of 14th century, altered second half of 18th century.

BARCZEWO (WARTEMBURG) MAP 16

Gothic hall **church**, 4th quarter of 14th century. Vaults and super-structure of tower after 1544. **Franciscan monastery** (Bernardine after 1597), late 14th century; rebuilt 1590s and converted into prison 1820s. Tomb of Cardinals Andrzej and Baltazar Batory (nephews of Stefan Batory, King of Poland), Mannerist, 1598, by *Willem van den Blocke*.

✦ ## BARDO MAP 13

Parish church, 1680–1700, by *Michael Klein*, important contemporary furniture; Baroque paintings, including one by *Michael Willman*. The 13th century wooden figure of the Enthroned Virgin is the object of local pilgrimages. Adjacent **monastery** houses good collection of sacral art, including paintings from the workshop of *Lucas Cranach*.

BARTOSZYCE MAP 16

Little medieval town, badly damaged in 1945, but restored. Gothic **basilica**, 14th–15th century. **Church** of St John 1485.

BARWAŁD DOLNY MAP 21

Church of Our Lady, wooden, late 18th century. Tower 16th century.

✦ ## BĘDZIN MAP 14

Castle founded by king Kazimierz the Great 1364. The massive central keep, 13th–14th centuries, is ringed by two outer defensive walls. Rebuilt in neo-Gothic style, 1834, by *Franciszek Maria Lanci*. Now houses a **museum** of archaeology, arms and armour, some coins and decorative arts. Town **walls** also 1364.

Parish church of St Nicholas, ca. 1400, with contemporary frescoes. Outstanding square domed mortuary chapel of Mikołaj Firlej, Palatine of Kraków and his wife Elżbieta, Mannerist, 1590s, by an architect associated with *Santi Gucci*. Wonderful marble sculpture and stucco. **Country House**, 1802 by *Jakub Kubicki*. A fine example of this important neo-Classical architect's work. Surprisingly substantial for its intimate size. Charming combination of the formal and the bucolic at the garden facade. Built for Marcin Badeni, a political supporter of the last king, Stanisław Augustus, and later Minister of Justice in the Kingdom of Poland, a universally respected and much-loved man.

The site of one of the largest extermination camps set up by the Germans, where some 800,000 people were murdered. The camp was destroyed by the Germans in 1943. There is only a monument there now.

Parish church, brick, Mannerist, 16th–17th century. Renaissance gravestone of Anna Rozdrażewska.

Neo-Classical **palace** of the Habsburg family, first half of 19th century.

Pauline monastery, 1407. Very fine brick church of SS Peter and Paul, expanded 17th century and later, but lovely and unspoilt.

Small **castle** of Teutonic Knights, late 14th century, converted into Gothic **church**, 1583. Tower 1726–30.

Important medieval market town. **Parish church**, 14th–15th century, expanded ca. 1550, and 18th and 20th centuries; furniture Baroque. **Castle**, Renaissance, 16th century, expanded in Baroque style ca. 1640. Town **walls** 15th century. Water tower 1606.

Private town built by the Radziwiłł family. They lavished care and money on it, establishing an academy or university there in the

1620s, but the town never recovered from its sack at the hands of Charles XII of Sweden, or indeed from the follies of its last owner, Prince Karol Radziwiłł, one of history's great buffoons. In an attempt to revive the town, the Radziwiłłs established a pottery there in the 18th century.

Church of St Anne, Renaissance, 1597–1602. Chapels 1625. Radziwiłł chapel with stucco and pictorial decoration, Baroque, early 18th century. **Reformed Franciscans' monastery** and **church** of St Anthony, 1671–8. **Basilian Friars' church** of the Nativity of the Blessed Virgin, 1747–9. Radziwiłł family **castle**, after 1622, by *Paolo Negroni*, demolished save for two Pavillions, outbuildings and treasure-houses, 1699–1701 by *Andrzej Józefat Jeziornicki*. Chapel, Renaissance, second quarter of 17th century. Gate Tower, 17th century, completed with addition of guard-houses 1696–1701 and connected by means of vaulted passage with fortress gate, 1699–1701, by *Andrzej Józefat Jeziornicki*. Earth bastion **fortifications**, late 17th century.

✦✦ BIAŁACZÓW   MAP 19
Elegant **country house** built for Stanisław Małachowski, marshal of the reforming Sejm that passed the Constitution of 3 May 1791. Neo-Classical, with curving colonnaded wings, 1797–1800, by *Jakub Kubicki*; good contemporary stucco and pictorial decoration. Neo-Gothic **orangery** and Romantic **ruins**, 1825, by *Franciszek Maria Lanci* in park. **Town hall**, neo-Classical, 1797. **Manor house**, partly wooden, late 18th century: a good example of this type of gentry residence.

BIAŁKA   MAP 21
Wooden **church**, ca. 1700, but still with late Gothic stylistic details.

BIAŁOGARD   MAP 2
Little medieval town, with **parish church** ca. 1310, rebuilt 19th century. **Church** of St George ca. 1510.

✦ BIAŁYSTOK   MAP 26
Private town of the Branicki family centred on the great Branicki **palace** 1697 by *Tilman van Gameren*. Rebuilt as a grand residence for Hetman Jan Klemens Branicki, 1728–58, by *Johann Sigismund Deybel* and *Jan Henryk Klemm*. Sculptures by *J. Redler*. Tower gate, 1755–8, by *Jan Henryk Klemm*. Formal **park** with parterres, espaliers and canals, mainly 1728–58. Two Rococo pavilions. Parish church of the Assumption, 1740s. Delightfully silly organ case 1752–62, by *Antoni Wierzbowski* and *Ignancy Żebrowski*. **Town Hall** 1745/6, by

Jan Henryk Klemm, now houses a museum concentrating of the history of the town. Jan Klemens Branicki was Grand Hetman of the Crown and Castellan of Kraków, and for a long time one of the principal supporters of the Saxon kings of Poland. Augustus III stayed at Białystok and took part in spectacular shoots organised for him there. Branicki later became leader of the pro-French party in Poland and, in spite of being married to Izabela Poniatowska (*Madame de Cracovie*), he opposed the election of her brother, Stanisław II Augustus, to the throne, and remained his political

enemy. In its heyday, Białystok was run on a very grand footing, and was often referred to as "the Versailles of the North" by the numerous aristocratic travellers who paused there on their way to or back from St Petersburg. After Branicki's death, Białystok was purchased by the king of Prussia and subsequently, in 1808, by Tsar Alexander I, who intended it as a country retreat, but nothing came of his plans and the palace became an institution. In the 19th century the town became an important and populous textile manufacturing centre, even beginning to rival Łódź by the beginning of this century. The town also had a large and vibrant Jewish population.

BIECHOWO   MAP 9
Oratorian church, 1734-65, with Rococo interior.

BIECZ   MAP 22 ✦✦
Market town and trading post close to the old border between the kingdoms of Poland and Hungary that grew rich on the Hungarian wine trade. In 1500 it had a population of 40,000 and 15 churches.
Parish church of Corpus Christi, late 15th century, completed 1521 by Italian builders from Milan; good Renaissance tombs and epitaphs; tomb of Mikołaj Ligęza, 1575; painting in high altar north Italian second half of 16th century; fortified belfry 15th/16th century, sgraffiti 16th century. Renaissance gate first half of 17th cen-

tury. A remarkably light building, considering its massive bulk. Lovely delicate brickwork on eastern gable. **Reformed Franciscans' church**, 1645–63, rebuilt 1739. **Town walls**, before 1399, expanded 16th century, gate tower, ca. 1520. **Town hall**, neo-Classical, ca. 1830, with Gothic/Renaissance tower, 1570s. Renaissance **merchant's house** 1612 (5 Kromera Street), housing Regional **Museum**, an eclectic jumble, not without interest, including exhibition of life and work of the historian Marcin Kromer, born in Biecz in 1512.

BIECZ (BEITSCH)   MAP 3
Parish church, Baroque, second half of 18th century. Baroque **palace** of Wittelsbach family, 1722/1802.

BIELAWY   MAP 17
Characteristic example of 15th-century village **church**. Wooden bell-tower 18th century.

BIELINY   MAP 27
Church of St Wojciech, founded by Elżbieta Zamoyska, 1763–70.

✦   BIELSK PODLASKI   MAP 26
Parish church founded by Izabela Branicka (see Białystok), 1783, facade and interior neo-Classical, 1796,by *Szymon Bogumił Zug*. **Town Hall**, Baroque, 1780s. Four wooden Orthodox **churches**, the earliest dating from the 16th century.

BIELSKO-BIAŁA   MAP 14
Medieval market town and centre of textile industry. Sułkowski

family **palace**, rebuilt from an earlier castle, dating from early 15th century, now local **museum** (little of interest). **Parish church**, ca. 1760. Neo-Classical **Protestant church**, 1790s; galleries and vaults 1832. **Town houses** with arcaded porches, 17th to 18th century.

BIENISZEW   MAP 10
Camaldolite church, 1747–81. Rococo frescoes.

BIERZGŁOWO (BIERGELAU)   MAP 10
Castle of Teutonic Knights, second half of 13th century; important gateway with ceramic decoration. Very good.

BIERZWNIK (MARIENWALDE)   MAP 2
Cistercian abbey founded 1282. Church 14th century. Monastery 15th century, rebuilt 1820.

BIEŻUŃ   MAP 17
Small town and residential complex built for Chancellor Andrzej Zamoyski. Baroque **country house**, third quarter of 18th century. It was on this estate in 1760 that Zamoyski experimentally freed his peasants from all their labour rents, and the success of the experiment led to the gradual emancipation of the peasantry on many other estates.

BINAROWA   MAP 22 ✦
Wooden **church** of St Michael the Archangel, ca. 1500, expanded 1640s; painted decoration of ceiling early 16th century, furniture 17th century. Very fine.

BISKUPIN   MAP 9
One of the most important archaeological sites in Poland, with remains reaching back to 3500 BC. The most interesting is the uncovered and partly reconstructed fortified lake-settlement, dating from 500 BC, consisting of over 100 houses. There is a museum on the history and development of the settlement. Pretty dull, unless you like that kind of thing.

BLIZNE   MAP 29 ✦
Wooden **church**, Gothic, first half of 16th century. Tower early 17th century. Wooden **vicarage** and **granary**, 19th century.

BŁONIE   MAP 18
Collegiate church, 1288, enlarged early 16th century, rebuilt in neo-Classical style 1812. Fine 'crystal' vaulting in chancel, ca. 1520.

Town hall, neo-Classical, late 18th century, by *Domenico Merlini*, rebuilt 1824 by *Bonifacy Witkowski*. On the eastern side of the town, well preserved remains of early medieval fortifications with earth ramparts, 11th-12th centuries.

BNIN   MAP 9
Ancient market town and seat of the Bniński family, later property of Działyński family, now part of Kórnik. **Town Hall**, Baroque, mid-18th century. See also KÓRNIK.

BOBOLICE   MAP 19
Impressive ruin of **castle** built by king Kazimierz the Great ca. 1350.

BOBOWA   MAP 22
Famous lace-making centre. Succursal **church**, second half of 15th century. Numerous examples of vernacular architecture (merchants' houses, manor house, synagogue, etc, 17th–19th centuries).

BOBRZA   MAP 20
Industrial village built by the state 1828–31. **Munitions factory**, neo-Classical, by *Wilhelm Lempe*, unfinished: ruin of factory hall and retaining wall, water engineering structures, and houses for staff.

BOCHNIA   MAP 21
Important centre of rock-salt mining since 13th century. According to legend, the deposits were discovered miraculously by the Blessed Kinga (Kunegunda), queen of Poland.
Parish church, 15th century, rebuilt 1665. Wooden belfry 1609, still in Gothic tradition. Houses in Market Square 18th century. **Dominican monastery**, now **Museum**: usual regional jumble, with some improbable objects from the Far East. See also WIELICZKA.

✦   BOĆKI   MAP 25
Reformed Franciscans' church founded by Sapieha family, 1730–9. Bell-Tower and enclosure contemporary.

✦✦   BODZENTYN   MAP 20
Collegiate church of the Assumption, founded by Cardinal Zbigniew Oleśnicki, Chancellor of Poland; a Gothic basilica 1440–52, with vaults dating from the first half of the 17th century. Rather heavy (one feels the architect was afraid it might fall down), but it has atmosphere. Renaissance altar from Kraków Cathedral, 1545–6, triptych before 1508, by Master *Marcin Czarny*.

Castle of the bishops of Kraków founded second half of 14th century, expanded 1657–1691.

BOGUCHWAŁA   MAP 29

Church of St Stanisław, early 18th century. Tower superstructure 1896. **Manor house** of Prince Teodor Lubomirski, mid-18th century, enlarged in neo-Classical style first half of 19th century.

BOGUSZOWICE   MAP 14

Wooden **parish church** on Greek Cross pattern, 1717.

BOGUSZYCE   MAP 19 ✦✦

Wooden **parish church**. Important painted ceiling and walls in Renaissance style, 1558. Polyptych of same date by *Jan Jantas*, and two interesting triptychs.

BOLESŁAW   MAP 22

Parish church, late Gothic, 1605; Ligęza family chapel, Mannerist, 1605.

BOLESŁAWIEC   MAP 6

Ruins of **castle** founded by Kazimierz the Great ca. 1335.

BOLESŁAWIEC (BÜNZLAU)   MAP 6

Important pottery centre since Middle Ages (Potters Guild founded 1543). Also the birthplace of Martin Opitz, the German poet, and the place where Marshal Kutuzov died in 1813.
Parish church, 1482–1521; interior rebuilt in Baroque style late 17th century by *Giulio Simonetti*. **Town Hall**, rebuilt in Baroque style in the 18th century from important late Gothic hall church 1525–35, with net vaulting by *Wendel Rosskopf*; three Renaissance portals, removed from destroyed merchant's house. Baroque gabled **houses** in market square, 17th–1st half of 18th century. **Museum**, concentrating on local ceramics industry, from 17th century to present day.

BOLIMÓW   MAP 17

Parish church, 1667. **Church** of St Anne, 1635.

BOLKÓW (BOLKENHAIN)   MAP 6 ✦

Castle of the Piast dukes of Świdnica. Built 1277–93 by Prince Bolko I, expanded first half of 14th century (with a tear-shaped tower, the only one of its kind in Poland). Lower courtyards with artillery fortifications, and decorative parapet walls, ca. 1540, by

Giacomo Pario for Salza family. Now houses **museum**, containing little of general interest. Parish church, ca. 1250, remodelled 14th century and 1846; sculptures, second half of 14th century. **Houses** in Market Square 16th–17th century.

✦✦ BOREK   MAP 11
Parish church, 1635–55, by *Cristoforo Bonadura the Elder*. Expanded late 17th century by *Giorgio Catenaci*.

BOREK STARY   MAP 29
Dominican church, 1684–1726; **monastery** 1712–38.

✦ BORONÓW   MAP 12
Wooden **parish church** on Greek Cross pattern, 1611.

BORYSŁAWICE   MAP 10
Parish church, wooden, 1759. Ruined **castle** of Jastrzębiec family, ca. 1425, expanded first half of 16th century. Rare example of a 15th-century minor nobleman's residence.

BOŻEWO   MAP 17
Parish church, 1453. Belfry 18th–19th century.

✦✦ BRALIN   MAP 12
Wooden **pilgrimage church**, 1711, surrounded by wooden porches and chapels for pilgrims. This kind of church, often lost in the middle of nowhere but coming to life once a year on the appointed pilgrimage day, is very much a feature of traditional Polish life.

✦✦ BRANIEWO (BRAUNSBERG)   MAP 15
An important Hanseatic town in the middle ages, badly damaged 1945. **Parish church** of the Holy Trinity, 1346–81, vaults 1442, tower superstructure 1536; destroyed 1945. **Jesuit college**, the first in Poland, founded 1565 by Cardinal Stanisław Hosius (1504–79) to spearhead the re-conversion of Polish youth to Catholicism. **Church**, Baroque, 1723–31. Neo-Classical **church**, originally Protestant, 1830–3, by *Karl Friedrich Schinkel*.

BRDÓW   MAP 10
Pauline church 1758, tower 1790.

✦✦ BROCHÓW   MAP 17
Fortified **parish church** of St Roch, 1551–61, by *Giovanni Battista di Venezia*; some alterations 1665. This is an astonishing structure: a

barrel-vaulted three-nave basilica with a facade reminiscent of the Romanesque, with towers and defensive wall forming a kind of castle. The composer Fryderyk Chopin was baptised in this church.

BRODNICA (STRASBURG)   MAP 17 ✦✦✦

Monastic **castle** of Teutonic Knights, 1305–39, including a monumental keep 50 metres high. Fortifications modernized 1415 by *Nikolaus Fellenstein*. Later additions, including **palace** of Princess Anna Vasa, 1526–45, rebuilt in Baroque style 1678–98, mostly destroyed 1945. **Parish church** of St Catherine, second quarter of 14th century,contemporary stone sculptures. Expanded up to 16th century. Some very fine elements of northern Gothic architecture. **Reformed Franciscans' church**, 1751–61, rebuilt 1840. **Town walls** 1320–30, expanded ca. 1370, wall of suburb 15th century. Chełmno Gate, ca. 1370. Tower and gable of **Town Hall**, late 14th century.

BRODY   MAP 20

Ironworks founded 1834 by Bank of Poland, neo-Classical. **Synagogue**, 18th century.

BRODY   MAP 4

Wooden **parish church**,Baroque, 1673. Enlarged 18th century, interior richly decorated.

BRODY(PFÖRTEN)   MAP 3 ✦

Palace-and-Town complex founded by Count Heinrich Brühl, the lackey who became favourite and chief minister to Augustus III King of Poland and Elector of Saxony, 1741–53, by *Johann Christoph Knoffel*: including palace, outbuildings, orangery, gate, farm buildings, park, barracks, inn, houses and town gate. **Church** (originally Protestant) 17th century; tower 1693; galleries ca. 1725, by *Georg Bahr*.

BROK   MAP 25 ✦✦

Parish church founded by Bishop Andrzej Noskowski in 1560, by *Giovanni Battista di Venezia*. As in Brochów (see above), some curious incorporation of Renaissance elements into an essentially Gothic structure.

BRZEG (BRIEG)   MAP 11 ✦✦✦

Castle of the dukes of Brzeg [1], founded ca. 1230, rebuilt 1541–60, by *Giacomo* and *Francesco Pario*, for Prince Frederick II of Brzeg. Fine gatehouse, 1550s, with elaborate stone decoration and sculptures depicting the descent of the dukes of Brzeg from the Polish royal house of Piast. The castle was devastated by Frederick II of Prussia in 1741, but restored in the 1970s, and now houses an interesting **museum** of local art and artefacts, mainly from the Middle Ages. Chapel, 1368–71, rebuilt ca. 1567 and 1783–4. Crypt under chapel containing richly decorated coffins of dukes of Brzeg. Fortifications, earth bastions, after 1620s and second half of 18th century. Gate 1596, by *Bernardo* and *Pietro Niuron*. Huge Gothic **parish church** of St Nicholas [2] 1370–1416; wall painting in sacristy, mid-15th century; epitaphs Renaissance and Mannerist. **Franciscan monastery** and **church** [3], before 1338, rebuilt after 1494 and 16th–20th centuries (since 1582 the church has been used as an armoury

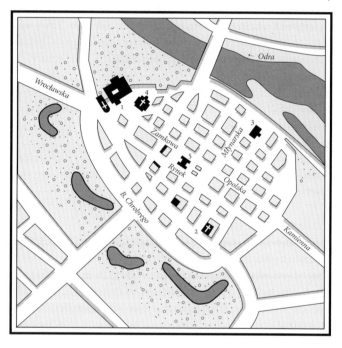

and warehouse). **Jesuit church** of the Holy Cross [4], 1734–9, by *Josef Frish*; painted decoration 1739–45, by *Johann Kuben*, furniture and wall painting contemporary. Impressive example of Silesian high baroque.

Town Hall [5] 1570–7, *Bernardo Niuron* and *Giacomo Pario*, with Gothic parts; interiors Baroque, ca. 1746. Also several substantial Renaissance and Baroque merchants' houses.

BRZESKO (BRIETZIG)   MAP 1
Parish church, originally 13th century, entirely rebuilt second half of 17th century, with Baroque wooden ceiling. Nine timber-framed **houses**, 18th century.

BRZEŚĆ KUJAWSKI   MAP 10
Parish church, mid-1300s, remodelled 1710.
Dominican church, 1383; rebuilt after 1584, in second half of 17th
century, and 1928. **Town Hall**, neo-Classical, 1824, by *Henryk
Marconi*.

BRZEŚCE   MAP 18 ✦
Wooden **manor house** of king Stanisław Augustus's courtier Jan
Kanty Fontana, 1784.

BRZEZINKI (BÜRGSDORF)   MAP 12 ✦
Wooden **church**, Gothic, ca. 1550, expanded 1693; painted decoration Baroque, 1693 and 1776; Gothic triptych. Enclosure and gates,
1753–4.

BRZEZINY   MAP 19 ✦
Parish church, 13th–16th century. Lasocki family chapel, 16th–17th
century; tombs of Stanisław Lasocki and his wife, by *Bernardino
Zanobi de Gianotis*, c1535. Tomb of Urszula Leżeńska by *Jan
Michałowicz*, 1563.
Reformed Franciscans' church and **monastery**, ca. 1700. **Bernardine
convent**, 18th century.
Wooden **vernacular builidngs**, 18th–19th centuries.

BRZEZINY   MAP 22
Parish church, wooden, ca. 1500, expanded 1933; painted decoration Renaissance, early 17th century; Gothic bas-relief. Bell-tower
16th century. **Manor house**, part wooden, turn of 18th and 19th centuries.

BRZOZÓW   MAP 29
Parish church, 1676–8, chapels 1758; rebuilt 19th–20th centuries.
Jesuit college, first half of 18th century.

BUK   MAP 9 ✦
Cemetery church, part wooden, 1760, painted decoration contemporary.

BUK (BÖCK)   MAP 1
Parish church, stone, late Romanesque, 13th century.

BYCINA (FICHTENRODE)   MAP 14
Country house, 1700; painted decoration of chapel 1730.

Historic royal burgh and provincial capital in Middle Ages, fought over by Poland and the Teutonic Order, destroyed by Swedes, its development was continually hampered, until the 19th century when it achieved quiet prosperity as German Bromberg.

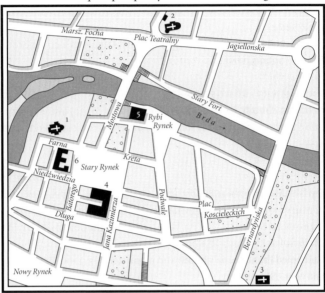

Parish church of St Nicholas and St Martin [1], 1460–1502, typical Pomeranian Gothic, with interesting pattern on western gable. **Poor Clares' church** [2]: chancel late 16th century, nave with tower 1615, painted ceiling 17th century. Monastic building now houses **museum**, concerned primarily with the works of the painter *Leon Wyczółkowski* (1852–1936), but containing also some local art and artefacts from earlier times. **Bernardine church** of St Mary and St George, with monastery [3], 1552–7. **Lawcourts** (now municipal Library), in Old Market Square [4], 1778. **Granaries** [5], timber, 18th–19th century. Jesuit College [6]. **Hotel** 'Pod Orłem', Art Nouveau.

BYSTRZYCA KŁODZKA   MAP 6

Medieval town with Gothic **parish church**, ca. 1300-15th century, expanded 1915. Renaissance and Baroque merchants' **houses**. Stone **pillory**, 1556. **Museum** of match-making industry.

BYTOM (BEUTHEN)   MAP 14

This town was an important silver and lead mining centre from the 12th century. **Parish church**: choir 13th and 14th century, nave 16th century, rebuilt 1678, expanded in neo-Gothic style 1857.

Franciscan church founded 1481, entirely remodelled 1783. In the park, there is a wooden **church** moved from the village of Mikulczyce, Gothic, mid-16th century.

Regional **museum** housing some interesting paintings of the Young Poland movement, and a wide range of foreign works, from the 15th century onwards, including some English and Scottish 19th century paintings.

Suburb of BOBREK.

Parish church, Baroque, 1790-98; vicarage neo-Classical, first half of 19th century.

Country house, neo-Classical, first half of 19th century; outbuildings 1782, wooden granary 1779.

BYTOM ODRZAŃSKI (BEUTHEN AM ODER)   MAP 4

Parish church, 1585, with earlier elements in west front ca. 1300, and tower, 15th century.

Town Hall, Renaissance, 1610. **Houses** in Market Square, ca. 1700.

BYTÓW (BÜTOW)   MAP 7 ✦

Castle of Teutonic Knights, by *Nicolaus Fellenstein* 1398–1406, expanded 16–17th century; fine rectangular fortress with early gun embrasures.

CEGŁÓW   MAP 18

Parish church, second quarter of 16th century, expanded first quarter of 17th century. Simple late Gothic village church, with unusual round buttresses. Also, good epitaph of the 15th century physician Wojciech Oczko.

CERADZ KOŚCIELNY (KIRCHEN CERADZ).   MAP 9

Parish church, Gothic, first half of 16th century; Renaissance chapel, late 16th century. Interesting knights' gravestones, second half of 16th century.

CHABÓWKA   MAP 21

Wooden **church**, rustic Baroque, 1757.

CHĘCINY   MAP 19 ✦

Old market town, centre of Jewish life 16th-19th centuries. On the hill above the town, ruins of royal **castle**, founded 1296, repeatedly rebuilt up to 15th century. In the 14th century this was considered the best fortified castle in Poland, and housed the Royal Treasury.

Parish church, Gothic ca. 1600, with earlier parts; square domed Mannerist chapel, 1614, by *Kasper Fodyga*.

Franciscan monastery founded 1368 by king Kazimierz the Great. Monastic building Renaissance, first half of 17th century, now a restaurant. Branicki chapel ca. 1640. Gate and farm buildings mid-17th century, and neo-Classical, 1820.

Poor Clares' church and **convent**, second half of 17th century. Baroque wooden **granary**, 18th century.

Synagogue, Renaissance/Baroque, ca. 1650. **Houses**, 16th – early 19th centuries.

◆◆ CHEŁM   MAP 28

Important provincial centre from 12th century, when it was the seat (and temporarily the capital) of the dukes of Halicz, and also the seat of an Uniate bishopric.

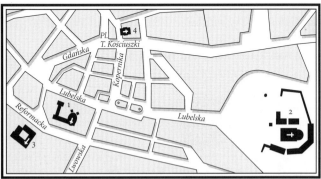

Piarist church of the Commission of the Apostles [1], on oval plan with radiating chapels, dating from the 1750s, by *Paweł Fontana*; a good example of Italianate Polish Baroque. Sculptures and furniture Rococo, painted decoration 1758, by *Józef Mayer*. Monastic buildings 1667–1726, by *Domenico Alessandro Belotti*. Now houses **museum;** usual jumble, but also some interesting Uniate religious paraphernalia.

Basilian Friars's monastery and **Uniate Cathedral** [2], 1735–56, by *Paweł Fontana*. Monastic buildings 17th century.

Reformed Franciscans' church of St Andrew the Apostle and **monastery** [3], 1730s. Orthodox Church [4].Ancient vaults and dungeons under the whole town.

◆◆◆ CHEŁMNO   MAP 10

Lovely thirteenth-century market town and provincial centre, also first base of the Teutonic Order in this part of Europe, granted to them by Duke Konrad of Mazovia in 1226. From then until it was recaptured by Poland in 1466, it was known under the German name of Cülm. It was also for a time a member of the Hanseatic

league. Contains a very important group of Gothic sacral architecture.

Town Hall [1], 1570 (tower 1595); a lovely and quintessential example of Polish Renaissance secular architecture with its charateristic decorative parapet.

Important **parish church** of the Assumption [2], 1290–1333; Niemojewski family chapel with Mannerist tomb, 1560–80. Substantial.

Dominican church of SS Peter and Paul [5], 1240s, expanded second half of 14th century and 17th century.

Cistercian Nuns' (later Benedictine nuns') **church** of St John the Baptist and St John the Evangelist [4] founded 1266, contains a rare early Gothic figural gravestone of Canon Lischoren. Organ 1613–19. Monastic building rebuilt 17th-18th centuries.

Franciscan church of St James [3], ca. 1290–1350, vaults 15th century

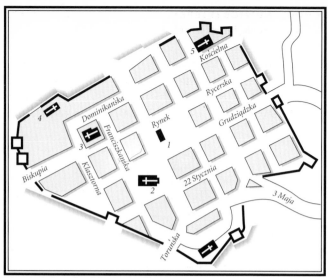

Hospital church of the Holy Ghost, ca. 1300.
Town walls with 17 towers and Grudziądz Gate, 14th–15th centuries.

✦ CHEŁMSKO ŚLĄSKIE (SCHÖMBERG)   MAP 6
Parish church, 1670s, by *Martin Urban*. Old vicarage 1575. New vicarage second quarter of 18th century.
Houses in market square, late 17th to early 19th century. Wooden **weavers' houses**, called the Twelve Apostles, 1707; very unusual

✦✦ CHEŁMŻA   MAP 10
Medieaval market town, and between 1251 and 1824 the seat of a bishopric.
Collegiate church (originally cathedral), very fine example of northern Gothic. Choir, transept and eastern towers 1251–63; vault ca. 1294; nave 1359. Furniture Baroque, 17th–18th centuries; sculpture Gothic.Tombs of bishops and canons 14th-18th centuries. Tomb of Bishop Kostka, Mannerist, late 16th century.

CHŁOPICE   MAP 29
Baroque wooden **church** (originally Orthodox), 1761–3. Bell-tower with chapel, 18th century.

✦✦ CHOCHOŁÓW   MAP 21
Well preserved highland village with remarkable ornamented wooden **houses**, 18th–19th centuries, as well as numerous little **chapels**, roadside shrines and figures of saints.

CHOCIANOWICE (KIEFERNRODE)   MAP 12

Wooden **parish church**, late Gothic tradition, 1662.

CHOCIANÓW (KOTZENAU)   MAP 6 ✦

Country house, ca. 1730, with remnants of Gothic/Renaissance castle and stuccoed interiors; outbuildings Baroque, 1777. Formal and
landscape **park** with neo-Classical pavilion. Interesting, but not
beautiful.

CHOCZ   MAP 12 ✦✦

Parish church; chancel 1629–34; main body and stucco decoration,
1790–3. Astonishing to find such a magnificent church being built
just as Poland was being partitioned. **Country house** buillt in 1780
by *Ephraim Schröger* for Kazimierz Lipski. **Palace** of mitred
prelates, Baroque, 1790, with interesting stuccoed interiors.
Reformed Franciscans' church and monastery, ca. 1733.

CHODEL   MAP 27 ✦✦

Parish church founded by Maciejowski family, 1541. Very unusual
late Gothic/Renaissance structure.

CHODZIEŻ   MAP 9

Small town of artisans and craftsmen. **Parish church**, late 15th century, rebuilt early 17th century; interior 1755. **Weavers' houses**, some
timber, 1798–1812.

CHOJNA (KÖNIGSBERG)   MAP 1 ✦✦

Parish church, brick with ceramic ornament, 1407, by *Heinrich
Brunsberg*, expanded 1459, tower reconstructed 19th century; gutted 1945. **Augustinian church** and **monastery**, 1290, damaged 1945.
Town walls and towers, ca. 1300; Main gate, early 1400s, like an
illustration from a fairy-tale. Town Hall 15th century.

CHOJNICA   MAP 9

Parish church, 1531, late Gothic with stellar vaulting.

CHOJNICE   MAP 7

Parish church, 1350s, extended second half of 15th century, reconstructed 1924. **Jesuit church**, 1718–44; painted decoration 1742, by
F.Haflich. **Jesuit college** 1744–55. **Town walls**, mid-14th century,
with regional **museum** in one of the towers.

CHOJNÓW (HAYNAU)   MAP 6

Parish church, 14th–15th century, nave vault 1468. Bożywój family chapel with tomb, Renaissance, mid-16th century. Priest's house first half of 16th century. **Castle,** founded 12th century by the dukes of Legnica, with Renaissance stone portal, 1546, by *Francesco Pario*. Houses regional **museum. Town walls** mid-14th century, Weavers' Tower ca. 1400, with decorative parapet wall mid-16th century, timber superstructure 1650.

CHOROSZCZ   MAP 25
Dominican monastery founded 1756 by Hetman Jan Klemens Branicki. **Park** of former residence laid out for Hetman Branicki, formal with cruciform canal, 1745. The scene of outrageous shoots organised for king Augustus III, with flying bears and bison. See also BIAŁYSTOK.

✦   CHOSZCZNO (ARNSWALDE)   MAP 2
Parish (formerly Templars') **church,** 14th century, tower ca. 1400. **Town walls** 14th century. Barbican late 15th century.

CHOTEL CZERWONY   MAP 20
Parish church founded by the historian Jan Długosz, 1443. Very picturesque stone church.

CHOTYNIEC   MAP 29
Wooden **church** (originally Orthodox), 1613.

✦   CHROBERZ   MAP 20
Parish church, Gothic, 1550–76, expanded 17th century. Renaissance/Mannerist tomb of Stanisław Tarnowski 1568, by *Jan Michałowicz of Urzędów*. Neo-Classical **residence** in landscape **park,** 1850 by *Henryk Marconi*.

CHRUŚLIN   MAP 17
Parish church, Gothic/Renaissance, workshop of *Joannes Baptista Venetus,* 1554, with coffered barrel vault similar to those at Brochów, Cieksyn and Pułtusk.

✦   CHRZELICE (SCHELITZ)   MAP 13
Castle of the dukes of Opole, 14th century, rebuilt as 3-winged Baroque palace with arcaded galleries, 1694.

✦✦ CHRZĘSNE   MAP 18
Late Renaissance **country house,** built 1635 for Stefan Dobrogost Grzybowski. Interiors altered mid-18th century.

CHWALĘCIN (STEGMANNSDORF) MAP 15
Pilgrimage church, 1728, by *Johann Christoph Reimers*. Facade neo-Classical, painted decoration 1748. Arcaded galleries with chapels and gate, 1822.

CHWARSZCZANY (QUÄRTSCHEN) MAP 3 ✦
Chapel of Knights Templar, later Hospitaller, then Joannitter (Protestant Order of St John), ca. 1250; murals Gothic. The only surviving part of a former castle. The parallel towers are an allusion to the pillars of the Temple of Solomon.

CIĄŻEŃ MAP 9 ✦✦
Palace of the bishops of Poznań, 1768, by *Giuseppe Sacco*, extended 1794–1818; interior Rococo. A very impressive pile. **Parish church**, originally Gothic, 1535, rebuilt 1760. Priest's house second half of 18th century.

CIECHANÓW MAP 18 ✦
Important regional centre from 13th century. Outside the town, **castle** of the dukes of Mazovia, ca. 1430, by master-mason *Mikołaj*, superstructure 15th–17th century; grand ruin. **Parish church** of the Nativity of the Blessed Virgin, 1516–25, rebuilt 1913.

CIECHANOWIEC MAP 25 ✦
Old trading post on Polish-Lithuanian border. **Parish church** founded by Ossoliński family, 1737–9, with contemporary belfries. **Country house** of Nowodwory, 1860, by *Franciszek Maria Lanci*, built for Count Michał Starzeński, now a **museum**. Also open-air **museum** of local wooden buildings (granaries, cottages, small manor-houses).

CIEKSYN MAP 18 ✦
Gothic/Renaissance **parish church**, mid-16th century, workshop of *Joannes Baptista Venetus*. Contemporary sculpted altarpiece by *Jan Jantas*.

CIEPLICE ŚLĄSKIE ZDRÓJ (BAD WARMBRÜNN) MAP 6 ✦
Health resort recognised since Middle Ages. **Parish church** 1712-4. Huge Schaffgotsch family **residence**, 1784–9, with stuccoed interiors. **Villa** in park, neo-Classical, ca. 1800. **Theatre**, neo-Classical, 1833 by *Albert Tollberg*.

CIESZKÓW (FREYHAN) MAP 11
Parish church founded by Katarzyna Sapieha, ca. 1750.

Capital of a duchy often disputed, most recently between Poland and Czechoslovakia, in 1919 and 1938.

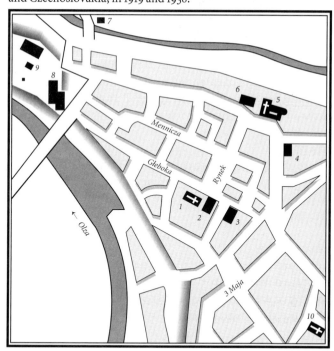

Dominican church of St Mary Magdalen [**1**], second half of 13th century, vaults and tower Baroque, 1790s. Tomb of Prince Przemysław I, ca. 1380. **Jesuit college** [**4**], early 18th century; church rebuilt 1781; college building remodelled 19th century. **Monastery of Hospitallers of St John of God** [**5**]1706, by *Michael Klein*. **Church** of the Holy Trinity [**6**], Gothic, 1594, expanded 1659. **Parish church** of St George [**7**], late 14th-early 15th centuries. **Protestant church** [**10**], 1709–50. **Castle** [**9**]on site of ancient fortified centre; Piast tower, second half of 14th century, superstructure 20th century. Chapel of St Nicholas, stone Romanesque rotunda, mid-11th century. **Palace** of Archduke Karl of Habsburg [**8**], neo-Classical, 1837, by *Josef Kornhausel*. **Town hall** with guardhouse [**2**], rebuilt 1836 by *Josef Kornhausel*. **Mint** (46 Mennicza Street), 1719, rebuilt ca. 1910. Baroque/neo-Classical **palace** of Larisch family [**3**], 1796; now **museum**. **Houses** in Market Square, arcaded, 15th-17th century.

CISÓW (ZISSENDORF)   MAP 6
Ruins of **castle** of the Piast dukes of Świdnica, late 13th century, enlarged 15th century.

ĆMIELÓW

MAP 20

A centre of pottery manufacture. **Castle** of Chancellor Krzysztof Szydłowiecki, Gothic/Renaissance, 1519-31; ruins of two palaces and chapel on island and of forecourt with gate tower. Earth bastion fortifications, first half of 17th century.

CYNKÓW

MAP 14 ✦

Wooden **church**, Gothic, 1631, by master-carpenter *Walenty Ruray*. Contains Gothic sculptures and paintings.

CZACZ

MAP 4 ✦

Parish church, 14th–15th centuries, rebuilt in Mannerist/Baroque style, 1653, by *Cristoforo Bonadura the Elder*; interior and furniture second half of 18th century. Tower 1682.

CZANIEC

MAP 21

Country house, first half of 17th century, remodelled second half of 18th century.

CZARNCA

MAP 19

Church founded by Hetman Stefan Czarniecki, 1640–59. Houses small **museum** devoted to Czarniecki, hero of the wars against the Swedes in the 1650s.

CZARNE

MAP 17

Wooden **church**, 1793; painted decoration ca. 1800.

CZARNKÓW

MAP 9 ✦

Collegiate church, Gothic, 1570s, altered first half of 17th century and 18th century. Tomb of Maciej Czarnkowski, Castellan of Bydgoszcz, and his wife Anna Opalińska, Italian school ca. 1550; brass tomb plate of Stanisław Czarnkowski, 1602.

CZARNOLAS

MAP 20

Manor house, built third quarter of 19th century on site of an earlier manor house belonging to Jan Kochanowski (1530–84), the greatest Polish poet of the Renaissance, who retired here from the court and sang the glories of quiet country life in his poems. Houses small **museum** devoted to his life and work. **Chapel**, neo-Gothic, 1826–46.

CZARNOWĄSY (KLOSTERBRÜCKE)

MAP 11 ✦✦

Magnificent **Premonstratensian convent** (founded 1228), 1682 by *Johann Fröhlich*; decoration added 1784; furniture late 18th century. Prelates' house, 1730.

Wooden **cemetery church**, 1687 frescoes and furniture 18th century.

✦ CZCHÓW   MAP 22
Medieval trading town on route between Poland and Hungary.
Parish church 1346, expanded 1430; murals 14th and 15th century,
Renaissance tombs, by *Girolamo Canavesi* and others. Ruins of **castle**, 13th century, with good round keep. Wooden **houses** in market
square, 18th–19th centuries.

✦✦ CZEMIERNIKI   MAP 27
Renaissance/Mannerist **parish church** of St Stanisław, 1603; interesting stucco decoration of vault 1614, by *Jan Wolff*. **Villa** of Bishop
Henryk Firlej, ca. 1620; decorative parapet wall neo-Gothic, 1852.
Good example of Mannerist summer residence with strong
Palladian influence. Italian bastion system fortifications with
Mannerist gateway, 1622.

✦ CZERNA   MAP 4
Discalced Carmelites' monastery ('Desertum') founded by
Tenczyński family 1630s. The layout of the four courtyards round
the church in the middle is an imitation of El Escorial. Remains of
Hermitages, 1671–95. Good carvings in local black marble.

CZERNICE BOROWE   MAP 18
Parish church, Gothic, early 16th century. Characteristic Mazovian
village church, with typical roof gables.

✦ CZERNIEJEWO   MAP 9
Country house of General Józef Lipski, Baroque concept, neo-
Classical aspect, 1770–1800, expanded 20th century. Not particularly beautiful, but masses of allure.

✦ CZERSK   MAP 18
Once the capital of a Piast duchy. Ruined **castle** of the dukes of
Mazovia, brick, early 1400s; upper parts of towers added 15th and
16th centuries. Gate tower second quarter of 16th century. More of a
fortified space than an organic castle.

✦✦ CZERWIŃSK   MAP 17
Old market town on the Vistula. **Monastery of Canons Regular**
founded 1148 by Bishop Alexander of Malonne. The church is a
Romanesque basilica, second quarter of 12th century, with some
contemporary murals and stone details (especially the west

entrance portal, ca. 1170), and some Gothic and Renaissance. Monastery ca. 1529, rebuilt in Baroque style before 1633, partly reconstructed 1950s; former refectory, now chapel, with stellar vaulting; murals Gothic. Gate-tower 1497.

CZĘSTOCHOWA

MAP 12 ◆◆◆

The most important religious shrine in Poland, the seat of the famous 'Black Madonna'. Also a magnificent example of a fortified monastery. The Pauline Fathers, founded in 13th century Hungary under the patronage of the Anjou dynasty, took their name from St Paul the Hermit of Thebes (hence the symbol of the two rampant lions repeatedly worked into the decoration). They came to the hill site of Jasna Góra at Częstochowa in 1382 at the invitation of Władysław Duke of Opole, a relative and protégé of Louis of Anjou King of Hungary, who was educated by them at one of their monasteries in Hungary. The painting of the Black Madonna would appear to have come to Częstochowa in 1384, but where it came from and how it got there is the subject of continuing controversy. The picture's legend, written down in 1474 but probably dating

Pauline Monastery on Jasna Góra: 1 - Basilica, 2 - Chapel of the Blessed Virgin, 3 - Sacristy, 4 - Courtyard & entrance to basilica, 5 - Entrance to chapel of of the Blessed Virgin, 6 - Monastery, 7 - Knights' Hall, 8 - Museum, 9 - Arsenal, 10 - St James' Bastion, 11 - Jagiellon Gate, 12 - Lubomirski Gate, 13 - St Barbara's Bastion, 14 - St Roch's Bastion, 15 - Bastion of the Holy Trinity, 16 - Western Gate.

from half a century earlier, holds that the picture is a portrait of the Mother of God painted by St Luke the Evangelist on the table-top of her house in Jerusalem. According to this legend, the picture was acquired by the Emperor Constantine, who venerated it in Constantinople. The legend is confusing about how it came from Constantinople to Kiev, but it is possible that it might have been part of the religious dowry of Princess Anna who married Vladimir of Kiev in the 10th century and brought Christianity to Russia. From Kiev, the picture was taken to Halicz, and, apparently, after the Tatar destruction of Kiev, hidden in the castle of Bełz. There Duke Władysław of Opole, who was made lieutenant of these territories for the Polish Crown, found it. According to the experts, the picture itself is either Byzantine, dating from anywhere between the 4th and 9th centuries, or North Italian ca. 1325, but neither of these

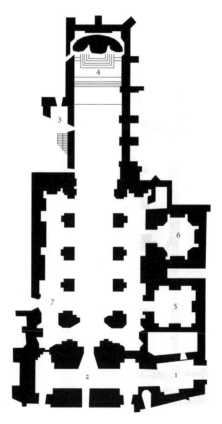

Basilica of the Holy Cross and the Nativity of the Blesssed Virgin: 1 - Porch, 2 - West porch, 3 - Sacristy, 4 - High altar, 5 - Dönhoff chapel, 6 - Jabłonowski chapel, 7 - Entrance to chapel of the Blessed Virgin.

theories can be tested in a satisfactory way; in 1430 a band of Hussite iconoclasts attacked Częstochowa and smashed all the ritual objects and images they could find, including the picture, which was broken into several pieces. As it was already an object of immense veneration, the picture was meticulously restored, which in effect meant that a new picture was painted over the remains of the old, incorporating some of the old elements, and adding some new ones, such as the two 'cuts' on the Madonna's cheek, which symbolise the desecration. The most important episode in the monastery's history was in 1655 when the monks and a handful of local nobles under the leadership of Father Augustyn Kordecki withstood a siege by overwhelming Swedish forces, a success that became the turning-point in the resistance to the Swedish invasion. This and various other moments have made Częstochowa synony-

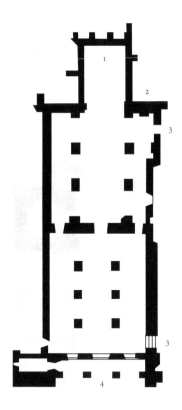

Chapel of the Blessed Virgin Mary: 1 - Altar with miraculous picture, 2 - Sacristy, 3 - Entrance to basilica, 4 - West door.

mous with the struggle for Polish independence.

The Gothic **church** of 1463 was rebuilt as a baroque basilica in the late 1600s, the original narrow shape giving it a very lofty appearance. Stuccoes and painted decoration by *Karl Dankwart*, 1690–3. High altar 1725–8, by *Giacomo Antonio Buzzini* and *Adam Karinger*; splendid rococo bishop's throne. Dönhoff chapel 1644–71, with fine stuccoes by *Franciszek Zaor*; chapel of the Holy Relics 1625; above it, Jabłonowski chapel, 1754.

Chapel of The Virgin Mary 1640–4, stuccoes after 1650; altar of ebony and silver framing miraculous picture of Black Virgin . Tower 1600–20, superstructure ca. 1700.

 Treasury museum – magnificent collection of liturgical and sacral art from 15th century to the present day, and a wide variety of objects deposited as votive offerings over the centuries, including jewels, Ottoman booty, arms and armour, and some 17th and 18th century painting and sculpture. The 'dresses' with whichthe picture is bedecked, are covered in an astonishing assemblage of fine jewels and ornaments, dating from the middle ages to the 17th century. Monastic buildings, first half of 17th century, rebuilt 18th century. Knights' Hall, 1647.Buildings around courtyard, 17th-18th centuries. Earth-and-masonry bastion fortifications, Dutch system, after 1620; St James' bastion 1674, by *Krzysztof Mieroszewski*, others 1720–9 and 1742–5, by *Christian Dahlke*; ravelin ca. 1676. Lubomirski Gate, stone, 1723; Stanisław Augustus Gate, 1767; Jagiellon Gate, first half of 17th centur.

Parish church of St Zygmunt, first half of 17th century, rebuilt 1780s. Church of St Barbara 1637–42, remodelled 1892–6.

CZOCHA (TSCHOCHA)   MAP 5

Sucha **Castle** of the Piast dukes of Świdnica, 14th century, destroyed by fire 1793; rebuilt early 20th century by *Bodo Eberhard* as a pseudo-historical residence.

CZORSZTYN   MAP 21

Ruins of **castle** founded by Kazimierz the Great, 14th century. Spectacular position commanding the gorge of the Dunajec river.

◆◆ CZYŻÓW SZLACHECKI   MAP 27

Country house of Castellan August Czyżowski, Baroque, 1740s, a refined and decorated version of a typical Polish manor-house of the period.

DĄBCZE   MAP 11

Timber **church**, Gothic 1668. Wooden **windmill** 1766.

DĄBROWA TARNOWSKA   MAP 22
Parish church, wooden, 1771. **Gate** of Lubomirski residence 1697.

DĄBRÓWKA POLSKA   MAP 22 ✦
Wooden **parish church**, ca. 1410, tower 1927. Painted ceiling second quarter of 17th century.

DĄBRÓWKA STARZEŃSKA   MAP 29
Renaissance **castle** of Kmita family, second half of 16th century, later the property of the Starzeński family. Gutted 1947. Park with neo-Romanesque Starzeński funerary **chapel**, ca. 1900.

DARŁOWO   MAP 7 ✦
Medieval town with **castle** of princes of Pomerania, third quarter of 14th century, expanded 16th–17th centuries (now **Museum**). **Parish church**, late 14th century, expanded 15th–16th centuries. **Church** of St George, 15th century, rebuilt 1502. Chapel of St Gertrude first half of 15th century: unusual central Gothic building. **Town Hall**, 1725.

DĘBINKI   MAP 18
Neo-Classical **manor house**, 19th century.

DĘBLIN   MAP 27
Grand **country residence** built 1779 by *Dominik Merlini* for Count Michał Wandalin Mniszech. In the elaborate **park**, laid out by *J.K.Szuch*, there is a very fine neo-Classical **mausoleum**. The house was inherited by Mniszech's son-in-law, Prince Jabłonowski, who was sent to Siberia for taking part in the Decembrist rising of 1825. In 1842 Tsar Nicholas I gave the estate to General Paskievich, Prince of Warsaw, for his part in putting down the Polish Insurrection of 1830–1. The Russian fortress of Iwangorod, one of the largest 19th–century fortification complexes, was begun nearby in 1837 and added to until the end of the century. Since 1928, this is the Polish Air Force officers' training school.

DĘBNO   MAP 22 ✦
Castle of Castellan Jakub Dębiński, 1470–80, with Renaissance sgraffiti, 1586, by *Jan de Simon*; some alterations 17th–19th centuries. One of very few surviving castles of this period. Houses small **museum** with one or two nice odds and ends. Also late Gothic **church**, 1500.

Highly important and spectacular wooden **church** of St Michael the Archangel, second half of 15th century; tower 1601; painted decoration and furniture ca. 1500, altar with triptych early 16th century. Everything inside and out is made of wood and painted all over, largely with the use of stencils.

DĘBNO   MAP 9
Parish church, 1447, restored 1910. Neo-Classical belfry, 1829, by *Sylwester Szpilowski.*

DOBCZYCE   MAP 21
Parish church, neo-Classical, 1834. **Castle** built by Kazimierz the Great, first half of 14th century, rebuilt late 16th century. Now houses small **museum** of regional interest as well as some archaeological objects, arms and armour, etc.

◆◆   DOBRE MIASTO   MAP 15
Collegiate church, 1357–91, a huge three-nave hall church with stellar vaulting. Tower superstructure ca. 1500. Collegiate buildings, with cloister, 1347. Chapel of St Nicholas ca. 1740. **Protestant church**, neo-Classical, 1830-3, by *Karl Friedrich Schinkel.*

DOBROWODA   MAP 20
Parish church, originally Gothic, rebuilt in Renaissance style 1524–5.

DOBRZEŃ WIELKI.   MAP 11
Wooden **church**, 1680.

Impressive and interesting, if not beautiful **country house** of
General August Gorzeński, with outbuildings, farm buildings, and,
in the landscape **park**, a circular Masonic Lodge and a lovely pavil-
lion, all neo-Classical, 1798–9, by *Stanisław Zawadzki*. Inside, frescoes by *Franciszek Smuglewicz*. Gorzeński, a huge man, was a
senior freemason, hence the groundplan of the house is a carpenter's square.

DOŁHOBYCZÓW   MAP 28
Ruin of **country house**, early 19th century, expanded for Edward
Rastawiecki with addition of curved colonnades and two outbuild-
ings, neo-Classical, 1837, by *Antonio Corazzi* and *Antoni Beck*, ruin.
Romantic pavilion and neo-Classical granary 1830s.

DOLSK   MAP 11 ✦✦
Parish church, 1474, with delightful Baroque vicarage, 1770.
Wooden succursal **church** in Gothic tradition, 1618. Ranges of
palace of the bishops of Poznań, Baroque, ca. 1670, rebuilt mid-19th
century.

DOMANIEWICE   MAP 17
Chapel of the Celesta family, Kraków merchant patricians,
Baroque, 1633. Charming Rococo organ case in shape of Polish
eagle, before 1759.

DOWSPUDA   MAP 23
Ruined **country house**, neo-Gothic, 1822–3, by *Henryk Marconi*,
built for the Napoleonic veteran General Ludwik Pac, a frantic
Anglophile who tried to import what he considered to be English
styles and even names on to his estate.

DROBIN   MAP 17
Parish church, 1477. Kryski family tombs, Mannerist, based on the
design of *Michelangelo* for the Medici tomb in florence.

DROGOSZE   MAP 16
Dönhoff family **country house**, Baroque, 1710–16, by *Jan de Bodt*
and *Jan van Collas*; chapel 1725, rebuilt in neo-Gothic style mid-
19th century.

DROHICZYN   MAP 25 ✦
Medieval market town on trade route to Russia. **Franciscan
monastery**, second half of 17th century. Bell-Tower 18th century

Jesuit college (later Piarist) **church**, 1696–1709. College building 1661–1710, Piarist college building 1747. **Church** and ruins of Benedictine convent, 1744.

DRWALEW   MAP 18
Country house, neo-Classical, early 19th century, by *Franciszek Lessel*. Late Baroque **church** 1768–74, by *Jakub Fontana*.

✦ DRZECZKOWO   MAP 11
Timber church, Baroque, 1775. In a landscape **park** nearby, two **manor houses**, one late Baroque, 18th century, the other neo-Gothic, 2nd half of 19th century.

✦ DRZEWICA   MAP 20
Castle of Primate Mikołaj Drzewicki, 1535. **Church** of St Luke, 1462, expanded 1914.

✦✦ DUKLA   MAP 22
Parish church founded by Mniszech family, Rococo, 1764–5; furniture contemporary; elegant figure tomb of Amalia Mniszech née Brühl, 1773. **Bernardine monastery**, 1761–4, rebuilt 1899–1902. **Mniszech country house**, 1638–1709, remodelled with addition of two outbuildings, 1764–5, modified 1875, burnt 1944.

DYNÓW   MAP 29
Parish church. Mannerist, 1604–17, rebuilt 1663. Artisans' **houses**, 18th and 19th centuries.

DYS   MAP 27
Parish church, second half of 16th century, remodelled in Renaissance style after 1610. Interesting stucco decoration.

DZIAŁDOWO (SOLDAU)   MAP 17
Ruined **castle** of Teutonic Knights, 1340s.

DZIEKANOWICE   MAP 21
Parish **church**, stone, Romanesque, 1220s, new nave 1645, expanded 18th century.

DZIEKTARZEWO   MAP 17
Parish church, first half of 16th century.

DZIERZGOŃ   MAP 15
Once the site of a Teutonic Knights' Castle. **Parish church**, first half

of 14th century. **Reformed Franciscans' monastery** and Church, originally 15th century, rebuilt in Baroque style 17th–18th centuries.

DZIERZĄŹNO WIELKIE   MAP 2 ✦

Church (originally Protestant) timber, 1595. Altars and furniture late Renaissance.

DZIERŻONIÓW   MAP 6

Medieval weaving centre. **Parish church**, 13th century, remodelled 1556–85; organ loft Mannerist, 1586. Neo-Classical **Protestant church**, with oval layout, 1795–8 by *Karl Gottfried Langhans*.

DZIĘGIELÓW   MAP 14

Baroque **country house**, 1770s and late 19th century.

ELBLĄG (ELBING)   MAP 15   ✦✦

Important Baltic trading port established as a counterbalance to the powerful city of Gdańsk. It was the centre of the English Baltic trade in the Middle Ages, and contained the largest community of Scotsmen outside Scotland until the 19th century. It never enjoyed the political autonomy of Gdańsk, and suffered as a result of changing hands between Polish and Prussian rulers several times in the course of history. But it never gave up trying to compete with Gdańsk, and was an architectural showpiece before the war.

Parish church, 13th century, expanded first half of 14th century, side chapels, 15th century. Gutted 1945. 4 Late Gothic triptychs. Bronze font 1387, Master *Bernhauser*.

Dominican monastery, founded 1238; chancel ca. 1250, nave 1320s; expanded ca. 1510. **Church** of Corpus Christi, ca. 1410, expanded 1696, ruin. **Town walls** 13th–14th century. Gate 1319, superstructure 1420–30. **School**, founded 1535, in which Jan Amos Komensky taught for a time, houses a small regional historical **museum**. The Old Town, virtually destroyed in 1945 is being rebuilt in a variety of modern styles, but keeping to the shapes and sizes of the original buildings, and incorporating whatever architectural elements have survived.

FALENTY   MAP 18

Country house built for Opacki family, ca. 1620, rebuilt in Romantic manner 1852–7, by *Franciszek Maria Lanci* for Count Aleksander Przeździecki. Landscape **park**, 1780s, by *Szymon Bogumił Zug*. The house was caught in the middle of the Battle of Raszyn in 1809, when Prince Józef Poniatowski leading the Army of the Duchy of Warsaw defeated the Austrians.

This small fortified town and fishing port, founded ca. 1270 by the bishops of Warmia (Ermeland) became their principal seat and capital - the prince-bishops of Warmia were temporal as well as spiritual rulers of their bishopric. The famous astronomer Mikołaj Kopernik (Copernicus) spent most of his life here, his post as canon of the cathedral giving him the time and the opportunity to carry on his work.

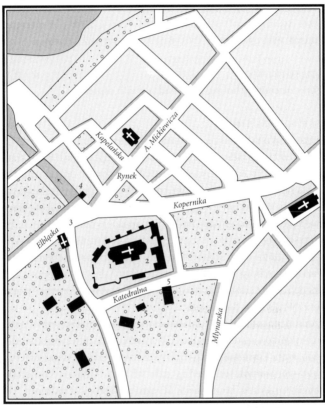

Cathedral of the Assumption and St Andrew [**1**], a huge brick hall church, 14th century. Chapel of Bishop Krzysztof Szembek 1732-5, with painted decoration by *Mathias Mayer*. Gothic polyptych 1504; altar painting of St Anne by *Bartłomiej Strobel*; Baroque furniture, 1630–1785; numerous tomb slabs, tombs and epitaphs, 14th–18th centuries. Amusing Baroque organ and gallery, 1683-5, by *Daniel Nitrowski*.

Palace of the bishops of Warmia [**2**], ca. 1530, remodelled 1727. Now houses **museum** dedicated to Copernicus, containing some of his instruments and books.

Canons' houses [**5**], 15th–18th century. Protestant church [**3**].

Water tower [4], **Fortifications** of cathedral hill with towers and gates, second half of 14th and later; southern gate with two towers, ca. 1530.

Very folkloric highland village. **Parish church**, ca. 1300, rebuilt 1750s, tower superstructure Renaissance, ca. 1600. Chapel of Our Lady of Carmel 1764. Furniture Rococo. Belfry ca. 1760. Renaissance **country house**, ca. 1600.

Parish church, mid-14th century, tower ca. 1500. **Country house**, 1589, repeatedly rebuilt up to 19th century.

Founded by the Polish king Mieszko I around the year 980 as a Polish outlet to the sea at the mouth of the Vistula, Gdańsk quickly became dominated by foreign traders, most notably Dutchmen and Germans. But in spite of adopting a somewhat Germanic culture and joining the Hansa, the city remained fiercely independent in outlook. In 1308 the Teutonic Knights put the city to fire and sword, and held on to it until 1454, when it reverted to Poland. In the 16th and 17th centuries, Gdańsk became one of the busiest seaports in Europe and by far the largest on the Baltic. Grain from all over Poland and shipbuilding materials (timber, tar, hemp, etc) from the forests of Lithuania were exported all over Europe, at huge profit to the merchants of Gdańsk. The city became an emporium in which the whole of Poland bought foreign and colonial produce. To satisfy its own inhabitants as well as the rest of Poland, Gdańsk became a flourishing centre of artistic craftsmanship, producing fine gold and silverware, clocks and furniture. Its renowned *Gymnasium Academicum* and *Collegium Medicum* earned it a strong position in the intellectual life of northern Europe. Its inhabitants included the great astronomer Johannes Hevelius and Jan Dantyszek, and it gave birth to Daniel Gabriel Fahrenheit and Arthur Schopenhauer. This great multi-ethnic metropolis acquired its own status within the Polish Commonwealth, and jealously guarded a number of privileges which gave it wide-ranging autonomy. This favoured status, which it would never enjoy in any other situation, accounts for the city's strong attachment to Poland, whenever it came under threat from outside.

In 1792 the Prussians attacked it once more, and it became part of first Prussia and then of the German Empire. In 1919 the Paris Peace Conference could not decide whether to award it to the newly independent Poland or to Germany, so it left it as a 'Free City'. This status made it all but useless to Poland, which built its own port at Gdynia along the coast, which harmed Gdańsk. And it was the 'Danzig Corridor' that was the ostensible bone of contention that led to the German invasion of Poland and the start of the Second World War. The first shots of the war were fired on the Polish military post of Westerplatte by the battlecruiser *Schleswig-Holstein*. In 1939 the city was incorporated into the Reich, but became Polish once again in 1945. Unfortunately, its 'liberation' by the Red Army in 1944 flattened most of the city, while virtually the entire German population fled westwards.

Gdańsk was resettled with a mixed population, mainly drawn from north-eastern parts of Poland that became Lithuania or the Byelorussian SSR in 1945. Between that and the extensive rebuilding that went on throughout the 1950s and 1960s, it was some time before the city forged a new identity for itself. This began to take shape very distinctly in the 1970s, on the twin rails of cultural revival and political dissent. This culminated in the great epos of Solidarity, which was born in Gdańsk in August 1980. Although things have moved on very rapidly since then, the city has retained a broad-shouldered quality, and is one of the most vibrant and exciting in Poland at the moment.

Large tracts of the old city were painstakingly reconstructed by the Poles after the war. This was done with such sensitivity that it does not jar, and it is very difficult to tell in some places which parts of a building are new and which are original (in the case of dwelling-houses, often only the facade was reconstructed, for obvious reasons). Gdańsk is a showpiece of northern Gothic architecture and also a unique example of Dutch Renaissance urban architecture in collision with Polish Renaissance and Mannerist styles. The end-result is delightful, and the facades of the merchants' houses lining the streets of the old town, dating from the 15th to the 18th centuries, are a pleasure to look at.

Main Town

✦✦✦ **Parish church** of St Mary [1] founded 1245 by Świętopełk II. The largest ecclesiastical edifice in Poland, and one of the most impressive. The aisles are the same height as the nave, which, combined with the huge and frequent windows, the slenderness of the pillars and the stellar and crystal vaulting, gives the building a sense of lightness. Chancel and transept completed 1447, nave and aisles 1484–98. Stellar vaulting 1498–1502, by *Heinrich Hetzel*. Altars and sculptures Gothic. Madonna and crucifix ca. 1415; free-standing tomb of the banker Simon Bahr and his wife Judith, Mannerist,

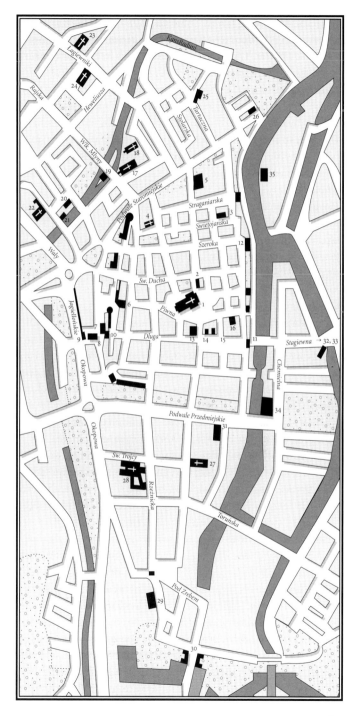

Łagiewniki
Kanalhadum
Rajska
Hewebiusza
Wlk. Młyny
Stolarska
Tartaczna
Podwale Staromiejskie
Straganiarska
Swietojanska
Szeroka
Wały
Jagiellonskie
Sw. Ducha
Piwna
Dluga
Okopowa
Chmielna
Stagiewna → 32, 33
Podwale Przedmiejskie
Okopowa
Sw. Trojcy
Rzeznicka
Toruńska
Pod Zrebem

23
24
25
26
18
19
17
5
20
22
21
4
3
12
2
6
1
16
10
13 14 15
9 8
11
34
31
27
28
29
30
35

1620, by *Abraham van den Blocke*; numerous epitaphs and tomb-slabs 15th–18th centuries, including a good group of 16th–17th century Mannerist epitaphs with figures and illustrations. Royal **chapel** [**2**]founded by king Jan III Sobieski, 1678–81, by *Bartholomäus Ranish* after *Tilman van Gameren*. Sculptural decoration by *Andreas Schlüter*. The only Italianate building in this northern and typically hanseatic city.

✦ **Church** of St John [**3**], 1371–c1415, expanded with addition of tower mid-15th century Altar early 17th century, *Abraham van den Blocke*.

✦ **Dominican church** of St Nicholas [**4**]; chancel 14th century, main body with side chapels 1487. Furniture Baroque and Rococo; paintings Mannerist-Baroque; crucifix Late Gothic, 1520, by master *Alexander*.

✦ **Hospital church** of the Holy Ghost [**5**], 14th–15th century. Hospital, Mannerist 1647.

✦✦ Great **Arsenal** [**6**], Mannerist, 1602-5, by *Anthonis van Opbergen*.

✦✦ **Seat of St George's Fraternity** [**7**], 1487–94, by *J.Glotau*, spires second half of 16th century. An interesting example of late Gothic 'neo-Romanesque' architecture.

✦ **City walls** ca. 1350, superstructure 14th-15th century; outer ring ca. 1380. Main (western) entrance to the city, with 'Więzienna' (Prison) Tower and foregate [**8**], ca. 1410, superstructure ca. 1507. 'Wyżynna' (Tall) Gate [**9**], 1586-8, by *Johann Kramer*, facade 1588, by *Willem van den Blocke*. 'Żuraw' (Crane) Gate [**12**], 1443-4, with wooden crane built in 1483 (now Maritime **Museum**). 'Zielona' (Green) Gate [**11**], built onto burgher's house, 1564-8, by *Johann Kramer* and *Regnier of Amsterdam*, rebuilt 1831. 'Złota' (Golden) Gate [**10**], Mannerist, 1612–14, by *Abraham van den Blocke*.

✦✦ Main **Town Hall** [**13**], 1379-82, expanded with addition of superstructure and tower, Gothic, 1465 and 1486-92; spire 1559-60, by *Dirk Daniels*; portal Baroque, 1768, by *Daniel Eggert*. Richly decorated interiors include the Great Council Chamber (Red Chamber), 1593-6 by *Jan Vredeman de Vries*.

✦✦ **Artus Court** [**14**], 1476-81, facade rebuilt in Mannerist style 1616-7 by *Abraham van den Blocke*. Facing it, Neptune Fountain, early 17th century.

Of the **town houses**, with their delightful facades, the following deserve attention: in Chlebnicka Street, no. 16, the Angel House [**16**], 1570, by *Johann Kramer*; in Długa Street, No. 12, Uphagen's House, 1776, by *J.B.Dreyer*, No. 28, the Ferber or Adam and Eve House, 1560, No. 35, 'the Lions' Castle', 1569, No. 41, the Golden or Steffens' House [**15**], 1609-17, by *Johann Voigt*, No. 43, Gdańsk Hall or Assessors' House, ca. 1500, rebuilt 17th-2nd half of 18th century;

and in Piwna Street, no. 1, Schlüter's House, 1640, by *Andreas Schlüter the Elder*.

Old Town:

Parish church of St Catherine [**17**], second half of 14th century; ✦✦ tower 1450–86, chancel and very ornate late Gothic vault first quarter of 16th century. Gothic triptych, early 16th century; painting Mannerist, 1609, by *Anton Moller*.

Brigittine Nuns' church [**18**], 1396–1402, expanded 1514; western ✦ chancel 1602.

Great Mill [**19**]on a bend in Radunia river, second half of 14th century. Old **Town Hall** [**20**], 1586–95, by *Antonis van Opbergen*; paint- ✦ ings mid-17th century, by *Adolf Boy*.

House of the Abbots of Pelplin [**21**] (3 Elżbietańska Street) with ✦ interesting front elevation, 1612.

Hospital church of St Elizabeth [**22**], ca. 1400. Hospital, 1752–3, by *Krzysztof Strzycki*.

Hospital church of St James [**23**], 1432.

Polish Post-Office [**25**], built as a hospital in 1844, this was the only Polish state building in the Free City, and the scene of a bloody battle on 1 September 1939.

Old Suburb:

Parish church of SS Peter and Paul [**27**], 1393–1486, expanded ca. ✦ 1500, vaulted 1514; tower 1486–1500.

Franciscan monastery church [**28**], chancel 1420–95, main body ✦✦ with side chapels ca. 1470–1514; pulpit 1541. Adjacent **chapel** of St Anne, 1484. Monastic building, first quarter of 16th century, rebuilt 17th and 19th century. Now houses Pomeranian **Museum** : Contains ✦✦✦ very good collection of Gothic sculpture and some painting; the works (mainly portraits) of Gdańsk artists of the Baroque era; and some works by Polish artists of the 19th century. There is also a surprisingly rich collection of Flemish, Dutch and Italian painting, including a very fine Last Judgment by *Hans Memling*. There is also a large collection of decorative arts from the middle ages to the present day, with a broad range of foreign works, as one might expect in a city with such wide international trade contacts.

Lesser **Arsenal** [**29**], Mannerist, 1643–5, and two gates, 1626–8, by ✦ *Jan Strakowski*.

Secondary school [**31**] (Targ Maślany Street), in German Gothic style, 1837, by *Karl Friedrich Schinkel*.

Lower Town and **Granary Islands:**

Church of St Barbara [**32**], ca. 1500, southern aisle Baroque, 1728, ✦✦ tower 1619. **Bastion** of St Gertrude, c 1600, by *Antonis van Opbergen*. Five **bastions** [**33**], 1621–36, by *Cornelis van dem Bosch*.

Granaries [**34**]: 'Mouth-of-the-Vistula', 18th century (53 Chmielna ✦

St); 'The Crown', 1755 (59 Chmielna St); Oliwa Granary, 15th century (11 Ołowianka St); Royal Granary, ca. 1620, by *Jan Strakowski* (14 Ołowianka St). **Maritime Museum [35]** in three former grain-stores.

Podgórze:
Hospital church of Corpus Christi, 15th century, expanded 1687–8 by *Bartholomäus Ränisch*. Hospital, 1780. Priest's house, 1762.

Wisłoujście:
At the straits leading into the port of Gdańsk, a unique **light-house**, dating from 1482. Circular building 1562, and adjacent barracks 1656. Fort with bastions 1572–1587 by *Anthonis van Opbergen*. Gate 1602. Outer ring of bastions 1626.

GĘBICE MAP 10
Parish church, ca. 1500.

GIDLE MAP 19 ✦✦
Dominican monastery and pilgrimage centre, 1632–44, by *Georg Burszt*; furniture 17th–18th century. Monastery building 1640–55. **Carthusian church**, 1754. Wooden **church** of St Mary Magdalen, 15th–16th century.

GIEBUŁTÓW MAP 21
Parish church Gothic/Renaissance 1600; murals 1616.

GIECZ MAP 9 ✦
Parish church of Our Lady and St Nicholas, stone, Romanesque, second half of 12th century.
In nearby GRODZISZCZKO, surviving foundations of 10th century pre-Romanesque **palatium** and **chapel** of the princes of Gniezno, destroyed 1038.

GIERAŁTOWICE MAP 14 ✦
Wooden **parish church**, 1534, tower 1844; painted ceiling ca. 1534.

GIERCZYCE MAP 20
Wooden **parish church** of St Nicholas, 1708; furniture Rococo.

GIŁOWICE MAP 21 ✦
Wooden **parish church** of St Andrew, before 1547. Surrounding chapels and figures 18th–19th centuries.

GIŻYCE MAP 12
Wooden **manor house**, Baroque, mid-18th century.

GŁADYSZE MAP 15 ✦✦
Dohna family **country house**, 1702–4, by *Jan de Bodt*, decoration Rococo, expanded 19th century. Kitchen, stables and riding school 18th century.

GŁĘBOWICE MAP 21
Country house, 1646, expanded 1773.
Wooden **church** of St Mary, 1518, rebuilt 1782.

GŁĘBOWICE MAP 11
Carmelite monastery, founded 1654, built 1676 and 1746–62; furniture Baroque, first half of 18th century.

Parish church, wooden, 1573 and 17th–18th centuries.

This busy industrial and mining centre can be said to be where the Second World War actually started. With his well-documented horror of appearing as the aggressor, Hitler contrived to get Poland to go to war on Germany. In a complex operation code-named 'Canned Goods', a dozen German convicts were taken out of their jail, dressed up in *Wehrmacht* uniforms and posted in and around the radio-station at Gleiwitz, then a few miles inside Germany. A dozen SS soldiers were dressed in Polish uniforms and in the early hours of 1 September 1939 they actually took a couple of steps on to Polish territory so as to be able literally to invade Germany. Having done so, they marched on Gleiwitz, attacked the radio-station, shot all the convicts and made a broadcast over the radio announcing that the Polish army had begun its invasion of the Reich. A million German soldiers tramped into Poland in righteous self-defence a couple of hours later. The radio-station seems to have disappeared.

Parish church, second half of 15th century, tower 1504; painted decoration in one of the chapels ca. 1470; furniture 17th–18th century.

Church of St Bartholomew: chancel 15th century, nave and tower early 17th century.

Reformed Franciscans' monastery [now Redemptorist), 1655-73; church expanded 1924–26.

✦ GŁOGÓW (GLOGAU)   MAP 4
Once an important market town and capital of a medieval duchy, it was badly damaged in 1945.

Collegiate church, 1413–66, with 13th-century Romanesque remnants. Side chapels 17th–18th centuries. Chapel of St Anne, 1441, rebuilt 17th–18th century.

Parish church of St Nicholas, late 14th century; aisles of chancel and chapels 15th century; Loreto chapel rebuilt 1672; carved portal mid-14th century. **Jesuit church**, 1694–1724, by *Giulio Simonetti*.

Tower of **castle** 13th century, rest 1652–69; rebuilt second half of 18th century. Town walls, 14th century. Bastion fortifications 1657-1720.

✦✦ GŁOGÓWEK (OBERGLOGAU)   MAP 13
Medieval seat of the Piast princes of Opole, from 1561 to 1945 property of the Oppersdorff family. Impressive Oppersdorff **castle**, Renaissance, 1560s and later; three wings added 1606-47. Gate 1671-2. Chapel 1645-68, rebuilt 1743-81. Important **parish church,** built

1380; chancel vault 15th–16th century; main body and towers Baroque, 1776–81. Stucco work by *Johann Schubert*, painted decoration by *Franz Sebastini*, and furniture Rococo, 1776–81. Oppersdorff chapel early 1400s, tomb Baroque, 1634, by *Sebastiano Sala*. **Franciscan monastery** (founded 1264). Church of St Bartholomew, 15th century, rebuilt in Baroque style, with addition of transept, tower and Loreto chapel, 1628–37. St Anthony's chapel, 1651, by *Peter Schuller*. Painted decoration and furniture Baroque and Rococo, ca. 1770, by *Franz Sebastini* and *Johann Schubert*. Monastery building, Baroque, 17th-18th century. **Church** and **hospital** of St Nicholas, Baroque, 1773. **Town Hall**, Renaissance, 1608. **House** in market square, Baroque, 18th century, and one, No. 18, Renaissance, first half of 17th century.

GŁOGOWIEC MAP 17
Parish church, Gothic and Renaissance, 1560s by *Giovanni Battista de Venezia*.

GŁUBCZYCE MAP 13 ✦
Medieval town on trade route to Bohemia. **Parish church**, late 13th–early 14th century, transept and chancel neo-Gothic, 1903–7. **Franciscan monastery** (founded 1448), 1753–70. Church, 1756–8, by *Josef Ignaz Topper*; furniture Rococo. Chapel of StFabian and St Sebastian, 1501.

GŁUCHOŁAZY MAP 13 ✦
Parish church; double-tower facade and portal second half of 13th century, main body 1731, by *Christoph Tausch*. Furniture Baroque and Rococo. Tower adjoining upper gate, late 14th century, superstructure 1631.

GŁUCHÓW
Parish church, Baroque, 1786. **Manor house**, 1793.

GŁUCHY MAP 18
Delightful wooden **manor house**, late 18th century. Birthplace of the poet Cyprian Kamil Norwid (1821–83). Almost unique in that, being privately owned throughout, it was never vandalised and, while being lovingly maintained by the present owners, it has not been over-restored, and preserves the natural atmosphere of a small manor-house of this type.

GNIEW (MEWE) MAP 8
Small town lying on the bank of the Vistula in the shadow of a

Teutonic Knights' **castle**, 1280s, rebuilt 1667–99 and after 1772, burnt 1922. **Parish church** of St Nicholas, after 1350, partly reconstructed 19th century.

This was the principal early stronghold of the Piast dynasty which in effect created Poland, and is therefore the cradle of the Polish state. It is also, importantly, a place of great religious significance. It was here, in the year 966, that the Polish prince Mieszko I accepted baptism for himself and his subjects. It was from here that the Bohemian bishop Wojciech (Adalbertus) set out to convert the heathen Prussians, who martyred him. And it was here that his body, ransomed by Mieszko's son Bolesław, was brought. Wojciech was canonised and became patron saint of Poland, and in the year 1000 Gniezno became the archbishopric which administered the Church in Poland (until a few years ago, the Archbishop of Gniezno was the Primate of Poland). In that same year 1000 the Emperor Otto III came on a pilgrimage to the grave of St Wojciech. He was so impressed by the bearing and competence of Bolesław the Brave that he named him '*Princeps Palatinus*' and crowned him with a tiara taken from his own brow. With the permission of the Pope, Bolesław was crowned King of Poland here in 1024. From

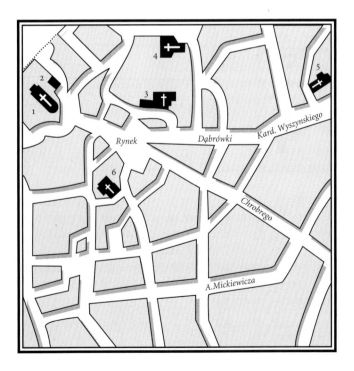

then on Gniezno was the place where kings of Poland were crowned until 1320, although already in 1138 the capital had in effect been moved to Kraków, and after that date the city declined in significance, becoming a sleepy backwater.

Cathedral of the Assumption and St Wojciech [1]. Choir with ✦✦✦ ambulatorium and radiating chapels 1342-72, by Archbishop Jarosław Skotnicki, main body 14th-15th century. Two Gothic portals and southern Tower comleted 1415, northern tower from 1528. The church was repeatedly altered and re-gothicised after the last war. Under the floor there are remnants of a pre-Romanesque basilica dating from ca. 977, whichbecame a cathedral in 1000, and of a second, Romanesque basilica from the 11th century.

1 – South door

2 – Towers

3 – North porch

4 – Potocki chapel

5 – Gembicki chapel

6 – Kołudzki chapel

7 – Baranowski chapel

8 – Dzierzgowski chapel

9 – Łubieński chapel

10 – Old chapter house

11 – Prelates' sacristy

Most of the chapels were rebuilt during the 17th–18th centuries as sepulchral chapels of bishops and canons, with portals, grilles, tombs and furniture. Baranowski chapel, ca. 1610; Kołudzki chapel, 1647; Potocki chapel, 1727–30, by *Pompeo Ferrari*; Łubieński chapel, ca. 1778. Prelates' sacristy, 1780, by *Ephraim Schröger*. The church contains some 70 tombs and epitaphs, including those of St Wojciech (replaced by the silver reliquiary below), 1478–86, by *Hans Brandt*; of Primate Jakub of Sienno, bronze relief, ca. 1480; the wonderful red marble tomb slab (now on the wall) of Primate

Zbigniew Oleśnicki, 1495, by *Veit Stoss*; 4 tomb slabs funded by Primate Jan Łaski, after 1537: that of Primate Andrzej Krzycki, after 1537, by *Giovanni-Maria Padovano*; of Primate Mikołaj Dzierzgowski, Renaissance, 1554, by *Girolamo Canavesi* and *Padovano*; of Primate Wojciech Baranowski, ca. 1615; of Primate Wawrzyniec Gembicki, 1636–42, by *Sebastiano Sala*. Cathedral **doors** with scenes depicting the life of St Wojciech, bronze, ca. 1170, one of the masterpieces of Romanesque art. Triptych ca. 1400;

splendid Berniniesque silver reliquary-coffin of St Wojciech, Baroque, 1662, by *Peter van den Rennen*. Treasury, with good collection of liturgical objects and silver, archives and chapter library with collection of illuminated manuscripts.

✦   **Collegiate church** of St George [2], Romanesque, 12th century, rebuilt in Baroque style 1782 by *Bernhard Langweber*.

✦   **Franciscan monastery** [3] founded ca. 1259 by Bolesław the Pious and the Blessed Jolanta. Church after 1270, southern aisle (Poor Clares' oratory) 13th–14th century, tower 15th century; reconstructed after 1613, rebuilt in Baroque style, facade second half of 18th century, interior re-Gothicized 1930–2. Monastery building after 1613, rebuilt in Baroque style 1755–72.

✦✦   **Monastery of Canons Regular** of the Holy Sepulchre with church of St John [4], brick with sculptural decoration of artificial stone, remodelled 1340s after a raid by the Teutonic Knights. Tower 15th–16th centuries. Important murals, third quarter of 14th century.

Church of St Michael [5], first quarter of 15th century, rebuilt 1811–5; tower 1900.

Church of the Holy Trinity [6], 1420-30, reconstructed 1613-32, altered 1687 and 1787.

GNOJNIK MAP 22
Parish church, stone, ca. 1380.

GOŁĄB MAP 27 ✦✦
Parish Church of St Florian and St Catherine, Mannerist, 1628–36.
Very ornate chapel supposedly modelled on the *Casa Santa* at
Loreto, commissioned by Chancellor Jerzy Ossoliński, with
ceramic sculptures of the prophets, Baroque, ca. 1640. Organ case
ca. 1641, by *Stefan Michelski.*

GOLCOWA MAP 29
Wooden **parish church** of St Barbara, before 1589, expanded 1885–7.

GOŁCZA MAP 21
Wooden **parish church** of St Francis Xavier, Baroque, 1657.

GOLISZEW MAP 12
Parish church, neo-Classical, 1825–37, by *Franciszek Reinstein.*

GOLUB-DOBRZYŃ MAP 10 ✦✦
Picturesque little town with a **castle** of theTeutonic Knights,
1302–6, rebuilt by Princess Anna Vasa; parapet wall, 1623.
Parish church, 1293–1350, with Baroque altar, 1640.
Town walls, early 1300s, expanded ca. 1425.

GOŁUCHÓW MAP 12 ✦
A rather unexpected sight in the Polish countryside. This **castle**,
built in the early 1600s in the Renaissance style by the Leszczyński
family, was transformed between 1872 and 1885 by Countess Izabela
Działyńska née Czartoryska in French Renaissance style, by
Zygmunt Gorgolewski and *Maurice Ouradou* after *Eugene Viollet-
le-Duc's* idea. Original architectural and sculptural elements and
even cordoba leather wall-coverings, 15th-17th centuries, brought
from France and Italy by Działyńska were incorporated into the
building, which is a very high-class pastiche. It stands in a finely
laid-out park, which contains an arboretum planted 1876-99. The
castle used to contain Countess Izabela's world-famous collection
of Etruscan vases, Limoges enamels, antique glass and ironwork,
but this was mostly pillaged during the war, and what is left is now
in the National Museums in Warszaw and Poznań. The exhibits on
view at the moment are little more than an overflow from the
Poznań National Museum.

✦ GÓRA MAP 4
Parish church, 1457–1552; hall church with radiating chapels.
Protestant church, 1744, incorporating tower of former town hall,
Gothic, 14th–15th century.

✦✦ GÓRA KALWARIA MAP 18
A typically counter-Reformation conceit of building a town supposedly following the ground-plan of Jerusalem, complete with
'Calvary', '*Via Dolorosa*' and other holy sites, 1666. (See also
Kalwaria Pacławska and Kalwaria Zebrzydowska). **Bernardine
church** and monastery founded by Marshal Franciszek Bieliński,
1755–9, by *Jakub Fontana*. **Church** of the Holy Cross, late 17th century, rebuilt 1791.
Town Hall, 1829–34; and **butchers' stalls**, 1836, neo-Classical, both
by *Bonifacy Witkowski*. In the 19th century, this little town became
an very important centre of cultural and spiritual life for Polish
Jews, as it was the seat of reputedly the wisest and the most venerated Tsaddyk.

GORUSZKI MAP 11
Reformed Franciscans' monastery. Baroque two-tier church with
chapel of St Francis' Sepulchre, 1742–5.

GÓRY WYSOKIE MAP 27
Parish church, Baroque, 1792–5, by *Józef Karśnicki*.

GORYSŁAWICE MAP 20
Succursal church, stone, Gothic/Renaissance, 1535, with square
domed chapel, 1696.

✦ GORZANÓW MAP 6
Renaissance **country house** with courtyard, second half of 16th century, rebuilt 1653–8 by *Carlo Lurago*. Original sgraffiti and painted
ceilings. Loggias, stairs and stucco Baroque, 1737. Partly in ruins.
Garden pavilion, 1637–40.

✦ GORZÓW WIELKOPOLSKI MAP 4
Cathedral (until recently parish church), ca. 1300; tower first quarter of 14th century, chancel 1489; murals and sculpture contemporary. **Town walls** 1325. Timber **granary** 1798.

✦✦ GOŚCIĘCIN MAP 14
Wooden **pilgrimage church** of St Brice, Baroque, 1661. Nearby is a
small wooden **hermitage**.

GOŚCIERADÓW   MAP 27
Country house built for Eligiusz Prażmowski, late 18th century
Formal **park** with triumphal arch.

GOŚCIKOWO   MAP 4 ✦✦
Cistercian abbey at Paradyż, founded 1230. Church of St Mary,
between 1234 and 1300, rebuilt late 18th century. High altar 1739.
Monastery building 1633, expanded 1750.

GOŚCISZÓW   MAP 6 ✦
Parish church, Romanesque, after 1233, tower 16th century; chancel
expanded early 17th century; ceiling 1595.
Renaissance **castle**, 1603, expanded from 14th-century Gothic original.

GOSŁAWICE   MAP 18 ✦
Church of St Andrew the Apostle, founded by Bishop Andrzej
Gosławski before 1426, thoroughly renovated 1898–1900. Most
unusual cruciform design with octagonal centre. Fortified **residence** of the same bishop, 1414–26.

GOSTKÓW   MAP 12
Neo-Classical **country house** built for the Skrzyński family, 1802;
painted decoration contemporary.

GOSTYŃ   MAP 11 ✦✦✦
Parish church of St Margaret, second half of 15th century; nave
vault after 1689. St Annes's chapel 1529–31. A substantial building.
Overlooking the town is a pilgrimage centre and **Oratorian
monastery**. Church modelled on *Baldassare Longhena's* project for
Santa Maria della Salute in Venice. It was actually begun in 1679, ten
years before the completion of the Venetian model, by *Giovanni*
and *Giorgio Catenaci*; dome and decoration 1726–8, by *Pompeo
Ferrari*. Painted decoration 1746, by *Georg Wilhelm Neunhertz*,
furniture Baroque and Rococo. Renaissance painting of the Virgin
Mary, 1540. Monastic building 1732–6, by *Pompeo Ferrrari*. Wall
with gates, monastery hospital and inn, late 18th century.
Octagonal crypt, containing coffins of local gentry 18th-early 19th
century, many with coffin portraits. A fascinating repository.

GOSZCZ   MAP 11 ✦
Country house, Rococo, 1749–55; stuccoed interiors.
Protestant church, Baroque, 1743–9.

GOSZCZANÓW   MAP 12
Parish church, Baroque, 1666, tower 18th–19th century.

✦✦ GRABARKA   MAP 26
Orthodox **pilgrimage centre** with wooden church and a famous hill
covered in crosses brought by pilgrims.

✦✦ GRABKI DUŻE   MAP 20
Utterly delightful baroque **country house**, 1742, by *Francesco
Placidi*. Neo-Classical outbuilding, early 19th century. Pity about
the surroundings.

GRABOSZEWO   MAP 9
Wooden **parish church** of St Margaret, 16th and 18th centuries.

✦ GRABOSZYCE   MAP 21
Wooden **church** of St Andrew, Gothic, 1585, tower after 1617.
Renaissance **manor house**, ca. 1575, by *Dziwisz Brandys*.

GRABOWO   MAP 15
Neo-Classical **parish church** , 1803–14, by *Hilary Szpilowski*.

GRABÓW N/PROSNĄ   MAP 12
Franciscan monastery, 1642–58, facade and furniture mid-18th century.

✦ GRANOWO   MAP 9
Wooden **parish church,** Baroque, 1729. Wooden windmill, early
19th century.

✦✦ GRĘBIEŃ   MAP 12
Wooden **church**, ca. 1500; important painted decoration of walls ca.
1500, and of ceiling 1520–30.

✦✦ GRODKÓW   MAP 11
Medieval town, owned by the bishops of Wrocław from the 14th
century. **Parish church**; chancel late 13th century, superstructure
14th–15th century, main body after 1450, chapels and tower late
15th-16th century; furniture Mannerist and Baroque. **Town walls**
1296, towers 1351; Lewin Gate superstructure ca. 1600.

✦ GRODNO (KYNSBURG)   MAP 6
Spectacularly situated **castle**, largely in ruins. Built 14th century by
Bolko II of Świdnica, rebuilt extensively 1545-87, at which time it

acquired its Renaissance garb and sgraffito decoration. The castle was acquired by the emperor Rudolph II in 1598, who gave it to Michael the Brave, Hospodar of Moldavia. It was ravaged by the Russians in 1945.

GRODZIEC   MAP 14

Grodzicki family **residence**, Renaissance, 16th–17th century, rebuilt 19th century. Formal **park** with fine oak trees, 17th century.

GRODZIEC (GRÖDITZ)   MAP 6   ✦✦

Castle of the dukes of Legnica, 1488. Palace and rondelles, Gothic/Renaissance, 1522–4, by *Wendel Rosskopf*. Blown up by the Swedes in 1642, partly reconstructed 1906–8, by *Bodo Ebhardt*. **Country house**, 1718–27, by *Johann Blasius Peinter*; with stucco work and painted ceilings.

GRODZISK MAZOWIECKI   MAP 18

Mokronowski family **manor house** (formerly in village of Jordanowice), Baroque, late 18th century; painted decoration neo-Classical, by *Jan Bogumił Plersch(?)*.

GRODZISK WIELKOPOLSKI   MAP 4   ✦✦

Parish church, Mannerist, 1648, by *Cristoforo Bonadura the Elder*. Painting of the Virgin Mary, ca. 1640, by *Bartłomiej Strobel*. Organist's house, 1645.
Bernardine monastery and church, 1662.

GRODZISKO   MAP 21   ✦✦

Church and Convent of the Poor Clares (founded 1228 on site of ancient fort), mid-17th century. Altars, enclosure with statues 1670s. Obelisk on elephant, modelled on *Bernini's* monument at Santa Maria Sopra Minerva in Rome, 1686. Grotto and hermitage of the Blessed Salomea, sister of Bolesław V the Chaste, perched on cliff, ca. 1650.

GRUDZIĄDZ   MAP 10   ✦

A small trading town, occupied by the Teutonic Order between 1241 and 1466. It became part of Prussia in 1772, and reverted to Poland in 1920.
Parish church of St Nicholas [1], first half of 14th century; tower superstructure 18th century.
Church of the Holy Ghost, 14th century. Benedictine convent [2], Baroque, late 17th century, expanded 18th century.
Jesuit church of St Francis Xavier [4] ca. 1650 and 1682–1715. Jesuit college 1648–80, expanded 1722–5.

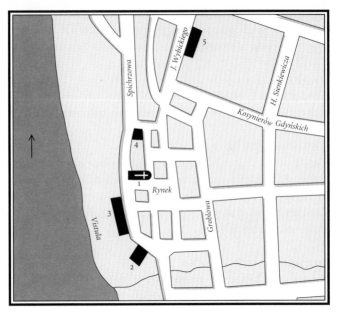

Reformed Franciscans' church [5], 1750–1; monastic buildings converted into prison 1804.

Town walls 14th century. Fortifications, earth-and-brick, 1776–86, by *von Gonzenbach*, later expanded.

Picturesque **granaries** [3] on steep bank of the Vistula, 17th–18th century.

GRUNWALD (TANNENBERG)   MAP 15

Scene of two dramatic battles. The first, fought on 15 July 1410, was one of the greatest battles of the Middle Ages. The King of Poland Władysław II Jagiełło led the combined forces of Poland and Lithuania (commanded by his brother Grand Duke Witold, or Vytautas) against the forces of the Teutonic Order. After a long and hard-fought battle, the might of the Order was shattered, and all but one of its senior knights lay dead on the field of battle, including the Grand Master, Ulrich von Jungingen.

The memory rankled over the centuries. In August 1914 the Germans under Ludendorff defeated two Russian armies under Samsonov and Rennenkampf not far away, and called their victory the Second Battle of Tannenberg in an attempt to wipe away the Slav insult.

The Polish monument of the 1410 battle is worth avoiding. More interesting are the ruins of the Hindenburg Mausoleum built as a monument to the 1914 battle. A strong sense that history was made here.

GRUSZÓW MAP 21

Parish church, wooden, early 16th century.

GRYFICE MAP 2

Parish church, 13th–14th century; chapels and tower 15th century, spire 1759; rebuilt 1658–68 and later.

GRYFINO MAP 1

Parish church, Romanesque/Gothic, 1250s, expanded 15th–16th century. Interesting Greek-Cross layout.

GRYFÓW ŚLĄSKI MAP 6 ✦

Parish church; chancel second half of 15th century, nave 1512, nave vault with Renaissance sgraffito, 1551; altered 17th century. Schaffgotsch tomb, Renaissance, 1585, by *Johann Klintsch*; high altar 1606.

Renaissance and Baroque town **houses**. Ruins of **castle** of the Piast dukes of Świdnica, second half of 13th century, rebuilt by the Schaffgotsch family in the 16th century; expanded 17th and 18th century.

GRYWAŁD MAP 21 ✦✦

Wooden **parish church**, 15th–16th century. One of the most important churches of its kind in this part of Poland.

GUŁTOWY MAP 9 ✦✦

Country house built for Ignacy Bniński,, 1780–6, by *Ignatz Graff*; stucco and pictorial decoration ca. 1800, by *Franciszek Smuglewicz*.

Timber **parish church**, 1738, tower 1834; Baroque painted decoration, 1750s

GUZÓW MAP 20

Manor house of the Łubieński, and later Sobański, families, in the French neo-Renaissance style, 1850.

HACZÓW MAP 29 ✦✦✦

Wooden **parish church** of the Assumption, 15th century, tower 1620s; painted decoration 1494. The largest wooden church in Poland and one of the best. It contains a miraculous 15th-century Pietà, crowned by Pope John Paul II in 1997.

Manor house, Baroque, second half of 18th century.

HAJDUKI   MAP 13
Succursal church, ca. 1300, rebuilt 18th century; murals 15th century.

✦✦ HARKLOWA   MAP 21
Wooden **parish church**, 15th–16th centuries; rebuilt second half of 19th century.

✦ HEBDÓW   MAP 21
Premonstratensian abbey (now Piarist monastery) on the Vistula, founded mid-12th century. Church second half of 13th century, completely rebuilt in the Baroque style, with addition of domed chapel, 1692–1727; towers 1650s, superstructure 1859. Monastery Baroque, 1644–64.

✦✦✦ HENRYKÓW   MAP 11
Magnificent **Cistercian abbey**, founded 1225 by Prince Henry the Bearded for monks from Lubiąż. Church of St Mary; chancel with ambulatory and chapels 1241–60; nave first half of 14th century; interior Baroque, 1692. Two chapels adjoining chancel 1506 and ca. 1560. Tower 1608. Three chapels behind chancel and facade 1692. Good paintings by *Michael Willmann*. Sepulchral monument of the dukes of Ziębice, mid-14th century. Monastic building 1681–1702, by *Mathias Kirchberger*. Ornate interiors, including refectory and Prince's Chamber, with portraits of Silesian Piast princes. **Park** with orangery and pavilions, 18th century.

HORODŁO   MAP 28
Dominican church with twin-tower facade, 1739–58; furniture Rococo. Nothing else in this somewhat God-forsaken place to remind one that it was where the Union of Horodło was signed in 1413, drawing Poland and Lithuania together.

✦ HORODYSZCZE   MAP 28
Palladian **country house**, early 19th century, probably by *Antonio Corazzi*, nusual for this region, where most of the gentry lived in small wooden manor houses.

✦✦ IGOŁOMIA   MAP 21
Important neo-Classical **country house** of Wodzicki family, ca. 1800, by *Christian Piotr Aigner*; stucco by *Fryderyk Baumann*. Nearby, small **archaeological reserve** with excavated furnaces of 3rd-5th-century pottery production centre.

IŁAWA (EYLAU) MAP 15
Parish church, 1317–25, tower superstructure after 1548. Not to be confused with Prüssisch Eylau, where Napoleon won a Pyrrhic victory against the Russians and the Prussians on 8 February 1807.

IŁŻA MAP 20
Parish church, 1603–34; chapel of Bishop Marcin Szyszkowski, Mannerist, 1629. Atop the limestone cliff, ruins of **castle** of the bishops of Kraków, ca. 1340, expanded 16th century.

IMBRAMOWICE MAP 21 ✦✦
Premonstratensian convent, founded 1223-6. Church of SS Peter and Paul, 1711-21, by *Kacper Bażanka*. Uniform furniture and painted decoration integrated with architecture, ca. 1719–25. A very fine baroque interior.

INOWŁÓDŹ MAP 19 ✦
On the bank of the Pilica river, **church** of St Giles, Romanesque, beginning of 12th century. Nice little building of chocolate-coloured sandstone, restored in the 1930s as a chapel for the President of Poland's nearby hunting longe. Ruins of Royal **castle**, 14th century.

INOWROCŁAW MAP 10 ✦
A centre of royal administration for the province of Kuyavia in the middle ages and then the seat of a palatine, this little town declined in importance in the seventeenth century.
Parish church, 15th–16th centuries, rebuilt 17th century and later.
Church of St Mary, granite and brick, Romanesque, early 13th century, reconstructed after fire 1901. The mysterious granite faces in the north portal are thought to be heads of pagan Slav gods.

INWAŁD MAP 21
Parish church, 1747–50. Neo-Classical **country house**, early 19th century.

IWNO MAP 9
Parish church, Baroque, 1778–89. Neo-Renaissance **country house** of Mielżyński family, ca. 1850.

JABŁONNA MAP 18 ✦
Villa built for Prince Michał Poniatowski, younger brother of the last king and himself Primate of Poland, 1775-9, by *Domenico Merlini* (partially remodelled in 1837 by *Henryk Marconi*). Four

neo-Classical pavilions, 1783, by *Szymon Bogumił Zug*. Park designed ca. 1783 by *Szymon Bogumił Zug* and redesigned first quarter of 19th century for Anna Dunin-Wąsowicz. Chinese Pavilion 1783 by *Szymon Bogumił Zug*. A good example of the late eighteenth-century fashion for suburban playgrounds. According to the account of an English traveller, the central salon had a fountain surrounded by flower-beds, around which were arranged day-beds in alcoves. The effect was said to be 'Turkish'. After the Primate's death in 1794, Jabłonna remained masterless for some time, but eventually passed to his nephew, Prince Józef Poniatowski, later Marshal of France but then just known as "Prince Pepi" and the favourite of the Warsaw ladies. After the last war, the interiors were partly reconstructed as they had been in the time of Prince Józef, and they now house a small collection of portraits, paintings and objects, including works by *Rosa da Tivoli* and *Jean Baptiste Pierre* (from the collection of Madame de Pompadour), *Baccio Bandinelli* and *Clodion*.

JAĆMIERZ   MAP 29
Wooden **parish church** of St Mary, Baroque, 1768.

JAKUBOWICE   MAP 21
Castle-type **manor house**, mid-16th century, rebuilt 1663.

JAKUBOWICE MUROWANE   MAP 27
Ruin of **country house**, originally built for Tenczyński family ca. 1600, expanded 18th century, and rebuilt in theRomantic manner after 1803. Original defensive wall with four angle pavilions.

JANISŁAWICE   MAP 17
Wooden **parish church**, ca. 1500, expanded 19th and 20th century.

JANKOWICE WIELKIE   MAP 11
Church, early 14th century, tower raised 1843. **Country house**, ca. 1800.

JANOWICE   MAP 22
Manor house in the Romantic manner, early 19th century.

✦   JANOWICE WIELKIE   MAP 6
Rather touristy village in the Sudety mountains. Late Gothic **church**, end of 15th century. Baroque **residence** ensemble, 17th–20th century. On hill overlooking village, ruins of Bolczów **castle**, end of 14th century.

Small town on Vistula, opposite Kazimierz Dolny. **Parish church**, Gothic, ca. 1537; expanded in Renaissance style 1585–1600 and 1610–15. Tomb of Andrzej Firlej and his wife Barbara, ca. 1587, by *Santi Gucci*.

Dominican church; chancel 1694–1700, by *Jan Michał Link*, nave 1715–20; rebuilt 1789 and 19th-20th century. Furniture Rococo. Monastery 1715–20.

Overlooking the town, ruins of Gothic/Renaissance **castle**, 1526–37, seat of the powerful Firlej family, which, like so many of the great families of the Middle Ages, died out in the sixteenth century. The castle was expanded, in Mannerist style ca. 1600 by *Santi Gucci* for its new owners, the Tarło family. It was rebuilt in Baroque style ca. 1675 by *Tilman van Gameren*, and mid-18th century for the Lubomirskis, who had acquired it subsequently.

This little town was the residence of the bishops of Łuck from 1423 to the 19th century.

Collegiate church of the Holy Trinity (Cathedral 1818–67), Baroque 1714–35. Belfry 1745. Many tombs of bishops. The poet and historian Adam Naruszewicz, Bishop of Smolensk, is buried here. Seminary, founded 1685, Baroque, mid-18th century.

The principal attraction of the place now is the state **Arab horse stud**, established in 1818 in some old outbuildings of the now nonexistent bishops' residence.

An important trading centre on the route to the Ukraine, which rather lost its sense of purpose. A delightful little town on the banks of the river San, full of lovely buildings, mostly strongly fortified. **Jesuit college** founded 1571. Very fine church 1582–94, by *Giuseppe Briccio S.J.*, modified by the incorporation of a Baroque staircase with statues 1625, rebuilt 1868.

Dominican monastery (formerly also Jesuit college). Church, 1629–35, expanded late 17th century–1708, by *Jacopo Solari*; eastern 2-tower facade Baroque, ca. 1715(?). Furniture Rococo. Remains of college building after 1678. Tenaille trace fortifications, 1674, expanded late 17th century. Chapel over "miraculous spring", Baroque, 1752.

Benedictine convent founded 1615 by Princess Anna Ostrogska: church, Mannerist, 1622–4, rebuilt in 1784. Convent building c 1650. Fortifications with rondelles after 1615.

Hospital church of the Holy Ghost, second half of 17th century.

Orthodox parish church, first half of 18th century. **Orthodox church** of St Mary, 16th century.

Synagogue ca. 1800.

Reformed Franciscans' church and monastery, Baroque, 1710–6, by *Tommaso Belotti*.

Houses, mainly Renaissance, expanded with addition of upper storeys, porches and rear rooms 17th–18th century. House of the Orsetti, a wealthy merchant family, ca. 1585, upper storey and porch 1646. This is now a **museum** containing a mixed bag of historical objects and decorative arts. Also of interest is the great network of underground vaults on several levels.

✦✦ JASIENICA ROSIELNA   MAP 29
Wooden **parish church** of St Mary, 1770.

JASIENIEC   MAP 18
Parish church, Baroque, 1747-54.

JAŚKOWO   MAP 15
Baroque **country house**, 1721 and 1776.

JASTRZĘBIA   MAP 22
Wooden **parish church** of St Bartholomew, 1520s, expanded 1606 and 1909.

✦✦ JAWOR   MAP 6
Capital of one of the Piast duchies in the Middle Ages. The **castle** and princely residence, built ca. 1250, was heavily rebuilt and expanded to house a prison in the 19th century.

Parish church, 14th century; richly carved portals ca. 1400 and 16th–17th century.

Bernardine monastery, 1486-92, western gable and tower early 16th century; remnants of 15th–16th-century murals. Important timber **Protestant church**, Baroque, 1654-6, by *Albrecht von Säbisch*, tower after 1709; painted decoration and furniture Baroque, early 18th century. One of only three surviving 'Peace Churches', sometimes also called 'Churches of Grace' - after the victory of the Catholic side in the Thirty Years' War, Protestant communities in Silesia (then part of the Empire) were obliged to hand their churches back to the Catholics, and had to obtain a special dispensation to build new ones for their own use. If such a dispensation was granted, the church could only be of timber, and it had to be situated outside the town walls. See also Świdnica.

Town walls, 14th century; outer ring with rondelles 1540. Town Hall

tower second half of 14th century, spire early 17th century.
Houses in market square Renaissance and Baroque, 16th–17th century.

JEDLEC   MAP 12

Wooden **parish church** of St Florian, 1745-53, connected with the Knights of Malta.

JEDLIŃSK   MAP 20

Parish **church**, Baroque, 1645, rebuilt 1752.

JĘDRZEJÓW   MAP 19 ✦✦✦

Important **Cistercian abbey**, founded 1140 by Janik Gryfita Archbishop of Gniezno, for monks from Morimond in Burgundy, and known locally as 'Little Morimond'. Church of St Mary and St Wojciech, Romanesque, ca. 1200, expanded and redecorated in Baroque style. Interior ca. 1730, two northern chapels 1733–42, two-tower facade 1751–4; painted decoration 1734–9, by *Andrzej Radwański*, sculpture by *Antoni Frąckiewicz* and others. Wonderful Rococo organ, with plenty of putti, 1745–60, by *Józef Sitarski*, and *Ignacy, Jakub* and *Joachim Kornecki*. An extraordinary juxtaposition of high baroque with low and severe Cistercian Gothic. Belfry mid-18th century. Note the tomb slab of Pakosław of Mstyczów with relief figure of the knight, 1319. Also, the grave of Wincenty Kadłubek (died 1223), a monk from Jędrzejów who became Bishop of Kraków, and an important chronicler. Surviving wings of monastery heavily rebuilt. In town, **parish church**, 15th century, rebuilt 16th–17th century, expanded 1754–62; murals 16th–17th century. On the main square of the town, there is an unusual **museum**, well worth a visit. It is essentially a private collection, put together by the Przypkowski family, whose forbears were prominent Polish Brethren in the 16th and 17th centuries. Apart from an interesting library and its own printing press, the museum contains one of the largest collections of old cookery books in Europe and the third largest collection of sundials in the world.

JELENIA GÓRA   MAP 6 ✦✦

Granted city rights in 1231, Jelenia Góra was famous for its fine-woven cloth. In 1392 it came under Bohemian rule, and from 1526 it was part of the Habsburg dominions. In 1742 it was captured by Prussia, and only reverted to Poland in 1920.
Parish church of St Erasmus and St Pancras [1], second half of 14th century, spire 1736; stalls and pulpit Renaissance.
Church of the Holy Cross (originally Protestant) [2], Baroque,

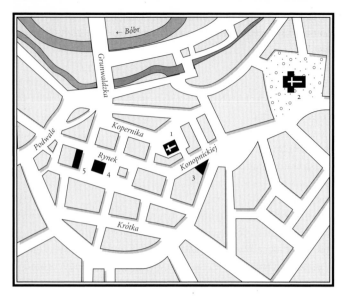

1709–18, by *Martin Frantz*; Baroque furniture and painted decoration by *Franz Hoffman*. Adjoining churchyard wall, and sepulchral chapels with grilles, 18th century. Chapel of St Anne [3].
Town houses [5], 17th–18th centuries.
Baroque **Town Hall** [4] and Neptune **well**.

JELONKI   MAP 15
Parish church, 1340s; Rococo painted ceiling.

✦✦   JEMIELNICA   MAP 14
Cistercian abbey founded in 1280 by Bolko I Duke of Opole. Church 13th–14th century, Baroque nave 1733–40 by *Friedrich Gans*; paintings by *Michael Willmann*. St Joseph's chapel ca. 1714. Monastery building after 1733, by *Friedrich Gans*. Farm buildings, 18th–19th centuries.
Cemetery church 14th century, murals third quarter of 14th century.

✦   JERZMANKI   MAP 5
Romanesque **parish church**, after 1250; nave vault Gothic, first quarter of 16th century.

✦   JEŻEWO POŚWIĘTNE   MAP 17
Parish church, 1530s, rebuilt 17th–18th century. Unusual polygonal layout for this part of Mazovia.

JEZIORANY MAP 16

Quiet little town, originally the property of the bishops of Warmia. **Parish church**, second half of 14th century, expanded 1913. Churchyard gate, second half of 18th century. Ruins of bishops' **castle** and defensive **town walls**, 14th century.

JEŻÓW MAP 19

Fortified **manor house**, early 1500s, expanded 1544, rebuilt 19th century; painted decoration Renaissance, 16th century.

JODŁOWNIK MAP 21 ✦

Wooden **parish church** of St Mary, Gothic, 1585; painted decoration Rococo.

JUTROSIN MAP 11 ✦✦

This village in the heart of Wielkopolska contains a surprising number of vernacular wooden and timber buildings. Timber **church** of the Holy Cross, Baroque, 1777. Belfry, end of 18th century. **Houses** around 1800. **Windmills** 1736 and 1746.

KACWIN MAP 21 ✦

Highland village with plenty of local architecture. **Parish church** of All Saints, early 15th century, rebuilt 1712 and 1767; ornate Baroque interior. Note the waterfall in the middle of the village.

KADŁUB MAP 12

Wooden **parish church** of St Andrew, 16th century, rebuilt 1949.

KALINÓWKA KOŚCIELNA MAP 23

Wooden **parish church**, Baroque, 1776. Wooden parish **granary**, Baroque, 1783.

KALISZ MAP 12 ✦✦✦

A very old trading settlement, marked as 'Calissia' on Ptolemy's map of the second century. Merchants from ancient Rome used to come here to buy amber, which they referred to as 'the gold of the north', collected on the Baltic shore. In the 13th century, Kalisz became the capital of one of the Piast duchies, and subsequently a royal town, with a strong castle and fortifications. From the 14th century Kalisz also became an important centre of Jewish life. The town experienced a minor boom at the beginning of the 19th century, but was badly shelled by the Germans in 1914.

Collegiate church of the Assumption [1]; choir 1353–45, main body Baroque, 1790. Tower reconstructed 1925–6. Important polyptych

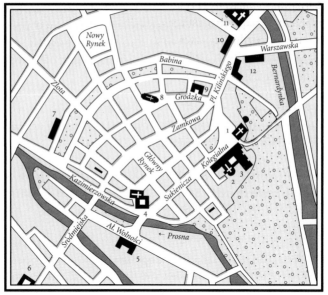

ca. 1500. Bell-tower, neo-Classical, ca. 1820, by *Sylwester Szpilowski*.

Jesuit college [2] founded 1581 by Primate Stanisław Karnkowski. Church of St Stanisław and St Wojciech, Mannerist, 1587–95, by *Giovanni Maria Bernardoni* and *Albin Fontana*; high altar, first quarter of 18th century, tomb of Primate Karnkowski, 1611. College, schools and printing office, 17th century, rebuilt for Cadet Corps in neo-Classical style 1795–7, by *David Gilly(?)*, and later.

Palace of the archbishops of Gniezno [3], linked with college, 1583–4, entirely rebuilt in neo-Classical style 1824–5 by *Sylwester Szpilowski* and *Franciszek Reinstein*, interior 1925.

Franciscan monastery [4] founded ca. 1250 by Bolesław the Pious and the Blessed Jolanta. Church of St Stanisław late 1250s, remodelled, with Renaissance/Mannerist stucco decoration, 1599–1632, by *Albin Fontana*. Chapel of the Passion, after 1250, remodelled 1632. Former bell-tower 1640, rebuilt 19th century. Monastic building , 1640-80, superstructure 1730, rebuilt 19th-20th century.

Parish church of St Nicholas [8], founded 1253 by Bolesław the Pious . Chancel second half of 13th century, with 16th century late Gothic vault; main body mid-14th century, rebuilt with Renaissance/Mannerist stucco decoration, 1612, by *Albin Fontana*. The church was partly re-Gothicized and the upper part of tower was added 1869–76. In the Baroque high altar there is now a copy of a painting of the Deposition, ca. 1620, by *Peter Paul Rubens*, destroyed by fire 1973.

Lateran Canons' house, 1448; rebuilt 1538–9 and 19th century.

Bernardine monastery [11] founded ca. 1465. Church 1594–1607, rebuilt in Baroque style 18th century; illusionistic painted decoration Rococo, third quarter of 18th century, by *Father Walenty Żebrowski*; furniture late Baroque, mid-18th century, by *Father Bonawentura Widawski*. Churchyard wall with gate and bell-tower Baroque, 18th century. Monastic building Baroque, 1594–1622.

Reformed Franciscans' church of St Joseph and St Peter of Alcantara and monastery [6], 1665–73, rebuilt 1919–36. Rococo furniture, mid-18th century, by *Józef Eglauer*. Triangular chapel in churchyard, 1717–36.

The old town also has an important group of neo-Classical buildings by *Sylwester Szpilowski*, including: **Courthouse** [5] 1820–4, **County college** [9] ca. 1819, **barracks** of Vistula Legion [7] ca. 1810, Wrocław **toll-gate** 1822, **bridge** on Prosna River 1825 (with *Franciszek Reinstein*), Pułaski **house** [10] 1820–30; and some town houses.

In the New Town: **Church** of St Gothard, neo-Gothic, 1908–10.

State prison, neo-Romanesque, 1844, by *Henryk Marconi* and *Franciszek Tournelle*.

KAŁKÓW (KALKAU)   MAP 13

Romanesque **parish church**, brick, mid-13th century, expanded 1931–3. Stone portals early Gothic. Murals Gothic and Mannerist.

Important pilgrimage centre. Fortified **Franciscan monastery** founded ca. 1668. Church 1770–5; painted decoration 1857. Monastery building second half of 18th century, expanded later. Calvary chapels, seven of them wooden, 1825–75. See also KALWARIA ZEBRZYDOWSKA

One of the finest examples of this particularly Polish phenomenon, the large open-air Way of the Cross with architectural Stations. It draws pilgrims from all over Poland, particularly at Easter, when the whole Passion of Christ is enacted in costume. When, in 1641, the founder's son acquired a miraculous painting of the Virgin, a secondary Way of the Cross, stressing the Mother of God's sufferings, was laid out alongside, and this generates its own historic rituals on the feast of the Assumption in mid-August. **Bernardine monastery** founded by Mikołaj Zebrzydowski. Church 1603-9, by

Giovanni Maria Bernardoni and *Paul Baudarth*; chapel of Miraculous Virgin Mary with impressive stucco work, 1658-1670; furniture Baroque, 1630s, high altar 1723. Organ case 1765–90. Monastic building completed 1654–66. Fortifications, 1624, with two rondelles rebuilt as chapels 1747. Farm building with gate, 1774. **Calvary**, laid out 1604 by *Feliks Żebrowski*, theologian, mathematician and magician, on the basis of drawings and descriptions of Jerusalem. 42 chapels, mostly Mannerist, some with good stucco work, 1605–16, by *Paul Baudarth*. In the little **church** of the Crucifixion, 1600–1, there is a series of paintings, before 1658, by *Father Franciszek Lekszycki*.

KAMIEŃ POMORSKI   MAP 1 ✦✦
Ancient Slav settlement and fishing port on the Pomeranian coast, and in the early days the site of an important pagan temple. In the 12th century it became the capital of a Slav duchy, and subsequently a Hanseatic town. The whole town was virtually destroyed by the Red Army in 1945.
Cathedral of Our Lady and St John the Baptist, founded before 1176, stone and brick Romanesque/Gothic, late 12th-13th centuries, rebuilt 1450s; portal and murals before 1300. Magnificent organ 1669–72. Chapter house with cloister, 14th–15th centuries. **Museum** in former cathedral treasury.
Bishop's palace 15th century, covered in ornate 16th-century decoration.
Town walls 13th–14th century. Wolin Gate, late 14th century. **Town Hall** 15th-16th centuries.

KAMIENIEC ZĄBKOWICKI (KAMENZ)   MAP 13 ✦✦
Ruin of one of the most spectacular and intensely Romantic of *Karl Friedrich Schinkel's* works, the **castle** built for Princess Marianna of Orange, granddaughter of Frederick William II of Prussia and wife of Frederick Albert of Prussia, between 1838 and 1872. A fire devastated the empty building in 1946 and after that the local communist authorities treated it as a mine of building materials. The ruin is still wonderfully imposing. It is now in private hands and there are some attempts being made to rebuild part of it.
Cistercian abbey founded 1249. Church ca. 1300, facades rebuilt ca. 1700, by *Matthäus Kirchberger*; furniture Baroque, 1701–12, paintings by *F.Liszka* and *Michael Willmann*.

KAMIENNA GÓRA (LANDESHUT)   MAP 6 ✦✦
Parish Church of SS Peter and Paul; choir Gothic, main body Renaissance, late 16th century.

On the hill, domed **Protestant church**, 1709–17, by *Martin Frantz*. Renaissance **castle**, ca. 1550-1588, with arcaded courtyard and tower. Baroque Town **houses.**

KAMIONNA MAP 4
Parish church, 1499. A simple rectangular layout with sophisticated star rib vaulting.

KAMPINOS MAP 18
Wooden **parish church**, Baroque, 1773–82. Nice setting in the Kampinos National Park.

KARCHOWICE MAP 14
Parish church ca. 1500. Tower first half of 19th century.

KARCZEW MAP 18
Parish church founded by Marshal Franciszek Bielinski, 1732–7, by *Jakub Fontana*; expanded 1911–3.

KARNIOWICE MAP 21
Manor house, mid-18th century; rebuilt ca. 1860.

✦ KARNKOWO MAP 17
Parish church founded by Karnkowski family, Gothic, after 1584, expanded and rebuilt in Baroque style 1761.

✦ KARPACZ-BIERUTOWICE (BRÜCKENBERG) MAP 6
Norwegian wooden **church**, dating from 1st half of 13th century, with carved decoration in Norman style. Saved from demolition and bought in 1841 by the Norwegian painter Joan Dahl, who lived in Dresden. He sold it to the Prussian king Frederick William IV, who wanted to erect it in Berlin, but in the end it was acquired by Count Reden, who had an estate there.

✦ KARSIBÓR MAP 1
Simple 15th-century village **church** with surprisingly good late Gothic triptych, ca. 1460.

✦✦ KARTUZY MAP 8
Carthusian monastery of Our Lady, founded 1380 (probably from Prague). Church, 1380–1405, contains Gothic altar sculptures from Gdańsk workshops 1444, interesting Baroque carved stalls and other furniture, 1638–83. Monastic buildings, including part of cloister, star-vaulted refectory and one hermitage. Also regional

centre for arts and crafts of the Kashubian people of the coast.

KĄSKI
MAP 17
Baroque **manor house**, second half of 18th century.

KĄTY WROCŁAWSKIE
MAP 11
Late Gothic hall **church** of SS Peter and Paul, ca. 1500. **Protestant church**, 1834–6, by *Karl Friedrich Schinkel*.

KAZIMIERZ BISKUPI
MAP 10 ✦✦
Romanesque **parish church** of St Martin, 12th century, expanded 1512 in Gothic style, and 1859. **Bernardine monastery** and church of the five Brother Martyrs founded by Bishop Jan Lubrański, 1518–20, rebuilt late 18th and 19th–20th century. Around churchyard, arcaded gallery with wooden gate belfry 18th century.

KAZIMIERZ DOLNY
MAP 27 ✦✦✦
An important trading-post on the Lwów-Zamość-Warsaw route. Also an inland port, where grain was brought in from the surrounding countryside to be bought by merchants and then floated down the Vistula to Gdansk for export. These contacts with the east are visible in the architecture of this picturesque little Renaissance town, which is largely unspoilt.

The **parish church** of St John and St Bartholomew [1], built in the late 1580s and expanded around 1610, by *Jacopo Balin*, is a fine and typical example of a style of late Renaissance church architecture that flourished in south-eastern areas of Poland proper. Note the Górski chapel, 1625–9, and the Royal chapel, 1653; the very fine organ, 1607–20, by *Szymon Liliusz(?)* as well as the good Mannerist furniture, ca. 1620. One of the most characteristic and beautiful buildings of its kind.

Reformed Franciscans' monastery [6]founded 1626 by the Firlej family. Church, 1680–90, rebuilt 1762–71. Monastery 1639–88. **Hospital church** of St Anne [3], ca. 1649–70. Hospital before 1635, rebuilt 20th century. Ruins of **castle** [2], 14th century around an earlier keep.

Extraordinarily ornate **houses** [5]in market square: Przybyła houses (St Christopher's and St Nicholas'), 1615; Gdańsk house, 17th–18th century, facade 1798. Houses in Senatorska Street: No. 3, Górski house, 1607; No. 11, Celej house, ca. 1635 (now housing regional **museum**). Renaissance **granaries** [7], on Puławska and Krakowska Streets, first half of 17th century.

KCYNIA   MAP 9
Carmelite church and monastery and arcaded pilgrimage gallery with Calvary chapels, Baroque, 1779–80.

KĘPNO   MAP 12
Neo-Classical **Synagogue**, 1814–5, by *Friedrich Wilhelm* and *Karl Friedrich Scheffler*.

Parish church of St George, 1360–70, expanded after 1470; chancel and "crystal" vaults, 1515, by master mason *Matz*. Very fine.
Castle of Teutonic Knights, ca. 1370, rebuilt 17th century.
Masonic Lodge, neo-Gothic, 1810.
A few kilometres away, in the woods, massive concrete remains of Hitler's '**Wolf's Lair**', from which he gave the order to launch 'Operation Barbarossa', the invasion of Russia. Mainly in ruins, but Goering's air-raid shelter and some of the offices are open. Also memorial to Colonel von Stauffenberg, who planted the bomb that was meant to kill Hitler here on 20 July 1944.

Birthplace of St John of Kęty, monk and savant, 1390–1473. **Parish church**, Baroque on Gothic remnants, with twin domed chapels, 1657–85; tower superstructure 1910.

From its foundation in the Middle Ages unitl 1789 this was a residence and private town belonging to the bishops of Kraków.
Palace founded by Bishop Jakub Zadzik, 1637–41, by *Tommaso Poncino* and others, one of the best examples of the 'Vasa' style; gallery wings Baroque, 1720–46, by *Kacper Bażanka(?)*. Interiors with stucco and painted decoration, ca. 1641, with ceilings from the workshop of *Tommaso Dolabella*.
Cathedral, formerly collegiate church, of the Assumption, 1632–5, with earlier remnants, rebuilt in neo-Baroque style, second half of 19th century. High altar with good altarpiece 1730 by *Szymon Czechowicz*; furniture original, 1726–65; sculpture from workshop of *Antoni Frąckiewicz*; tomb of Elżbieta Zebrzydowska, ca. 1553, by *Giovanni Maria Padovano*. Important **treasury**.
Church of the Holy Trinity, 1640–4, apse with altar ca. 1725, by *Kacper Bażanka*.
Seminary, 1724–6, by *Kacper Bażanka*.
Neo-Classical **Record Office**, 1824, and **Post-Office**, ca. 1825. **Villa** of Tomasz Zieliński and Romantic garden pavilions, 1846–58.
Bernardine church and monastery on Karczówka Hill founded by Bishop Marcin Szyszkowski, 1624–31, partly rebuilt ca. 1720–30 by *Kacper Bażanka(?)*. In the market square, there is a **museum** with a reasonably good gallery of Polish painting.

Old weaving town. **Parish church**, 1563–77, rebuilt 1720–2; tower superstructure 1772.

KIJE
MAP 20

Parish church, first half of 17th century; the original 12th-century stone Romanesque church now forms the presbytery. Chapels 18th century.

KIKÓŁ
MAP 10

Neo-Classical **country house** built for Ignacy Zboiński, ca. 1790.

✦✦ ### KIWITY
MAP 16

Parish church of SS Peter and Paul, 15th century. One of the most picturesque Gothic village churches of Warmia.

✦ ### KLEMENSÓW
MAP 28

Country **residence** of the Zamoyski family, a comfortable rather than grand house, used as a retreat from their palace in Zamość. Original Baroque house built 1744-6 for Tomasz Zamoyski by *Andrzej Bem* and *Jerzy de Kawe(?)*, remodelled 1826–41 by *Henryk Marconi*. Neo-Classical orangery added 1810–3 by *Henryk Ittar*.

✦ ### KLĘPSK
MAP 4

Wooden **church** of St Mary, ca. 1581, tower 1657(?); painted decoration, galleries and furniture Renaissance and Mannerist, 1581–1614. Gothic triptych and sculpture of the Virgin Mary early 14th century.

KLESZTÓW
MAP 28

Parish (formerly Orthodox) **church**, 1773; painted decoration Rococo, 1773, by *Gabriel Sławiński*.

✦✦ ### KLIMONTÓW
MAP 20

In the most lovely unspoilt setting, a wonderful Mannerist **collegiate church**, founded by Chancellor Jerzy Ossoliński. Elliptical,

with ambulatory and two towers, 1643–50, by *Lorenzo Senes*. Stuccoes by *Giovanni Battista Falconi*. Drum with dome 1732. Baroque facade completed 1775–9.

Dominican monastery founded 1613 by Castellan Jan Zbigniew Ossoliński. Church with stucco and carved-stone decoration, Mannerist, 1617–after 1623. Organ case ca. 1620-30. Monastic building 1620-3, with 18th-century alterations.

KŁOBUCK   MAP 12 ✦

Monastery of Canons Regular founded in 1454 by the famous Polish historian Jan Długosz (1415–80). Church expanded ca. 1620 by *Valentin von Säbisch*, rebuilt 1670 and 1796–1810. Monastic building repeatedly remodelled.

Neo-Gothic **residence** in Zagórze, 1795–1800, rebuilt in 1891.

KŁOCZEW   MAP 27

Parish church, Baroque, 1643–1737; furniture ca. 1750. Bell-towers ca. 1737.

KŁODAWA   MAP 10

Carmelite monastery, 1718–55. Church 1765.

KŁODZKO   MAP 6 ✦

Important stronghold and market town on medieval trade route between Poland and Bohemia.

Church of the Knights Hospitallers of St John of Jerusalem, 15th century; northern tower 1487, by *Johann Strausberger*; aisle vaults 1487–90; nave vault 1552–5. Taken over by Jesuits 1624 and rebuilt in Baroque style 1673–5. Impressive interior with high altar 1727–9, by *Christoph Tausch*, and Baroque furniture, late 17th-1st half of 18th centuries. Tomb of Bishop Ernest of Pardubice, second half of 14th century. **Jesuit college**, 1655–90, by *Carlo Lurago*.

Franciscan church 1628–31, completed second half of 17th century. Monastic building 1678–1731, painted decoration of refectory, 1744, by *Felix Anton Scheffler*.

Dominating the town, on site of 10th-century fort, there is a **fortress**, 1680–1702, by *Giacomo Carove*, expanded 1741–4 and later by Frederick II of Prussia after his conquest of Silesia. **Town Hall**, 16th–18th centuries, rebuilt 1890s; tower Renaissance, 1653–4. Rare Gothic **bridge** over canal, 1390, with Baroque statues, first half of 18th century.

KLUCZBORK   MAP 12 ✦

Medieval market town on salt route between Kraków and

Wrocław. **Parish church** 14th century; interior rebuilt in Baroque style 1743–5; tower superstructure after 1795.

Town Hall and adjacent houses, known as 'the Twelve Apostles', 18th century. Almshouse, 1778, by *Karl Gottfried Langhans*. The town also boasts the only **museum** of beekeeping in Poland.

KLUKOWO   MAP 25

Parish church, Baroque, second half of 18th century.

KMIECIN   MAP 15

Church (now **museum**), 14th–15th centuries; wooden tower, 1679. Timber **house,** ca.1850.

KNYCHÓWEK   MAP 25

Parish church, Renaissance, 1631–46. Vicarage 1790.

✦   KOBYLIN   MAP 11

Parish church of St Stanisław, 1512–7, tower 16th–17th century, Baroque chapel, before 1701; Gothic triptych 1518.

Bernardine monastery church, founded 1456, second half of 15th–early 16th centuries, facade and vaults remodelled ca. 1720.

✦✦ KOBYŁKA   MAP 18

Beautiful **Jesuit church** of the Holy Trinity, 1741–63, by *Guido Longhi* and *Jakub Fontana*; painted decoration and furniture Rococo.

KOBYLNIKI   MAP 17

Parish church, ca. 1521. Interesting Renaissance Kobylnicki tombs.

✦   KOCK   MAP 27

Originally a market town, the property of the Firlej family, the town was transformed in the second half of the 18th century to harmonise with the new palatial scheme introduced by Princess Anna Jabłonowska. Neo-Classical **country residence** with curved colonnades and a pair of outbuildings, ca. 1780, by *Szymon Bogumił Zug*, rebuilt before 1840 by *Henryk Marconi*.

Parish church, neo-Classical, 1779, by *Szymon Bogumił Zug*.

✦✦✦ KODEŃ   MAP 26

Headquarters of the senior branch of the Sapieha family. The only part of the original stronghold to survive is the **church** (originally Orthodox) founded by theSapiehas, ca. 1540. In the town, **parish church** of St Anne, founded by Mikołaj Sapieha, an unusual

Renaissance/Mannerist building, 1629-35, with Baroque facade, 1709. The painting of the Virgin Mary in the high altar, a Spanish madonna from the first quarter of 17th century, erroneously thought at the time to represent Our Lady of Guadelupe, is one of the most venerated miraculous Madonnas in Poland. It was brought from Rome by Mikołaj Sapieha (1581–1644), Palatine of Minsk and Castellan of Wilno, himself a convert from the Orthodox faith. He had gone to Rome in poor health and experienced a miraculous improvement while praying before this painting, which hung in a chapel in the Vatican. He begged the Pope to give or sell him the picture, to no avail. So Sapieha bribed the sacristan, who cut the picture out of its frame and passed it to him, and he left the Papal dominions before the theft was discovered. The sacristan was burnt at the stake for sacrilege and Sapieha excommunicated. He nevertheless built a church for the painting and continued to venerate it, and he was eventually received back into the fold by the Pope.

KODENIEC MAP 28

Wooden **parish** (formerly Uniate) **church** of St Mary, triple-aisled, Baroque, 1791.

KOŁACZKOWO MAP 9

Parish church, 1830-6. Neo-Classical **country house**, first half of 19th century. The writer and Nobel Prize winner Władysław Reymont lived here 1920–5, and there is a memorial room of his in the house.

KOŁBACZ MAP 1 ✦✦

Cistercian abbey founded in 1173 for monks from Esröm in Denmark. Church, Romanesque, 1210–30, and Gothic, ca. 1300, chancel completed 1347. Very fine rose window. In 1535, after its dissolution, the monastery buildings were converted into a residence, and then pulled down. Only the 15th-century barn survives.

KOŁO MAP 10 ✦

Parish church, late 14th century, southern chapel early 16th century; nave vault and northern chapel 1863.
Bernardine monastery, founded 1456. Church, 1773–82, painted decoration second half of 18th century. Monastic building, 1755–64, with Gothic remnants.
In the nearby meadow, ruin of **castle** founded ca. 1360 by Kazimierz the Great.
Town Hall, neo-Classical, ca. 1815, with brick tower ca. 1390.

This old port became the seat of a bishopric in the year 1000, but was subsequently downgraded and the bishopric moved to Kamień Pomorski.

Collegiate church of the Immaculate Conception, 1301–21, expanded second half of 14th century, towers 15th century; remnants of Gothic murals, second half of 14th century. Bronze font, 1355, by *Johann Alart*; bronze candelabrum, 1327, by *Johann Apengheter* from Lübeck; Gothic triptychs, early 16th century; Gothic stalls, sculpture and paintings. Impressive neo-Gothic **Town Hall**, 1829–32, by *Karl Friedrich Schinkel*, incorporating some authentic elements from the 15th century.

Parish church, rebuilt before 1628 by Konarzewski family, eastern part and tower 1695. Radomicki **country house**, 1697, later belonged to younger branch of Czartoryski family.

Cradle of the Koniecpolski family, developed as a private town from 1403. **Parish church** of the Holy Trinity, founded by Hetman Stanisław Koniecpolski, Baroque, 1632–44; Koniecpolski's tomb 1653. Organ case and gallery before 1659. Churchyard wall with gate and two bell-towers, ca. 1650.

At nearby CHRZĄSTÓW: **Parish church**, 1767. **Country house** of Koniecpolski, and later of Potocki, families, first half of 17th century, remodelled late 18th century. Neo-Classical outbuildings.

Old market town, exactly halfway between Kalisz and Kruszwica, as attested by the only surviving milestone of this period in Poland, dating from 1151. The town's pre-war Jewish community has been immortalized in the book *Konin* by Theo Richmond.

In the Old Town, simple ashlar Romanesque **church**, 13th century, with carved stone portal and baptismal font.

Parish church of St Bartholomew, second half of 14th century. Zemeliusz chapel, square, domed, Renaissance, 1595–1607. **Reformed Franciscans' church** 1727; monastic building 1733, by *Mateusz Osiecki*. **Town Hall**, neo-Classical, early 19th century.

Residence of Chancellor Jacek Małachowski who, as Marshal of the Crown contributed a great deal to cleaning up, paving and lighting Warsaw in the 1780s. The house itself was never built, but the

Baroque ensemble, started after 1740, includes: a regular **park** with canal, viewing mound and parterres; summer-house, second half of 18th century; bower, neo-Classical, 18th–19th century; Greek Temple, early 19th century; Romantic Egyptian orangery, 1825, by *Franciszek Maria Lanci*; Grandchildrens' cottage and wall with towers, neo-Gothic, before 1850, by *Franciszek Maria Lanci*.

KOŃSKOWOLA   MAP 27 ✦

Parish church, 1627, expanded 17th–18th century, facade 1730–1; monument to Princess Zofia Lubomirska, by *Tilman van Gameren*. **Church** of St Anne, ca. 1610. Lovely example of Lublin-Zamość type of Renaissance/Mannerist church.

KONSTANTYNÓW   MAP 26

Manor house of Sedlnicki family, neo-Gothic, early 19th century.

KOPRZYWNICA   MAP 20 ✦✦

Important **Cistercian abbey** founded 1185 for monks from Morimond in Burgundy by Kazimierz the Just. Stone church of St Mary and St Florian, 1207–40. Gables ca. 1507, chapel and sacristy ca. 1697. Facade and tower, 1770–90. *Father Józef Karśnicki*. Murals late 14th century. Painting of the Virgin Mary in high altar, 1646, by *Bartłomiej Strobel*. Only surviving wing of monastery ca. 1250. Abbot's house ca. 1615–20.

KÓRNIK   MAP 9 ✦✦

Castle of the Górka family, originally 16th century, passed to Działyński family 1676 and to Zamoyski family in 1852. In the late 1820s Count Tytus Działyński, an ardent patriot who was imprisoned by the Prussians more than once, commissioned several architects, including *Karl Friedrich Schinkel*, to produce drawings for a transformation of the old residence into a neo-Gothic castle. Although Działyński contributed much himself, it seems that Schinkel's project was the basis for the reconstruction. The result (English neo-Gothic with Moorish elements) is interesting, but hardly beautiful. The castle is furnished and hung with some fairly good pictures. It also contains the famous archive and library put together by Działyński, as well as a collection of arms and armour, decorative arts and even, rather improbably, of ethnographic art from Australasia and Polynesia brought back in 1880 by Count Władysław Zamoyski, the last owner of Kórnik, who bequeathed it to the nation in 1925. The park is an arboretum. **Parish church** founded by Górka family, ca. 1437, workshop of *Heinrich Brünsberg*, rebuilt second half of 18th century. Neo-Gothic facade and interior, 1838, by *Franciszek Maria Lanci*. Renaissance tombs of Górka family.

✦ KORONOWO   MAP 10
Cistercian abbey of the Assumption, begun 1289. Stucco vault decoration, 1687; furniture second half of 17th century, paintings by *Bartłomiej Strobel*. Organ and gallery after 1754. Wooden **water mill**, 18th century, with well-preserved interior.

KOŚCIAN   MAP 9
Parish church, early 14th century, chancel late 15th century, tower and chapels 15th-16th century. Continuously rebuilt and not very beautiful. Gothic tryptich 1507.

✦ KOŚCIELEC KUJAWSKI   MAP 10
Romanesque **parish church**, ca. 1200. Chancel vaulting end of 15th century, nave vault 1894. Kościelecki chapel with Renaissance tomb ca. 1565, by *Giovanni Battista Quadro(?)*; north chapel 1861-2.

✦ KOŚCIELEC PROSZOWICKI   MAP 21
Romanesque **church** of St Wojciech, founded by Bishop Wisław of Kraków, ca. 1230, rebuilt later. Impressive but not attractive.

KOŚCIELEC KOLSKI   MAP 10
Romanesque **parish church**, ca. 1150; sacristy before 1600, brick nave 1790, by *Jeremi Królikowski*.
Neo-Classical **Mailcoach Station**, early 19th century. Landscape **park** with Romantic structures, including a Mosque, second half of 19th century.

✦ KOSTRZYN (KÜSTRIN)   MAP 3
Castle, originally of the princes of Poland, later of the Knights Templar, finally of the margraves of Brandenburg, brick, Renaissance/Mannerist, ca. 1550, by *Kaspar Theutz* and *Giromello*, with remnants of Gothic castle, 14th–15th century, north-eastern wing 1598–1608. Largely in ruins. Fortifications ca. 1540, by *Giromello*.

KOSZALIN   MAP 2
Medieval seaport and residence of the bishops of Kamień. **Parish church** of St Mary, 1300–33, partly reconstructed 1842–5 and later. Octagonal **chapel** of St Gertrude, 1383.
Town walls 1292–1310.

KOSZUTY
MAP 9

Wooden **manor house**, Baroque, late 18th century.

KOWALEWO
MAP 10

Wooden **parish church** of SS Peter and Paul, triple-aisled, 1784.

KOWALEWO POMORSKIE
MAP 10

Parish church, 1286–1330, with Baroque interior. Tower early 18th century. Ruined **castle** of Teutonic Knights, 1280–1303.

KOWARY
MAP 6

Parish church, early 16th century, ceilings after 1633.

KOZIEGŁOWY
MAP 14

Parish church: chancel ca. 1460, nave before 1595, rebuilt 1679. Kawiecki chapel second half of 17th century.

KOŹLE
MAP 14

Inland port on the salt route. **Parish church**, 15th century, tower 1570, facade neo-Gothic, 1897–9. Earth-and-brick **fortifications** with bastions, 1743–5, by *Gerhard Cornelis van Wallrave*, expanded second half of 18th century, and 1806.

KOZŁOWICE
MAP 12 ♦♦

Wooden **church** of St John the Baptist, second half of 17th century.

KOZŁÓWKA
MAP 27 ♦♦♦

Splendid Baroque **residence** built for Bieliński family 1735–42, by *Józef Fontana(?)*, rebuilt for Zamoyski family 1879–1907, by *Jan Heurich Jr*. Furnished in 19th-century furniture and hung almost exclusively with portraits of the Zamoyski family, almost all of them 19th-century copies. Lovely building. One of the ranges now houses a makeshift **museum** of Socialist Realist sculpture - dozens of monstrous Lenins and Stalins dating from the 1950s stored here after Stalin's fall. Probably the best collection in the world.

✦ KOŹMIN MAP 11

Parish church, 1670s. Przyjemski chapel, Renaissance, early 17th century. Sculpture representing the Dormition of the Virgin, Gothic, first half of 16th century.

Bernardine monastery founded 1628. Church 1648–70. Organ 1770-2, by *Andrzej Majeronowicz*. Monastic building second half of 17th century-1725.

Wooden **church** of Holy Trinity, 1570.

Renaissance **castle**, third quarter of 16th century, by *Giovanni Battista di Quadro(?)*, cellars and lower part of tower 15th century; rebuilt 17th–18th century and 1865.

KOŻUCHÓW MAP 4

Parish church, 15th century, vaulting second half of 16th century. **Castle**, originally stronghold of Piast princes of Fłogów , built before 1415, rebuilt several times; of little interest. Well preserved **town walls** 15th century, rebuilt with addition of rondelles mid-16th century.

✦✦✦ KRAKÓW MAP 21

According to legend, the settlement on Wawel Hill was founded by a prince of the Wiślanie (Vistulans) by the name of Krak. The city became an important trade centre, and was first mentioned as such in the year 965. In the year 1000 Kraków became a bishopric, which enhanced its political significance, and after 1138 it became the principal royal seat. But it was vulnerable to destruction by Tatar raids, and suffered particularly badly during that of 1241. In 1257 the city was rebuilt and organised under 'Magdeburg Law', a well-tried and practical form of incorporation. It was not until the reign of Kazimierz the Great (1333–1370) that the city, finally restored to its proper political importance and ringed by fine defensive walls and towers, came into its own as the capital of Poland. The following century saw its heyday, and it was then one of the grandest and most beautiful cities in central Europe. The wealth of its merchant patricians as well as the noble magnates who kept palaces here encouraged the evolution of a large number of local architects, painters and craftsmen, and attracted prominent talent from other countries. The increasingly lively contacts with Hungary and the cities of northern Italy in the 1400s brought the Renaissance to

Kraków early. The city also made its mark as a centre of learning with the establishment in 1364 of the Jagiellon University.

The transfer of capital status to Warsaw in 1596 did not immediately affect Kraków, which continued to thrive on its wealth and cultural heritage, and remained an important power-nexus for south-eastern Poland. But the decline in importance began to make itself felt in the late 1600s, and by the eighteenth century the city had become a backwater – by the 1760s its population had fallen to no more than 10,000. By the end of the century it had become so decrepit that most of the old city had to be rebuilt, hence the large numbers of town houses dating from earlier periods that have late eighteenth-century or early nineteenth-century facades.

The city's fortunes revived somewhat at the beginning of the nineteenth century, helped by the revival of interest in history. In 1815 the Congress of Vienna left it as an independent republic, but this status was liquidated in 1848, when the Austrians incorporated it into their slice of Polish lands. After Austria's defeat by Prussia in 1866, Vienna was prepared to buy the docility of its provinces with concessions, and allowed its Polish ones far-reaching autonomy. As the other two regimes ruling Poland at the time (Russia and Germany) were moving in the opposite direction, Kraków naturally became the centre of Polish cultural and political life. This second flowering came to an end with independence in 1918, but it has revived faintly after the Second War, mainly because, almost uniquely among Polish cities, Kraków did not suffer any material damage.

✦✦✦   The **Wawel** hill, a natural defensive site, bears traces of a 10th
century fortified centre and the ground-plan of a pre-Romanesque
chapel of the Virgin Mary, clearly visible in the cellars of the present
castle [1]. This was built by Kazimierz the Great in the 1340s, and
expanded for Zygmunt I into a large palace with three wings and an
arcaded courtyard in the Renaissance style by *Francesco Fiorentino*
(1507–16), Master *Benedykt* (1524–9) and *Bartolomeo Berrecci*
(1530–6). Completed in 1536, it was the first major Renaissance
building north of the Alps. The east wing contains interiors with
painted friezes, one 1534 by *Hans Dürer*, and the Deputies' Hall,
with coffered ceiling with sculpted heads 1535, by *Sebastian
Tauerbach* and *Jan Janda*. The north wing was redecorated for
Zygmunt III in the Baroque style, 1590s–1620s, by *Giovanni
Trevano*, with the addition of two angle towers. The hall was redecorated in neo-Classical style 1787 by *Domenico Merlini*. The castle
was converted into barracks by the Austrians in 1804. Restoration
began in 1905. Of minor interest is the west wing, formerly the
kitchens, refurbished in high Nazi style for Hans Frank, the
German governor of Poland, who lived there during the Second
World War. The Castle interiors contain 136 Brussels tapestries
commissioned 1550–65 by king Zygmunt Augustus, in sets representing: the Garden of Eden, the story of Noah, the story of the
Tower of Babel, landscapes with animals, coats of arms, mono-
grams and grotesques – probably the greatest single collection in
existence. Also some earlier and later tapestries; painting (Italian,
Flemish, Dutch, French, English); and a fine collection of

Renaissance furniture, mainly Italian. There is also a treasury (not much in the way of crown jewels, as these were removed by the Prussians in 1796 and melted down; but some important objects connected with the crown, including the 'Szczerbiec' coronation sword, ca. 1270); an armoury (with fine Polish and oriental arms and armour); and a remarkable set of Turkish tents, banners and saddlery, captured at the battle of Vienna in 1683.

Cathedral of St Wacław and St Stanisław [2]. Remnants of a ✦✦✦ Romanesque cathedral, 1075–1150, of which only the western part with St Leonard's crypt, ca. 1120, survives. The present church was built between 1320 and 1346. Spire of clock tower 1715 by *Kacper Bażanka.*

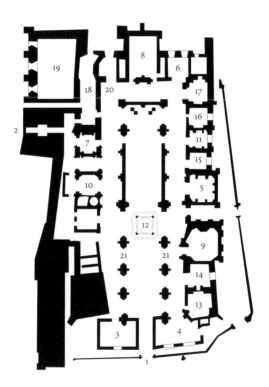

1 - West door, 2 - Clock tower, 3 - Chapel of the Holy Trinity, 4 - Holy Cross chapel, 5 - King Zygmunt's chapel, 6 - Tomicki chapel, 7 - Zebrzydowski chapel, 8 - St Mary's chapel, 9 - Vasa chapel, 10 - Lipski chapel, 11 - Zadzik chapel, 12 - Mausoleum of St Stanisław, 13 - Potocki chapel, 14 - Szafraniec chapel, 15 - Konarski chapel, 16 - Corpus Christi chapel, 17 - Załuski chapel, 18 - Sacristy, 19 - Treasury, 20 - Blessed Jadwiga's crucifix, 21 - Royal tombs.

Holy Trinity chapel, 1431. Holy Cross chapel, late 15th century, with Ruthene painted decoration ca. 1470 and marble tomb of king Kazimierz the Jagiellon by *Veit Stoss*, 1492. Zygmunt chapel, a magnificent example of Florentine Renaissance, 1517–33, by *Bartolomeo Berrecci*, with sculptural decoration by *Berecci*, *Giovanni Cini*, and tombs of Zygmunt I, 1526–31, by *Bartolomeo Berrecci*; Zygmunt Augustus, 1574, and Anna Jagiellon, 1575, by *Santi Gucci*; small silver altar, 1530s, by *Pankraz Labenwolf*, with paintings by *Georg Pencz*. Tomicki chapel, 1530, by *Bartolomeo Berrecci*; tomb of Piotr Tomicki, 1535, by *Bartolomeo Berrecci*. Zebrzydowski chapel, 1562–3, by *Jan Michałowicz of Urzedów*; tomb of Andrzej Zebrzydowski, 1563, by *Jan Michałowicz*. St Mary's (Batory) chapel, 1595, by *Santi Gucci*, some alterations 1649, with tomb of king Stefan Batory, 1595, by *Santi Gucci*. Vasa Chapel, begun 1605, by *Giovanni Battista Gisleni(?)*, and *Sebastiano Sala(?)*. Lipski Chapel, 1632, expanded 1746, by *Francesco Placidi*. Zadzik Chapel, 1766, by *Francesco Placidi*. Padniewski Chapel, 1840, by *Pietro Nobile*; tomb of Franciszek Padniewski, 1575, by *Jan Michałowicz*. In main body of church: mausoleum of St Stanisław, 1629, by *Giovanni Trevano*, with silver coffin, 1671, by *Peter van der Rennen*; high altar mid-17th century; organ loft 1761, by *Francesco Placidi*. In the ambulatory, black crucifix known as 'Blessed Jadwiga's Crucifix', late 15th century, with a number of ex-voto offerings, including the stirrup of Grand Vizir Kara Mustafa, sent to Kraków by courier after the Battle of Vienna, 1683, by king Jan III Sobieski as a token of victory; two Gothic triptychs, Holy Trinity, 1467, and Mater Dolorosa, late 15th century, by *Stanisław Durink*. Other paintings 15th–18th century, by *Jan Tretko, Tommaso Dolabella, Guercino, Tadeusz Kuntze*; portrait of Anna Jagiellon by *Nikolaus Martin Kober*. Grilles and chandeliers 16th–17th century, from Nuremberg and Gdańsk. Tapestries from Flanders, 17th century.

Royal tombs between pillars of ambulatory: Władysław the Short, second quarter of 14th century; Kazimierz the Great, 1370s; queen Jadwiga and king Władysław III, 1902 and 1906 respectively, both by *Antoni Madeyski*. Between nave pillars: Władysław Jagiełło, second quarter of 15th century, with Renaissance canopy, 1524, by *Giovanni Cini*. In Corpus Christi chapel: Jan Olbracht, 1501, workshop of *Veit Stoss*, in Renaissance setting, 1505 by *Francesco Fiorentino* (first work of the Renaissance in Poland); Michał Korybut Wiśniowiecki and Jan III Sobieski, both 1760, by *Francesco Placidi*. Also tombs or monuments of: Piotr Kmita, 1505, *Vischer foundry*; Cardinal Fryderyk Jagiellon, 1510 by *Peter Vischer*; J. Konarski, 1521, by *Bartolomeo Berrecci*; Piotr Gamrat, 1547, by

Giovanni-Maria Padovano; M. Szyszkowski, ca. 1630, by *Giovanni Trevano*; Piotr Gembicki, 1654–7, by *Giovanni Battista Gisleni(?)* and *Giovanni F. Rossi*; Potocki family, 1830 and 1833–40, with statue by *Bertel Thorvaldsen*. In **crypts**, royal tombs with metal sarcophagi, Mannerist and Baroque, 16th–17th century, mostly made in Gdańsk. Also tombs of various national heroes, including Tadeusz Kościuszko, Prince Józef Poniatowski, the poet Adam Mickiewicz, Marshal Piłsudski and, most recently brought over from Newark in England, General Władysław Sikorski. Cathedral **treasury** (not normally open to public, but a few of the objects are on show in the little museum opposite the cathedral), contains very impressive collection of chalices, monstrances, reliquiaries and other sacral objects, all the more remarkable for being only a fraction of a fraction of the cathedral's original equipment.

Houses of canons, choristers and cathedral vicars, 15th century with some remodelling up to end of 18th century. **Fortifications** 14th–15th century, bastions added 1790–4. Władysław IV Gate, after 1595, preceded by rondelle, ca. 1580, (on it, equestrian monument to Tadeusz Kościuszko).

Old Town (laid out 1257 on site of earlier settlements)
Achpresbyterial church of the Virgin Mary [3]. Traditionally the ♦♦♦ church of the German merchant community. A wonderful building, with a delightful exterior and a splendidly murky interior, with the atmosphere of a temple. Choir with carved decoration, 1355–65, vault 1442, nave 1392–7. Towers 1288–1320, superstructure of northern tower 1408, spire 1478 by *Mathias Heringk*; spire of southern tower ca. 1550. West porch 1750–3, by *Francesco Placidi*. Painted decoration of choir designed 1889–91 by *Jan Matejko*. Stained glass

second half of 14th century. High altar, huge wooden polyptych, 1477–89, by *Veit Stoss,* one of the wonders of the world. Stalls 1586 and 1635; altars 1723–61, by *Kacper Bażanka* and *Francesco Placidi*; paintings by *Giovanni Battista Pittoni*; ciborium 1554, by *Giovanni-Maria Padovano*. On right side of choir, in south aisle, crucifix, ca. 1491, by *Veit Stoss.* Bronze epitaphs, of Peter Salomon, 1516, by *Hans Vischer the Elder,* and of Boner family, 1538; over 100 other tombs and epitaphs. Behind it, **church** of St Barbara (since 1583 Jesuit) [4], 1390s, undistinguished. Interior redecorated ca. 1687 and 1742. By entrance, amusing Gothic Gethsemane with stone sculptures, 1488–1515. Jesus chapel, stone, Mannerist, 1609; painted vault 1765, by *Piotr Franciszek Molitor*; paintings ca. 1618, workshop of *Tommaso Dolabella*; very good stone Pietà, 1410, by *the Master of the Beautiful Madonnas.*

◆◆ In the middle of the Market Square, **Cloth Hall** [5], 14th century with decorative parapet, 1556–60, by *Santi Gucci,* restored 1870s. Houses the National Museum's gallery of 19th century Polish painting – a very mixed bag, poorly hung, but well worth a visit. **Tower** of non-existent Town Hall [6], before 1383, partly rebuilt 15th–16th century, spire 1784. Also in square, little **church** of St Wojciech [7], a delightful concoction of a square Romanesque chapel, 12th century, with Baroque superstructure and dome, 1611; a sacristy, 1711; and a chapel 1778.

Almost every house within the area enclosed by the old city walls dates from between the 14th and 16th centuries, and many are built on far older foundations. Although many were remodelled later or rebuilt quite drastically in the 18th or 19th centuries, most contain some original elements, such as portals, staircases, vaulting, beams and even frescoes. Most are privately owned, but it is generally possible to penetrate into the courtyard or the stairwell, where one can sometimes discover some delightful details. Of note in the **Market Square**: No. 6, Zborowski palace; No. 7, Montelupi palace, Renaissance portals mid-16th century; No. 8, Salamander house, with stone vaults, 14th century; No. 9, Boner-Firlej palace, 15th century, Mannerist decorative parapet wall, third quarter of 16th century; No. 10, Golden Carp house, painted coffered ceilings and friezes, late 16th century; (No 16, otherwise of little note, was the scene of a banquet given on the occasion of an international congress in 1364 by its wealthy patrician owner, Kazimierz Wierzynek, and attended by the Emperor Charles IV, the kings of Hungary, Denmark, Cyprus and Sicily, and by half-a-dozen other sovereign princes); No. 17, Hetman's palace, with carved stone vaults and heraldic keystones, ca. 1390, portals second half of 15th century, and 17th–18th century; No. 19, Picture house, facade early 18th century;

No. 20, Zbaraski, later Jabłonowski, later Wodzicki palace, 1620s, facade and upper-storey suite with Baroque Classical decoration, 1783.; No. 21, Lanckoroński palace, with carved beam ceilings and stucco in chapel, 17th century; No. 22, with Mannerist portal, early 17th century, with contemporary stucco; No. 26, St John of Capistrano house, stuccoed interior, 17th century; No. 27, Potocki palace, called the Ram house on account of the figures on the 18th-century facade; interiors rebuilt with neo-Classical decoration early 19th century, and later (one of the grandest Kraków society residences in the old days); No. 28, with painted ceiling, 17th century; No. 35, Wodzicki palace, called "Krzysztofory", 1682 by *Jakub Solari*, rebuilt repeatedly, interior with stucco, 17th–18th centuries, by *Baldassare Fontana*. No. 44, vaults 15th century, stone-carving and remnants of loggia, 16th century, now Historical **Museum** of the City of Krakow.

Dominican monastery [8], founded 1221, with church of the Holy ✦✦ Trinity. Traditionally the church of the Krakovian gentry and aristocracy. The least atmospheric church in Kraków, but still the largest sacral interior in the city. Begun 1241, rebuilt second half of 14th century, considerably reconstructed after fire 1850; west portal late 14th century. Myszkowski chapel, with sculpted busts in dome, 1614, from the Pińczów workshop. St Jacek's chapel 1583, rebuilt 1618, with paintings, 1625, by *Tommaso Dolabella*, stucco in dome by *Baldassare Fontana* and paintings by *Karl Dankwart*, ca. 1700, altar first quarter of 18th century, by *Antoni Frąckiewicz*. Zbaraski chapel, black marble interior with altar and tombs of Princes Krzysztof and Jerzy Zbaraski, and elliptical dome, 1633. Chapel of Our Lady of the Rosary with Greek-cross floor-plan, Baroque, 1688. In church, paintings, first quarter of 17th century, by *Tommaso Dolabella*; brass epitaph plaque to Filippo Buonaccorsi, known as Callimachus, ca. 1496 by *Peter Vischer the Elder* after a design by *Veit Stoss*; tomb of salt-mine administrator Prospero Provano, ca. 1584, and many others. Monastery buildings with three cloister gardens: original stone refectory and remnants of Romanesque monastery, ca. 1225. Chapter house, ca. 1250. Cloister, mid-14th century; new wings 15th–18th century, upper storey 17th century. Refectory murals, end of 15th century.

Jesuit college with **church** of SS Peter and Paul [9], founded by ✦ Zygmunt III. Church begun 1597, completed 1605–19 by *Giovanni Trevano*, on model of *Il Gesù* in Rome. Some marvellous rich stucco 1633, by *Giovanni Battista Falconi*. High altar, 1726–35, by *Kacper Bażanka*. Organ ca. 1765. Tomb of Bishop Andrzej Trzebicki, ca. 1679; of Brzechffa and Branicki families, 1716 and 1720–27 respectively, by *Kacper Bażanka*. A magnificent, but rather

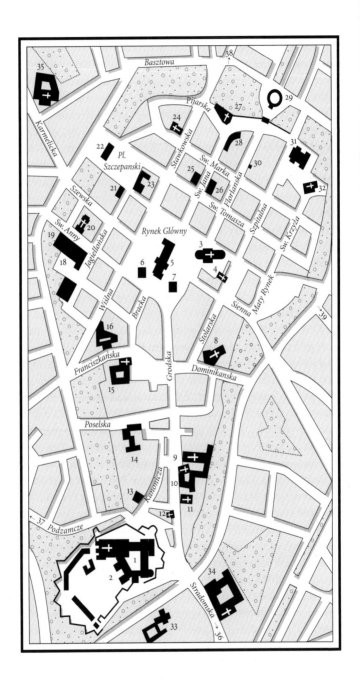

Basztowa
Pijarska
Karmelicka
35
38
29
27
28
24
Sw. Marka
31
30
22
Pl.
Szczepanski
Stawkowska
Sw. Jana
25
26
Floriariska
32
21
23
Szewska
Sw. Tomasza
Szpitalna
Sw. Krzyza
Sw. Anny
Rynek Glówny
20
19
Jagiellonska
3
18
6
5
4
7
Wislna
Maly Rynek
Sienna
Bracka
39
16
Stolarska
8
Franciszkanska
Dominikanska
15
Grodska
Poselska
14
9
10
Kanonicza
13
11
37
12
Podzamcze
1
2
34
Stradomska
33
36

cold church which does not quite work architecturally

Church of St Andrew [**10**], after 1086, rebuilt ca. 1150. This is a curi- ✦✦
ous building, as it is a classic Romanesque basilica in miniature,
with twin-towers, a great west front, a nave with two aisles and side
galleries, a transept, presbytery and an apse, all crowded into a tiny
space. Given to thePoor Clares (ca. 1318), who added an oratory
(now sacristy). Spires 1639. Interior redecorated in Baroque style
1701, by *Baldassare Fontana*. Monastic building ca. 1325, expanded
16th century and later. Loreto chapel 1642.

Church of St Giles [**12**] at the foot of the Wawel hill, ca. 1320,
expanded after 1595. Stalls from dismantled shrine of St Jacek in
Dominican church, ca. 1580.

Canons' houses on Kanonicza Street mostly early 16th century,
Renaissance and Mannerist, some with lovely stone portals and
window-embrasures, many of them bearing shield with two
crossed sceptres, the arms of the Jagiellon University. No. 18, 4th
quarter of 14th century, rebuilt in Renaissance style, 1563, by *Jan
Michałowicz of Urzędów*; No. 21, Deanery [**13**], third quarter of 14th
century, expanded in Mannerist style with addition of arcaded galleries around courtyard and portals, 1580s, workshop of *Santi
Gucci*.

Collegium Juridicum of the Jagiellon University, first half of 17th
century, with a charming arcaded courtyard.

Discalced Carmelites' monastery [**14**], 1611, converted into prison
1797, now **Archaeological Museum**, containing some good Slav
idols and a hoard of Hunnish gold.

Franciscan monastery [**15**], founded 1237 by Henry the Pious. ✦✦
Church 1260s, expanded 1400s, remodelled 1650s and reconstructed 1850–1912. A bit of a mess, but worth it for the astonishing
Secession style painted decoration and exceptional stained glass
designed, 1900, by *Stanisław Wyspiański* (particularly the west
window of God the Creator, magnificent when viewed at sunset). In
side-chapel, good picture of sorrowing Virgin, early 16th century.
Monastic building begun 14th century, cloisters 1423–55, with contemporary murals; gallery of portraits of Kraków bishops,
15th–19th century, tombs and epitaphs 15th–17th century; library
after 1630, stucco 17th/18th century, by *Baldassare Fontana*.

Archbishop's palace [**16**], 16th century, rebuilt 1640s, and 19th century. **Collegium Novum** [**17**] **and Collegium Maius** [**18**] of the ✦✦
Jagiellon University. Cluster of earlier buildings unified and linked
with arcades in 1490s. Some academic re-gothicising in 19th century. Library 1518–40, by the masters *Stefan* and *Benedykt*. Legend
has it that Dr Faustus, whom Goethe made famous, studied here,
and Copernicus certainly studied astronomy here. The richly deco-

rated interiors are open to the public, and there is a good collections of portraits of kings, rectors, professors; of university regalia; clocks, objects, textiles, tapestries and carpets. Above all, there is an exceptional collection of chemistry and physics equipment, astronomical instruments and geographical and celestial globes dating from the 15th–17th centuries. Nowodworski College [19].

♦♦♦ University **church** of St Anne [20], 1689–1703, by *Tilman van Gameren*. Spires ca. 1778, by Father *Sebastian Sierakowski*. Uniform furniture, altars, mausoleum of St Jan Kanty, with sculptural stucco by *Baldassare Fontana*, and painted decoration by *Carlo* and *Innocenzo Monti* and *Karl Dankwart*, 1703. Paintings by *Jerzy Eleuter Siemiginowski* and *Szymon Czechowicz*. Organ 1723-7, by *Szymon Sadkowski*. Beautiful baroque interior, luscious but graceful and light.

♦ **Stary Theatre** [21], founded 1843, rebuilt entirely 1903–7 by *Franciszek Mączyński* and *Tadeusz Stryjeński*, a good example of early Modernism. Decorative frieze 1906 by *Józef Gardecki*. On

♦ other side of square, **Palace of Art** gallery [22], Art Nouveau, 1901, by *Franciszek Mączynski*.

♦♦ **Szołajski House** [23], branch of **National Museum**, containing Polish painting and sculpture from 14th–18th century. Includes a stunning collection of 15–16th century Krakovian painting, as well as sculpture by Veit Stoss and others, and the iconic Madonna of Kruźlowa.

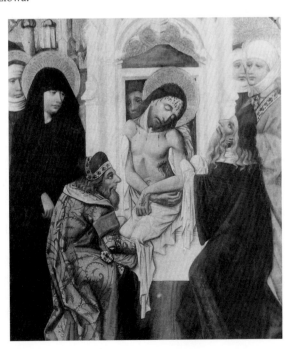

Church of St Mark [**24**], begun 1263. Nave 16th century, redecorated ✦
1621–47. St Sophia's chapel 1542, superstructure of belfry 1617.

No 12 Św Jana Street, mid-17th century facade, now houses Kraków **Historical Museum** [**25**].

Church of St John [**26**], mid-17th century, with 12th century stone Romanesque remnants, redecorated 1723. Behind, **convent of the nuns of the Presentation**, 1715–38, by *Kacper Bażanka*, expanded 1807.

Piarist monastery with **church** of the Transfiguration [**27**], 1718–27, by *Kacper Bażanka*, facade 1760 by *Francesco Placidi*. Illusionist vault painting 1731 by *Franciszek Eckstein*, decoration after 1732, *Jakub Hoffman* and others. Monastery building, along with Arsenal and other neighbouring buildings, rebuilt in the neo-Gothic style, 1879–84, by *Maurice Ouradou*, to house the ✦✦✦ **Czartoryski Museum** [**28**].

This is one of the world's most delightful private collections, and has a remarkable history. It was the brainchild of a patriotic 18th-century lady, Princess Izabela Czartoryska, who liked the idea of having objects which had belonged to great figures of the past or had some close association with them on the one hand, and who was fired by the idea of creating a hall of memory and fame of Poland's past greatness on the other. The collection thus comprises a mixed bag of everything from antiquities to nineteenth-century art, from sculpture and painting to textiles and jewels. Some objects are of slight artistic merit but of great affective worth, some are downright spurious, some magnificent. What purports to be Shakespeare's chair is juxtaposed with high-quality objects of vertu, Captain Cook's cutlass with *Rembrandt*'s haunting 'Landscape with the Good Samaritan'. The flavour is unique. Dominating the collection is *Leonardo da Vinci*'s 'Lady with the Ermine', without doubt his most beautiful painting, knocking spots off the 'Mona Lisa', and the most important work of western art in Poland. See also PUŁAWY

City walls 13th–14th century. Outer ring early 15th century demolished after 1806. St Florian's Gate [**29**] ca. 1305, superstructure 1498, spire, 1660. In front of it, Barbican, 1499.

Floriańska Street: No. 41, House of Jan Matejko [**30**], now **museum** dedicated to the life and work of the painter, but also with many works of art and decorative objects he used as 'props' in his paintings. No. 45, "Jama Michalika", Art Nouveau coffee-house, 1910, by *Karol Frycz*. Słowacki **theatre** [**31**], a miniature version of *Garnier's* ✦ Paris Opera, 1891–3, by *Jan Zawiejski*.

Church of the Holy Cross [**32**], early 1300s, nave and tower ca. 1400, murals ca. 1420 and later. Bronze font 1423. A rare example of ✦

a centrally-supported Gothic church, with its single pillar and square nave.

Town houses in **Mariacki Square**: No. 3, called Hippolitus house, portals 15th and mid-16th century, ceilings second half of 17th century, stucco 17th or 18th century, by *Baldassare Fontana*; in courtyard, wooden galleries, first half of 17th century. No. 4, Prelates' house, with inner courtyard, 1625, by *Maciej Litwinkowicz* and *Jan Zatorczyk*, decorative parapet wall.

In **Mikołajska Street**: No. 5, passage with stucco decoration, 1675. No. 18, facade Gothic/Renaissance, first half of 16th century, upper part added with Baroque portal mid-17th century.

In **Sienna Street**: No 5, house of the Fraternity of Charity, rebuilt 1595 from Gothic house, expanded 17th or18th century; portal Rococo; Baroque painted interiors, late 17th-18th century.

Former suburb of STRADOM:

◆◆ **Bernardine monastery [33]**, founded 1453. **Church** of St Bernard, 1659–80 by *Krzysztof Mieroszewski*. Paintings third quarter of 17th century, by *Franciszek Lekszycki*. Gothic sculptures of St Anne, end of 15th century, *Workshop of Veit Stoss*, and of Sorrowing Christ early 16th century. 'Dance of Death' ca. 1650. Baroque organ and gallery 1701-2, by *Euzebiusz Pasierbski*. **Missionaries' monastery** with **church** of Conversion of St Paul [34], 1719-28, by *Kacper Bażanka*; interior with sophisticated light-effects. Epitaph of Jan Sakran, 1527, from the *Cranach workshop*.

Former town of KAZIMIERZ:

Founded by Kazimierz the Great for the large numbers of Jews who had fled the pogroms attendant on the Black Death in western Europe and sought refuge in Poland. It gave the Jews special privileges, thereby attracting them here, but it was in no sense a ghetto, as the many churches proclaim.

◆◆ **Augustinian monastery** and **church** of St Catherine [36], founded 1342 by Kazimierz the Great. Spectacular chancel 1345–78, vaults after 1443, by Master *Hanusz*, nave turn of 14th century. Hungarian chapel, with central pillar supporting vault, 1403-14. South porch with decorative portals 1426; high altar 1634; tomb of Castellan Spytek Jordan ca. 1603. Monastery, chapter house and cloister second half of 14th century. Cloister murals, Gothic and Renaissance, 14th-16th centuries. Bell-tower 15th century.

◆◆ **Pauline monastery** on Skalka Hill, founded 1472 on the site of the martyrdom of St Stanisław. **Church** of St Stanisław, 1733–40, *Georg Muntzer*, completed 1740-2 by *Antoni Solari*. Stucco 1744 by *Johann Georg Lehnert*, and 1749, by *Wojciech Rojowski*. Spires 1762. Side altars by *Antonio Solari*, with sculpture by *Wojciech Rojowski*.

Monastic building mid-17th century, by *Jan Zaor*. Pool with enclosure and gate, 1683–90, stairs 1723, and statue of St Stanisław 1731. It has been suggested that this pool was originally a sacred place in heathen times.

Trinitarian monastery (now Hospitallers of St John of God) with **church** of the Holy Trinity 1758 by *Francesco Placidi* - an important Baroque facade. Painted vault 1757–8 by *Józef Piltz*.

Church of Corpus Christi. Choir 1369-87, by *Hans Czipser*; nave ♦♦♦ after 1405, by *Nikolaus Czipser*; superstructure, nave vault and gable ca. 1500. Tower 1582, spire 17th century. Three galilees, first half of 17th century. Chapel of Our Lady with stuccoed dome 1662. Stained glass ca. 1420; high altar 1634 and stalls, 1629, by Master *Stefan*, with paintings by Master *Marcin*. Renaissance painting of the Virgin Mary first half of 16th century. A wonderful building, its severe, slender Gothic pillars making an exciting contrast with the Rococo furniture. Monastery of the Canons Regular 16th century, three wings with arcaded gallery, rebuilt 17th–18th century.

✦✦ **Old Synagogue** (now **Museum** of Jewish History), Gothic, early 16th century, rebuilt with Renaissance architectural detail, 1557–70 by *Matteo Gucci*, devastated by Nazis, reconstructed 1959. **Jordan house**, first half of 16th century, rebuilt turn of 16th century. **R'emuh Synagogue**, 1557, repeatedly rebuilt and expanded; R'emuh **Jewish cemetery**, laid out 1553, with Renaissance and Baroque tombstones, 16–17th century. **High Synagogue**, 1590, repeatedly rebuilt. **Isaac's Synagogue**, 1640.

Former suburb of ZWIERZYNIEC:

✦✦ **Premonstratensian convent** [37], founded 1162. Original Romanesque **church of St Augustine** rebuilt in Baroque style 1596–1626, and interior of chancel in Classical style, late 18th century, by *Sebastian Sierakowski*. Monastic building with Renaissance decorative parapet wall, 16th–17th century.

Church of the Holy Redeemer, with Romanesque chancel, 12th century; nave and tower Gothic, 1622. Painting of Crucifixion, 1605 by *Kasper Kurcz*. Octagonal wooden **chapel** of St Margaret, 1690.

Former suburb of PIASEK:

Capuchin church, 1690s, by *Giovanni Ceroni* and *Martino Pellegrini*. Monastic building 1746. Loreto shrine, 1715 by *Kacper Bażanka*.

Carmelite monastery, 1657–79. **Church** of the Visitation, with Gothic remnants, 1390, towers adjoining chancel 1760. Stalls and high altar 1699 by *Jerzy Hankisz*; organ early 18th century; chapel of the Virgin Mary, 16th century, enlarged 1634; stucco and painted decoration, by *Jan Piotr Molitor(?)*, Rococo, 1756.

Former suburb of KLEPARZ:

Convent of the Nuns of the Visitation, with **church** of St Francis of Sales [**38**], 1695, by *Francesco Solari*. **Collegiate church** of St Florian, on Romanesque remnants, rebuilt after 1655, expanded 1760, tower superstructure 1902.

Former suburb of WESOŁA:

Discalced Carmelites' monastery [**39**] (since 1780 St Lazarus' Hospital). **Church** of the Immaculate Conception, after 1634, nave flanked by chapels. Black marble altars 1686. **Discalced Carmelites' convent** with **church** of St Theresa, 1719–33, by *Kacper Bażanka*; fine black marble late Baroque interior. Sculpture of Virgin Mary, ca. 1380.

Astronomical observatory, 1787 by *Stanisław Zawadzki* and *Feliks Radwański*.

Former suburb of PŁASZÓW:

Concentration-camp built by the Germans in 1942 on site of two Jewish cemeteries. Nearby stands the celebrated factory of Oskar Schindler.

Former suburb of MOGIŁA:

Cistercian abbey of St Wacław, founded 1225 by Bishop Iwo ✦✦ Odrowąż for monks from Lubiąż. Church begun 1243. Nave vault and furniture second half of 18th century; facade 1780, by *Franciszek Moser*; murals Renaissance, 1537–8, by *Stanisław Samostrzelnik*. East wing of monastery with chapter-house, third quarter of 13th century. Cloister mid-14th century. Library 1533, by Master *Benedykt*. Painted decoration 1538 by *Stanisław Samostrzelnik*. Abbot's palace 15th century, expanded 1569. Wooden **parish church**, 1466 by *Maciej Mączka*; rebuilt after 1587 ✦✦ and 1761. Baroque wooden belfry-gate, 1752.

Former suburb of PRĄDNIK BIAŁY:

Neo-Classical **manor house**, rebuilt first quarter of 19th century, from palace of bishops of Kraków.

Former suburb of RUSZCZA:

Parish church, ca. 1420; altered 17th and 20th century. Inside, tomb slab, ca. 1425, of Wierzbięta of Branice.

Other Museums in Kraków:

National Museum 'New Building', 1936–9, by *Bołesaw Szmit*, ✦✦ houses Polish 20th century painting and earlier decorative arts, as well as some militaria.

Jagiellon University Library, with exhibition of incunabula, includ- ✦✦ ing Baltazar Behem's beautiful illuminated *Codex* of 1505.

Czartoryski Library (Św Jana St), with a fine collection of illuminated manuscripts and incunabula.

Archdiocesan Museum (Kanonicza St).

Polish Air Museum, Rakowice. A motley collection of mementos and wrecks, and also the only surviving Polish pre-war PZL P-11 fighter.

In environs of Kraków:

WOLA JUSTOWSKA:

Renaissance **Villa**, first half of 17th century, with Gothic parts, rebuilt early 19th century and 1882.

BRANICE:

Manor house, Renaissance/Mannerist, 1603. A typical semi-fortified gentleman's residence of the period.

KOŚCIELNIKI:

Country house of Wodzicki family, 1708–27, by *Giuseppe Piola* and *Antonio Bay*, altered after 1773, by *Józef Lebrun(?)*, and, in neo-Classical style, early 19th century.

BIELANY:

✦✦✦ **Camaldolite monastery** founded 1605 by Mikołaj Wolski, Grand Marshal of Poland, Baroque, 1610–30, by *Orazio Turiani* and *Valentin von Säbisch*. Church of the Assumption 1622–42, with a fine stone facade by Wallenstein's architect *Andrea Spezza*. Inside, remains of very fine stucco work by *Giovanni Battista Falconi*, paintings by *Tomaso Dolabella*. 14 monastic hermitages, 1605–9. A most impressive building, redolent of the Counter-Reformation, in a magnificent position.

NOWA HUTA:

Specially-built socialist industrial town, begun 1948. The huge steelworks at its core were sited far from either ore or coal, specifically in order to create what was assumed would be a vigorously socialist proletariat on the doorstep of traditional 'bourgeois' Kraków. The plan misfired catastrophically. The workers of Nowa Huta proved remarkably resistant to socialist principles and waged a running battle to obtain permission for building a church (something that had not been taken into consideration when the central planning office had designed the town). As permission was not forthcoming, the workers turned a brick hut into a chapel and then, in 1977, began to 'repair' it. This 'repair work', punctuated with the occasional Militia attack, culminated in one of the largest churches in Poland, the **church** of Our Lady Queen of Poland, 1967-1977, by *Wojciech Pietrzyk*, known as the 'Ark' on account of its sweeping shape. Not beautiful, but impressive. The rest of the town is a show-piece of Stalinist architecture, with its inimitable blend of crushing heaviness with prissy 'tastefulness'.

Originally headquarters of the Krasicki family, this magnificent **castle** was built in Renaissance/Mannerist style between 1592 and 1618 by *Galeazzo Appiani* and others; partly rebuilt 1860s by the Sapieha family, to whom it had passed. A spectacular sight.

Original headquarters of the Krasiński family, the only great magnatial family of Mazovia (see also Opinogóra and Sterdyń). Nothing remains of the earlier castle or houses, except for a much-restored gate-tower. The last residence, a hideous 19th century house, was demolished during the German occupation by no less distinguished a person than Erich Koch, then Gauleiter of East Prussia, who built in its stead a bomb-proof palace, complete with subterranean cinemas and swimming-pool. **Parish church** founded by Krasiński family, Mannerist, 1575, interior Baroque, ca. 1739. Fine Krasiński tombs, 16th-17th century; painted decoration 1747 by *Sebastian Eckstein.*

Originally a trade settlement on the route between Poland and Russia, later a royal burgh, and from the 17th century a private town of the Zamoyski family. **Monastery of Canons Regular. Church** of Our Lady and St Augustine, begun 1469, altered 1527–41. Squat and lacking in grace, but full of atmosphere. Tenczyński tombs, workshop of *Santi Gucci* - of particular note that of Jan Tenczyński and his betrothed, the Swedish Princess Cecilia Vasa, 1604–5, with the legend of the love of two children dissolved by death. Paintings commemorating the Battle of Lepanto, 1627, workshop of *Tommaso Dolabella.* Neo-Classical organ case, 1804.

KRASNOBRÓD   MAP 28
Dominican church 1690s by *Jan Michał Link*, facade rebuilt 1769.

KRASNOSIELC   MAP 18
Neo-Classical **church**, 1792, by *Hilary Szpilowski*.

✦   KRASNYSTAW   MAP 28
Trading settlement, from 1490 to 1826 residence of the bishops of
Chełm.
Jesuit church of St Cecilia, 1695–1717, by *Jan Huss*, facade 1730–41;
stucco first quarter of 18th century, painted decoration ca. 1723, by
Adam Swach; furniture 18th century; organ case third quarter of
18th century, by *J. Maucher*. College building 1695, expanded 1730,
rebuilt 1902.
Bishop's palace 1826. **Seminary** 1739, rebuilt turn of the 19th/20th
century.

✦ · KREMPACHY   MAP 21
Highland village **parish church** of St Martin, mid-16th century .
Cemetery church of St Valentine, in Renaissance tradition, 1761.

✦   KREMPNA   MAP 22
Church of SS Cosmas and Damian (originally Orthodox), wooden,
16th–17th centuries, tower 1771.

✦   KROBIA   MAP 11
Romanesque **church** of St Giles, ca. 1250, facade ca. 1605.

KRÓLIKÓW   MAP 12
Parish church, Baroque; stuccoes, painted decoration and furniture Rococo, 1790–7.

KROMOŁÓW   MAP 19
Jewish cemetery with 18th–19th century toombstones.

KROŚCIENKO   MAP 22
Parish church, choir 14th century, with contemporary and ca. 1490
murals; nave 1546, with Renaissance murals, 1589; rebuilt in
Baroque style.

✦   KROŚNIEWICE   MAP 17
Jerzy Dunin-Borkowski **Museum**. The varied remains of the collection of a great hoarder, including paintings, works of art, manuscripts, books, coins, arms and armour.

Pilgrimage church with rectangle of arcaded galleries and chapels, founded by Bishop Teodor Potocki, 1715. Furniture ca. 1725. **Almshouse**, ca. 1720.

KROSNO   MAP 29 ✦✦
Important glass-making centre, still exporting all over the world, also the site of the sinking of the first oil-well in Poland (1854). **Parish church** of the Holy Trinity, last quarter of 15th century, vaults, gables and domed chapels with Baroque decoration, 1638–46, by *Vincenzo Petroni*. Chapel of Portius family (of Scots ancestry), second quarter of 17th century, by *Vincenzo Petroni*. Furniture 1640s. Exceptional collection of 20 mid-17th century paintings, some by *Tomasso Dolabella*, on the subject of death. Belfry 1651.
Franciscan monastery, founded 1378. **Church** of St Martin, 15th–16th century, reconstructed ca. 1900. Oświęcim chapel, 1647 by *Vincenzo Petroni*, with ornate stucco work by *Giovanni Battista Falconi*, portraits of Stanisław and Anna Oświęcim. Renaissance tombs by *Giovanni-Maria Padovano*. Mannerist tombs by *Jakub Trwały*. Baroque tombs by *Giovanni Reitino*. Wing of monastery, 1591, rebuilt end of 18th century. **Capuchin church** and monastery, 1771–1811. **Houses** in market square, 16th–18th century. **Museum** of the Polish oil industry.

KROTOSZYN   MAP 11 ✦✦
Major centre of the Bohemian Brethren, later Polish Brethren. **Meeting House**, now Catholic church, 1597, reconstructed 1774–82. Very fine **Trinitarian monastery**, 1733. Church 1766–72, designed by *Karl Martin Frantz*. Wooden **church** of St Fabian and St Sebastian, 1572, rebuilt 1813. Small local **museum**.

KRUPE   MAP 28 ✦
Ruins of Orzechowski **castle**, late 16th century, expanded 1608. **Manor house** of Rey family, last quarter of 18th century, rebuilt ca. 1840, and ca. 1880.

KRUSZWICA   MAP 10 ✦✦
Ancient centre of one of the western Slav tribes at the head of lake Gopło, and, from 10th to 12th centuries, important religious site. Romanesque **collegiate church** of SS Peter and Paul, 1120–40. Relicts of **castle** founded by Kazimierz the Great, mid-14th century, including the 'Mouse' Tower, in which, the legend goes, after a life of indulgence and cruelty the wicked prince Popiel was eaten alive

by mice, as a result of which an honest wheelwright named Piast was invited to found a new dynasty.

◆ KRUSZYNA   MAP 19
Dönhoff **country house**, 1630, restored ca. 1870 for Lubomirski family. Original formal **park** with pavilions, grotto and hermitage. **Parish church** of St Matthew, ca. 1650–96.

◆ KRUSZYNIANY   MAP 26
Village of Tatar soldiers granted land by king Jan III Sobieski. Wooden **mosque**, 18th century.

◆ KRUŹLOWA WYŻNA   MAP 22
Wooden **church** with painted ceiling, 1520. The famous wooden Madonna now in the National Museum in Kraków comes from here.

◆◆ KRZCIĘCICE   MAP 19
Church of St Procopius, 1531–42 by Master *Albert*. Lovely gothic gables. Interesting combination of red brick Gothic structure with Renaissance details. Renaissance tomb of Jan Niemsta, the founder of the church, 1542.

KRZEMIENICA   MAP 19
Parish church, Gothic/Renaissance, 1598.

KRZEMIENICA   MAP 29
Wooden **parish church**, 1754.

KRZEPICE   MAP 12
Small royal town with iron mining origins. **Church** of Canons Regular, founded 1466, rebuilt before 1628 by *Valentin von Säbisch*.

◆◆◆ KRZESZÓW (GRÜSSAU)   MAP 6
Magnificent **Cistercian abbey**, founded 1292 from Jędrzejów. Church 1728–35. Painted decoration 1735, by *Georg Wilhelm Neunhertz*, and uniform furniture, integrated with architecture, completed before 1775. Sculpture by *Anton Dorasil* and *Ferdinand Maxmilian Brokoff*. Behind chancel, sepulchral chapel of the Piast Dukes of Świdnica, 1735–47, painted decoration by *Georg Wilhelm Neunhertz*, 1736; tombs of Bolko I and Bolko II, 14th century Monastic building 1662, expanded in 1768. **Parish church** of St Joseph 1690s; good painted decoration 1695, by *Michael Willmann*.

KRZESZOWICE   MAP 21 ✦✦
Neo-Gothic **parish church**, designed by *Karl Friedrich Schinkel*,
begun 1832. Potocki **country house**, 1850–8, *Franciszek Maria Lanci*
and *Feliks Pokutyński*, rebuilt late 19th century - a mess. Neo-
Classical **villa** of Princess Izabela Lubomirska, called Vauxhall,
1789 by *Szczepan Humbert*, rebuilt late 19th century.

KRZYCKO WIELKIE   MAP 4
Baroque **manor house**, ca. 1750.

KRZYDLINA WIELKA (GROSS-KREIDEL)   MAP 6
Church, early 16th century, painted ceiling Renaissance, mid-16th
century.

KRZYWACZKA   MAP 21
Neo-Classical **manor house**, first half of 19th century.

KRZYWIN   MAP 11
Church: chancel 1450, nave first half of 16th century.

KRZYŻANOWICE   MAP 20 ✦✦
Parish church, founded in 1789 by the priest turned reformer and
later Jacobin Hugo Kołłataj. Small but monumental neo-
Classicism by *Stanisław Zawadzki*. Furniture contemporary.

KSIĄŻ (FÜRSTENBERG)   MAP 6 ✦✦
Magnificent Hochberg family **castle** in wonderfule setting, still very
grand, though badly damaged by the war and post-war neglect.
Original structure Gothic/Renaissance, 1548–55, with remnants of
earlier castle of the dukes of Świdnica (1292). Front block Baroque,
1718–34, by *Felix Anton Hammerschmidt*; thoroughly rebuilt early
20th century. Contains fine hall of mirrors. Ruined romantic Old
Castle, 1797, by *Christian Wilhelm Tischbein*. Of interest too are the
bunkers built for Hitler, who took a fancy to the place, and saw it as
another lair for himself in the east. He forced the occupant, Princess
Daisy of Pless, to move out and began work in 1941.

KSIĄŻ WIELKI   MAP 19 ✦✦
Very good, mostly stone **parish church**, 15th century,
expanded first half of 17th century. Myszkowski chapel, first half of
17th century.
Palace of Bishop Piotr Myszkowski, 1585–95 by *Santi Gucci*, superstructure neo-Gothic, 1846, designed by *Friedrich August Stuler*.
An unusual Mannerist construction, with two symmetrical pavil-

ions, housing the chapel and library respectively, with artillery emplacements below.

KSIĄŻNICE WIELKIE MAP 22

Parish church of the Assumption; chancel 1680, chapel 1733, nave 1864. Very important Gothic polyptych, 1491 by Master *Michał of Kraków*, a pupil of *Veit Stoss*.

♦♦ KSIĘŻY LAS MAP 14

Charming wooden **church**, 1494, with 18th-century chapel attached.

♦♦ KUROZWĘKI MAP 20

Lovely Baroque/Classical **country house** of the Sołtyk family, ca. 1770, by *Ferdynand F. Nax(?)*, expanded from small oval castle of Kurozwęcki family (14th–17th century). Later home of Popiel family, and recently re-occupied.

Monastery of Canons Regular founded 1487. Church rebuilt in Baroque style first half of 17th century. Lanckoroński Chapel 1676–97, stuccoes 17th–18th century. Monastic building expanded first half of 17th and 19th century.

♦ KURZELÓW MAP 19

Collegiate church of St Mary, built by *Archbishop Jarosław Skotnicki*, 1360. The single pier vault of the nave is in contrast to the rather heavy exterior.

KUTNO MAP 17

Baroque **country house**, 1781–55. Originally a small timber palace, 1750s, by *J.M.Walter* and *J.F.Knobel*, built as a staging-post for king Augustus III on his journeys between his court capital in Dresden and his state capital in Warsaw.

♦ KWIATOŃ MAP 22

Fine wooden **church** of St Prakseva (originally Orthodox), 1700.

♦♦ KWIDZYŃ (MARIENWERDER) MAP 8

Cathedral (now parish church). Choir and crypt ca. 1340, main body and tower after 1350. Mosaic 1380, murals second half of 14th century. Very good late Gothic bishop's throne, 1510. Cathedral chapter, 1322–84, now a **museum**, of mainly local interest.

♦ KWILCZ MAP 4

The cradle of the Kwilecki family and its property in unbroken line of descent from the 14th century to 1939. **Country house**, 1828, by *Karl Friedrich Schinkel*. **Parish church**, 1766–81.

ŁABĘDNIK MAP 16

Church, 14th century, rebuilt 16th century.

ŁABISZYN MAP 10

Reformed Franciscans' church, chancel 1690, by *Pietro Fontana*, nave 1731, expanded 1911. Monastery (now priory), 1731.

ŁABUNIE MAP 28 ✦

Baroque **country house** of the Zamoyski family , after 1744, by *Jerzy de Kawe*, rebuilt, with addition of semicircular colonnaded ranges, after 1770. Farm buildings 1776. **Church**, Baroque, first half of 17th century, remodelled 18th century.

LACHOWICE MAP 21 ✦

Wooden **parish church** of SS Peter and Paul, Baroque, 1789. Wooden **watermill**, ca. 1850.

ŁĄCZA MAP 14

Wooden **church** of St Mary, before 1499, tower later.

ŁĄCZNIK MAP 13

Church, 1723, western part expanded 1877. Painted decoration Rococo, 1761 by *Francesco Sebastini*; furniture Rococo.

LĄD MAP 10 ✦✦✦

Important **Cistercian abbey** founded ca. 1175. Church of St Mary and St Nicholas, originally ca. 1200, rebuilt 1651–89 by *Tomaso Poncino, Giorgio Catenaci, Jan Koński* and *Giuseppe Belotti*; tower superstructure 1725. The wonderful domed octagonal nave by *Pompeo Ferrari* dates from 1735. Polychromy by *Adam Swach*, 1711, and *Georg Wilhelm Neunhertz*, 1732. Interesting organ case, 1732-5, by *Pompeo Ferrari*. The fine chapter house with central pillar, cloister and oratory murals of ca. 1370 are all that remains of the original Gothic monastery, which was heavily rebuilt in the 17th–18th century. Ceiling in Abbots' hall, 1722 by *Adam Swach*.

ŁAGÓW MAP 4

Old fortified settlement, with **castle** of the Knights Hospitallers of St John of Jerusalem, mid-14th century. Outer ring of fortifications 16th century, expanded late 17th century, rebuilt late 19th century. Now a hotel.

ŁĄKA MAP 29
Church, 1713–44 by *Jan Chomkiewicz*. Lubomirski **country house**, turn of 17th century, by *Tilman van Gameren*, lowered and rebuilt 1850–4.

ŁĄKA PRUDNICKA MAP 13
Renaissance **castle**, 16th century, rebuilt 1727, and in neo-Gothic style, 1874.

LANCKORONA MAP 21
Medieval village beside ruins of royal **castle**. **Parish church** 14th–16th centuries.

✦✦✦ ŁAŃCUT MAP 29
Originally the lair of one of the Stadnicki family, who was little more than a brigand, Łańcut was acquired from his family along with Wiśnicz by the Lubomirskis around 1600. In 1753 Prince Stanisław Lubomirski, Marshal of the Crown, married Princess Elżbieta Czartoryska, a great patroness of the arts, who recast Łańcut in her own way. Through one of her daughters it passed to the Potocki family, in whose possession it remained until 1944, when the last owner, Alfred Potocki, took as many works of art as he could pack into 14 railway freight wagons and escaped from the advancing Soviets. Under the Potocki regime Łańcut became a byword for slightly vulgar show and manic entertaining. Distinguished guests who stayed here included the Comte de Provence (later Louis XVIII), the Emperor Franz Jozef II, Archduke Rudolf, Archduke Charles, Joachim von Ribbentrop, the

Duke and Duchess of Kent, and an assortment of Afghan monarchs and Rumanian princesses. Important castle-type magnate's **residence** erected 1629–41 by *Mattia Trapola* for Prince Stanisław Lubomirski. Stucco by *Giovanni Battista Falconi*. Spires 1680s by *Tilman van Gameren*. Extensive reworking for Princess Elżbieta Lubomirska of second floor, new wing and decoration of facades and interiors 18th–19th century by *Piotr Aigner*, stuccoes by *Fryderyk Baumann*, painted decoration by *Vinzenzo Brenna* and *Antoni Smuglewicz*. Some redecoration in neo-Baroque style 1894–1903 for Potocki family. Neo-Classical orangery, ca. 1800 by *Piotr Aigner*. The house has some magnificent interiors, including the ballroom and the theatre, furnished with good French and Polish 18th-century and English 19th-century furniture, some good pictures, antique marbles and a fine statue of Prince Henryk Lubomirski as a boy, 1787, by *Antonio Canova*. There are also some interesting turn-of-the-century 'Chinese' rooms with matching furniture. Fortifications 1629–41, restored 1894–1903. Romantic "Little Castle", ca. 1800 by *Piotr Aigner* and *Fryderyk Baumann*, restored 1903. Riding School 1831, by *L. Bogochwalski*; now houses largest collection of carriages and harnesses in Poland.
Synagogue, 1761, with **museum** of Judaica.

ŁAPCZYCA   MAP 21
Church of St Mary, 1340 and 15th century. One of many founded by king Kazimierz the Great.

ŁAPSZE WYŻNE   MAP 21
Parish church, 1760.

ŁASIN   MAP 10
Church, ca. 1300, gables 1647, nave rebuilt 1710, 1889–92 and 1912. Wooden bell-tower, 18th century.

ŁASK   MAP 12 ✦✦
Collegiate church founded by Primate Jan Łaski, brick with rich ceramic decoration (only partly preserved), 1525; remodelled after 1749. Marble bas-relief late 15th century, by *Andrea della Robbia,* in south chapel. Wooden **church** of the Holy Ghost (now Protestant), Baroque, 1666.

ŁASZEW   MAP 12 ✦
Wooden Gothic **church**, first half of 16th century; painted ceiling Renaissance, mid-16th century; Pietà, ca. 1430.

ŁAZANY   MAP 21
Parish church, Gothic/Renaissance, 1586–90. Treasury with many Lubomirski bequests.

ŁAŻANY   MAP 6
Renaissance **castle** with arcaded courtyard, late 16th century, rebuilt 17th and mid-18th century. Now in ruins.

ŁAZISKA   MAP 14
Wooden **church** of St John the Baptist, first half of 16th century.

LĘBORK (LAUENBURG)   MAP 8
Church of St James, 15th century, rebuilt 1910.

ŁĘCZNA   MAP 27
Old market town, famous for its horse-fairs. **Church**, 1618–31, rebuilt after 1730. **Synagogue**, 1648, expanded 1846, now a **museum**.

◆◆ ŁĘCZYCA   MAP 17
An off-shoot of the ancient Piast princely residence at nearby TUM, which was also the site of the first Benedictine abbey in Poland, founded 996 by St Wojciech on a palisaded defensive mound. Of this, only the **collegiate church** of St Alexis survives, a stone basilica with galleries, two choirs and four towers, one of the best preserved Romanesque churches in Poland, dating from 1161. Carved portal and remnants of murals also Romanesque. Beside it, wooden **parish church**, 1761.

In 1331 a castle was built half a mile away at Łęczyca, the site of a small market town. The remains of the royal **castle**, rebuilt by

Kazimierz the Great, 1357–70, now house a local **museum**.
Church, before 1425, redecorated mid-17th–18th century.
Bernardine monastery and **church**, 1636–43 and 1677–86, in
Gothic/Renaissance tradition, painted decoration and furniture
Rococo, third quarter of 18th century. Organ 1764-6, by *Michał
Engler jr.* and *Franz Eytner*.

LEGNICA (LIEGNITZ)   MAP 6 ✦✦✦

Rebuilt after the Tatar invasion of 1241, Legnica becme the capital of
the Piast dukes of Legnica-Brzeg, who did not die out until 1675. It
was a thriving trading town, with some mining and metalworking
industry. It also saw the foundation of the first Lutheran university
in Europe (1526).

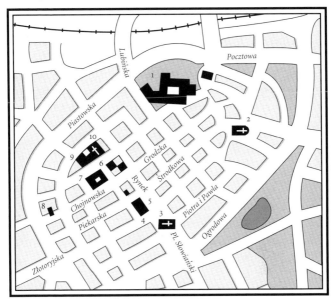

Castle of the dukes of Legnica [1], founded before 1238 by Henry
the Bearded, expanded 16th–17th century and 1835 by *Karl
Friedrich Schinkel*. Remnants of Romanesque *Palatium*, in south
wing and traces of stone chapel in west wing, early 13th century.
Eastern Gate 1533, by *Georg von Amberg*. In town, **church** of SS
Peter and Paul [3], begun 1328 by Master *Wieland*, vaults 1420–30,
side chapels 15th-16th century, exterior rebuilt 1894. Brass font ca.
1300, polyptych 1498, tombs and epitaphs 14th-17th century. **Jesuit
college** (up to 1698 Franciscan monastery) [9]; **church** of St John
[10] 1714–30; Piast sepulchral chapel (rebuilt from Gothic chancel),
circular, domed, with sculpture and painted decoration, 1676–9 by
Carlo Rossi, and *Mathias Raüchmuller*, restored 1960. College

building 1700–6, by *Johann Georg Knoll*. **Church** of St Mary (since 1524 Protestant) [**2**], 14th century, rebuilt 1828 by *Karl Friedrich Schinkel*. Town **walls**, first half 14th century. **Town Hall** [**4**] 1737–41, by *Franz Michael Scharhoffer*. **Military Academy** [**7**] 1726–35, by *Johann Christian Hertel* and others. **Palace** of Lubiąż abbots [**6**] 1745, by *Martin Frantz(?)*, now houses **museum**. "Herring stalls" in market square [**5**], some facades with sgraffito decoration, Renaissance, others baroque or neo-Classical. Chojnów gate [**8**].

✦✦ LEGNICKIE POLE   MAP 6
Site of a critical battle, fought on 9 April 1241, in which Henry the Pious of Poland stood up to the Tatar Horde which had swept through the whole of eastern and southern Poland. The Tatars retreated from the field, but it was a Pyrrhic victory for the Poles, the flower of whose knighthood died on the field. In the little Gothic **church** there is a **museum** dedicated to the battle. Fine **Benedictine abbey**, 1727–31 by *Kilian Ignaz Dientzenhofer*. Church of St Jadwiga, on a groundplan which is a combination of intersecting ellipses. painted decoration by *Cosmas Damianus Asam*, sculpture by *Karl Josef Hiernl*, pictures by *Christian Philipp Bentum* and *Vavrinec Vaclav Reiner*.

✦✦ ŁĘGOWO   MAP 15
Protestant **church**, 1599–1604. Pictures by *Anton Möller*.

✦ ŁĘKI GÓRNE   MAP 22
Wooden **church**, late 15th century, expanded 17th century. Painting late 15th century. **Manor house** of Lubieniecki family, early 17th century, attic storey 19th century; stucco 18th century.

LEMBARG   MAP 15
Church, second half 14th century, rebuilt early 18th century. Painted decoration ca. 1700 by *S. Cichonowski*.

✦✦ LESKO   MAP 29
Church, Gothic, 1534, interior redecorated before 1760, tower rebuilt 1889. **Castle** of Kmita family, 1507, residential tower, mid-16th century; rebuilt 1656 and 1837; reconstructed after 1945. The **Synagogue** is one of the most interesting left in Poland, now a **museum. Jewish Cemetery** with numerous stone 'macevas'.

✦ LEŚNA PODLASKA   MAP 25
Notable **pilgrimage centre**, venerating a round red rock with an image of the Virgin, allegedly sent down from heaven. Pauline

church, 1731–52 by *Karol Bay*, rebuilt late 19th century. St Mary's chapel with well, 1718.

LEŚNO   MAP 7
Timber **church** in Gothic style, 1650.

LESZNO   MAP 11 ✦✦
This private market town was founded in 1547 in the cradle of the Leszczyński family, and, thanks to their conversion to Calvinism during the Reformation, it also became a haven for Protestants and, even after they had converted back to Rome, for Bohemian Brethren. The College of Leszno (founded 1555) was, along with the Academy of Raków, a leading centre of Arian thought, and was greatly enhanced when the Czech philosopher Jan Amos Komensky became its rector in 1620. The city and the college were sacked in 1655 during the Swedish invasion, and three years later the Arian sect was banished from Poland for having sided with the Protestant Swedes.

Church of St Nicholas, founded by Bogusław Leszczyński, 1685–96 by *Giovanni* and *Giorgio Catenaci*, and 1707–9, by *Pompeo Ferrari*. Good vigorous Jesuit Baroque. Leszczyński tombs by *Pompeo Ferrari*.

Church of the Bohemian Brethren, 1652–4. Gruszczyński chapel 1711, by *Pompeo Ferrari*. **Lutheran church** of the Holy Cross, begun 1707 by *Pompeo Ferrari*; external walls 1711–mid-18th century, by *Johann Adam Stier*, interior 1792. Tower 1782 by *Karl Martin Frantz*. The design does not quite work, but the effect is grand. **Pastor's house**, first half of 18th century, now **museum** of local history and the Arian movement. Impressive **Town Hall** 1709 by *Pompeo Ferrari*. **School** of the Bohemian Brethren, 17th century and 1714.

LEWIN BRZESKI   MAP 11
Church (later Protestant church), 14th century, remodelled 1593 and 1660. Baroque **residence**, first half of 18th century, gates and outbuildings later.

LEWKÓW   MAP 12 ✦✦
Elegant Palladian **country house** of General Wojciech Lipski, with traces of Baroque in its shape and ornamentation, 1788–91; stucco and pictorial decoration ca. 1800, probably by *Antoni Smuglewicz*.

LEŻAJSK   MAP 29 ✦✦✦
Magnificent fortified **Bernardine monastery** founded 1608 by

Łukasz Opaliński, Marshal of the Court. Church of the Annunciation 1618-28, by *Antonio Pellacini* of Lublin, painted decoration 1752, mainly by *Stanisław Stroiński*. Good Baroque/Rococo furniture, great organ (one of the few surviving original instruments of this period in Poland and one of the best of its kind in Europe), 1678-1729, by *Stefan Studziński* and *Jan Fłowiński*. A riot of angels, saints and dragons, plus Hercules and the Hydra. Stalls ca. 1650. Miraculous painting of Madonna of the Consolation, 17th century by *Father Erasmus*. Monastic building, 1637 and 1670; stuccoed and painted interiors, 17th–18th century. Fortifications first half of 17th century and 1675, by *J. Wałowicz*. **Parish church** 1619, also fortified.

✦✦ LIBUSZA   MAP 22

Wooden **church** of the Nativity of the Virgin, ca. 1510, tower 1607. Very good painted ceiling and murals 1523.

✦✦✦ LIDZBARK WARMIŃSKI (HEILSBERG)   MAP 16

A residence of the bishops of Warmia. Copernicus lived and worked here for a time. Bishops' **castle**, 1350–1400, superstructure of angle turrets after 1497;arcaded inner courtyard; star vaulted interiros, murals 15th–16th century. Forecourt 15th century, fortifications expanded 1589. East wing rebuilt as palace of Bishop Adam Grabowski, 1766; expanded ca. 1770 by Bishop Ignacy Krasicki, the wit and poet, who had a particular affection for this place. Now Regional **Museum.**
Parish church, second half of 14th century, eastern part 1891–6. Spire 1718. Timber **Orthodox** church (originally Protestant), 1821–3. Town **walls** with towers, ca. 1350, two-tower Tall Gate 1532.

✦ LIPKÓW   MAP 18

Manor house, 1792, that belonged to Paschalis Jakubowicz, one of the most popular manufacturers of the silk sash belts that were an essential part of the Polish nobleman's costume, whose factory was in this village.

✦✦ LIPNICA MUROWANA   MAP 22

Picturesque little highland town full of vernacular architecture. Wooden **cemetery church** of St Leonard, end of 15th century. Painted decoration Gothic and Baroque. Three Gothic triptychs.

LISEWO   MAP 10

Church of the Holy Cross, end of 13th century. Tower with decorative parapet second half of 16th century.

Sleepy little town, with many old wooden houses, set in meadows on Liwiec river, once the border between Mazovia and Lithuania.

Castle of the dukes of Mazovia, 1420s, by Master *Mikołaj*, on to which was built a small Baroque country house in the 1780s. This now houses a **museum**, mainly of militaria from all over the world; an incredible hotch-potch, but some people like rows of bayonets. A place of rustic charm.

ŁODYGOWICE   MAP 14

Wooden **church**, 1634–7, chapels and tower added 1797. Fortified **manor house**, Mannerist, ca. 1630, re-gothicised 19th century.

ŁÓDŹ   MAP 19 ✦

This city is a unique phenomenon in Poland. In 1821 it was a village with a small spinning cottage industry, but that year the Polish government assisted the expansion of this industry, and by 1830, Łódź had 4,000 inhabitants and a number of steam-powered spinning machines. The production of wool here tripled between 1823 and 1829, and the production of cotton quintupled between 1825 and 1830. By 1845, when Łódź was linked to Warsaw by rail, it had become the principal supplier of cotton to Russia and China. By then Łódź had 20,000 inhabitants, and by 1900 it had 300,000. It had become one of the three cotton "L"s; Lancashire supplied the

British Empire with cotton, Lille supplied the French colonies and much of Africa and South America, Łódź supplied the Russian Empire and China. The terrible working conditions that accompanied the city's vertiginous development spawned strong workers' movements at the turn of the century, which played a major part in the unrest of 1905, and carried on into the inter-war period and more recent times. During the last war, Łódź was renamed Litzmannstadt, in honour of a Nazi worthy, and it was where the implementation of the Nazis' 'Final Solution' began. Łódź had a large Jewish population, and it was the first place in Poland where a ghetto was created, in 1941, as a preliminary to its concentration. The ghetto was then emptied by regular shipments to the extermination camps.

Since the war, Łódź has gained fresh fame as the home of the Polish Film School, which has turned out half-a-dozen of the greatest filmmakers of our time, including Andrzej Wajda, Roman Polański and Krzysztof Kieślowski. Like many North American industrial cities of the same period, Łódź was built on a grid pattern, and has no real organic centre - only a four-kilometre long main street.

Town Hall, 1827. Geyer **Weaving Mill** 1837, housing Historical **Museum** of the Textile Industry, fascinating and well worth a visit. Poznański family **palace,** 1888, now **Museum** of the City of Łódź. **Franciscan church** in Łągiewniki, 1702–23. Monastic building second half of 18th century.

Muzeum Sztuki, the first museum dedicated expressly to modern art, founded 1928, in another of the Poznański family palaces. An important collection of modern art. Many other splendid palaces, in every style under the sun, often mixed together, mainly 1870–90, run up by industrial tycoons, who often crashed before they were completed. Most are neglected, but still present an amazing sight. Also, very fine cemetery, full of highly theatrical and magnificent mortuary chapels, tombs and monuments. See also OZORKÓW

◆◆   ŁOMŻA   MAP 25
Small town built up by the princes of Mazovia in the Middle Ages. **Parish church** of St Michael the Archangel and St John the Baptist (now cathedral), 1504–25, remodelled 1692, by *Giuseppe Simone Belotti*. Lovely crystal vaulting in aisles.
Capuchin church of Our Lady of Sorrows 1770–89, expanded 1859. Monastery 1770–2, rebuilt 1862.

◆   ŁOPIENNO   MAP 9
Church, ca. 1670, by *Giorgio Catenaci*.

ŁOPUSZNA   MAP 21

Wooden **church**, early 16th century, rebuilt 20th century. Good
Gothic triptych, ca. 1440. **Manor house** of Tetmajer family, wooden,
ca. 1800. Houses curious **museum** of Szlachta culture.

ŁOWICZ   MAP 17 ◆◆◆

From the 13th century, this was one of the main residences of the
archbishops of Gniezno.

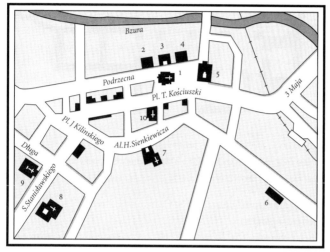

Collegiate church of the Assumption [1], 1652–68 by *Tommaso* and
Andrea Poncino; towers 1624, spires third quarter of 18th century,
by *Ephraim Schröger*. St Victoria's chapel with tomb of Primate
Jakub Uchański, 1580–3 by *Jan Michałowicz of Urzędów*, redeco-
rated in neo-Classical style 1783 by *Ephraim Schröger*. Tarnowski
chapel, 1611, with tomb of Paweł Tarnowski, by *Willem van den
Blocke*. Primate Adam Komorowski's chapel with his tomb and
Rococo decoration, 1759 by *Ephraim Schröger*. Primate Jan
Wężyk's chapel with Renaissance/Mannerist vault decoration,
1640. Lipski chapel, domed, 1647, with painted decoration, 1718 by
Adam Swach. High altar Rococo, after 1761, by *Ephraim Schröger*,
with sculpture by *Jan Jerzy Plersch*. Tombs of Jan Przerembski, ca.
1562 by *Girolamo Canavesi*, and Henryk Firlej, ca. 1626 by *Willem
van den Blocke*(?). Canons' houses [3] 16th–17th century, one
wooden, second half of 18th century.
Parish church of the Holy Ghost [9], early 16th century, western
facade 1778, tower 1620; rebuilt 19th century.
Bernardine monastery [8] founded 1464, converted into barracks
1823. Former church, ca. 1582. Monastic buildings, late 16th century–1603, expanded ca. 1762 by *Samuel Fischer* of Gdańsk.

141

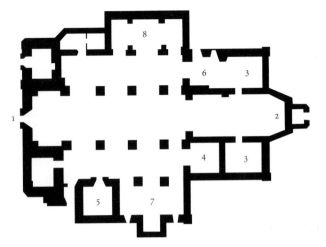

1 - West door, 2 - High altar, 3 - Sacristies, 4 - St Victoria's chapel, 5 - Tarnowski chapel, 6 - Komorowski chapel, 7 - Wężyk chapel, 8 - Lipski chapel.

Bernardine nuns' church of St Clare and convent [7], ca. 1650, by *Tommaso Poncino*.

Piarist church of St Wojciech [10], 1672–80, expanded with addition of two-tower facade, in mid-18th century; painted vault and furniture, ca. 1725.

Remains of Missionaries' **seminary** (now branch of Warsaw National Museum) [5] founded by Primate Michał Radziejowski, 1701 by *Tilman van Gameren*; chapel, with stuccoes and painted decoration, after 1695 by *Michelangelo Palloni*.

Town Hall [4] 1828 by *Bonifacy Witkowski*. Some nice little town houses on triangular market place, 16th-19th centuries.

Romantic **villa** of General Stanisław Klicki [6] with chapel, doorkeeper's lodge and tower, brick and iron ore masonry with use of 15th–18th century stone fragments from former castle, 1824 by *Karol Krauze*.

♦♦ LUBARTÓW   MAP 27

Church of St Anne, on oval groundplan, founded by Sanguszko family 1733, by *Paweł Fontana*. Belfry and enclosure mid-18th century.

Capuchin church and monastery 1741.

Lubomirski, later Sanguszko **residence**, first half of 17th century, expanded 1690s by *Tilman van Gameren*, rebuilt 1747 by *Paweł Fontana*. Orangery second half of 18th century.

LUBAWA (LOBAU)   MAP 15

Church, ca. 1330, rebuilt ca. 1550. Mortęski chapel 1581.
Bernardine monastery founded 1580, redecorated several times.
Wooden **hospital church** of St Barbara, Baroque, 1779.

LUBAWKA   MAP 6 ✦

Parish church, 14th century, rebuilt 1615 and 1735. **Calvary chapels**
on 'Holy Hill', 18th–19th century. **Houses** in market square,
17th–18th century.

LUBERADZ   MAP 18

Neo-Classical **country house** of Dembowski family, 1789 by *Hilary
Szpilowski*. Some restorations 1870s and 1902.

LUBIĄŻ (LEUBUS)   MAP 6 ✦✦✦

Magnificent **Cistercian abbey** founded 1163 by Duke Bolesław I of
Silesia, for monks from Schulpforte in Saxony. Burnt by Hussites in
1432, damaged in the Thirty Years' War, and after secularisation in
1810. Used as a luntatic asylum by the German government, then as
a military hospital by the Red Army. Church, first half of 14th century. Ducal chapel 1312. Aisle and ambulatory vaults, porch and 2-
tower facade, 1681–1700. Tombs first half of 14th century. Abbots'
palace, 1690s. Monastery (with the longest facade in Silesia, a mas-
terpiece of the Baroque), 1690–1720. Late 17th–century stucco in
reception halls. Ducal hall, 1731, with painted decoration by
Christian Philipp Bentum, sculpture by *Franz Josef Mangold*.
Painted decoration of refectory, 1733, by *Felix Anton Scheffler*; of
library 1734–8, by *Bentum*. **Parish church** of St Valentine, ca. 1700.

LUBIN (LUBEN)   MAP 6 ✦

Parish church of St Mary, 14th century, expanded 1446–1515. Good
stalls. Ruins of **castle** , mid-14th century, chapel with carved portal
1349, expanded 18th century

LUBIŃ   MAP 11 ✦✦

Benedictine abbey, founded ca. 1070 by monks from Belgium.
Romanesque **church**, before 1111; chancel Gothic, 1444–62. Interior
redecorated ca. 1730, vault painting 1732, by *Wacław Groff*. Organ
1670-90, by *Wojciech Libawicz*. Monastery 1617, rebuilt mid-18th
century.
Stone Romanesque **church** of St Leonard, early 13th century, superstructure and nave 1556.

A city with a curious profile; important both economically and strategically, Lublin never quite achieved the importance in Polish life that it might be considered to deserve. Although it had been a thriving trading post for centuries, Lublin was not incorporated as a town until 1317. In the 16th century it flourished as a centre of cultural and intellectual life, giving rise to its own form of Renaissance architecture. It was also the home of many prominent Hussites and at the time of the Reformation became the centre of much religious argument. Its position on the border between Poland and Lithuania made it a convenient place for the Sejm of 1569 to meet, considering its business was to formalise the union between the two crowns into one between the two states. The Union of Lublin created the Commonwealth of Two Nations. For the same reasons, the city was the seat of the Crown Courts for the south and east of the country.

Lublin suffered badly from Nazi extermination policies, and from military action in 1944. In that year, on 22 July, the 'Committee of National Liberation', Stalin's puppet proto-government for Poland, issued its manifesto from Lublin, which it turned into the de facto capital of Poland for the next six months.

One of the curiosities of Lublin is the existence of two universities in the town. One, the Catholic University, founded in 1919, the only one of its kind in Eastern Europe, has a unique reputation for excellence, and was the only free seat of learning throughout the Communist period. The other, the Marie Curie-Skłodowska University, founded in 1944, is the state university.

Lublin was also a very important centre of Jewish life and above all intellectual and religious culture. Its Yeschiva or High School was famous all over Europe during the Renaissance, when it had eminent refugees from as far afield as Spain among its teachers. In 1581, Lublin also became the seat of the Council of the Four Lands, the parliament of the Jewish state-within-the-state, which functioned until 1764.

♦♦   Royal **castle** [1], built around 13th–century keep expanded by Kazimierz the Great mid-14th century. Altered several times up to the first half of the 17th century, and turned into prison 1820s. Rebuilt in the Romantic manner 1826, by *Ignacy Stompf*. Castle **chapel** of Holy Trinity founded by Władysław Jagiełło, with vault supported by central pillar, ca. 1395. Renaissance portal, second quarter of 16th century. Frescoes Ruthenian-Byzantine. Those of chancel, 1418 by Master *Andrzej*, those in nave, Balkan school. The castle now houses a **museum**, with a rich archaeological section, giving a good idea of the ethnic migrations and the trading links in this part of the world in early Medieval times. It also has a large

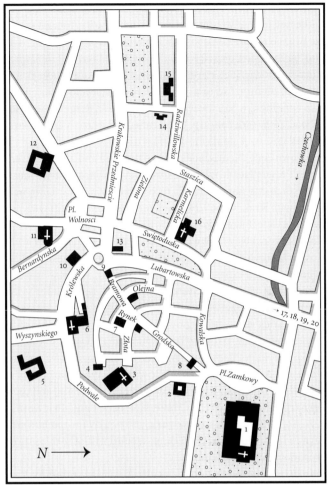

gallery of Polish painting from the 15th to the 19th centuries, decorative arts, and numismatic collections. Worth a look.

Hospital of St Lazarus with **church** of St Wojciech [**2**], 1630, with Renaissance stucco decoration.

Dominican monastery church of St Stanisław [**3**] 1574(?), gable early ✦✦ 17th century; interior redecorated and two towers added mid-17th century; chancel lengthened by means of Tyszkiewicz chapel, with stucco decoration, 1645–58 by *Giovanni Battista Falconi*. Contemporary painted decoration of dome by *Tomasz Muszyński*. Firlej chapel, octagonal, 1630 by *Jan Wolff*. Rosary chapel, rectangular, early 17th century. Sgraffiti on facade, 1668. Furniture Rococo, ca. 1760. Sculpture by *Sebastian Zeisel*. Paintings, mid-17th century, by workshop of *Tomaso Dolabella, Albin Kuczewicz, Tomasz Muszyński*, Friar *Reginald* and others. Monastery building, mid-17th century. Chapter house after 1574.

✦ Neo-Classical ' **Old Theatre**' [4], 1822 by *Łukasz Rodakiewicz*.

✦✦ **Cathedral**, formerly Jesuit church of St John the Baptist and St John the Evangelist [6], 1592–1604. Facade rebuilt in neo-Classical style, 1819, by *Antonio Corazzi*. Painted decoration 1757, by *Józef Mayer*. Stucco after 1633. Pictorial decoration of Olelkowicz-Słucki chapel, 16th/17th century. Sacristies 1684–97. High altar mid-17th century. Two paintings, ca. 1667 by *Franciszek Lekszycki*. Remnants of **Jesuit college**, 16th–18th century. Gate, called Trinitarian Tower, neo-Gothic, 1819, by *Antonio Corazzi(?)*.

Old **Town Hall** [7], originally 1389, expanded and altered several times. Present facade 1781, by *Domenico Merlini*, and 1836. Square with merchants' **houses**, mostly reconstructed in 1950s. Town **walls** 1340s, with Kraków Gate [9], mid-16th century, rebuilt 1782, and Grodzka Gate [8], redecorated 1785 by *Domenico Merlini*.

Neo-Classical New **Town Hall** [13], 1828 by *Aleksander Groffe*. **Hospital church** of the Holy Ghost, 15th century. Dome over chancel 1608. Church expanded 1730s.

Bernardine (now Jesuit) church [10] 1636-58, redecorated 1770s. Painting of the Virgin Mary early 16th century.

✦✦ **Missionaries' monastery** (now Seminary) [5] founded 1696 by Anna Zbąska. Church of the Transfiguration 1719–30. Paintings ca. 1735, by *Szymon Czechowicz*. Monastic building first half of 18th century, incorporating older palace with elevation bearing stucco bas-reliefs of Polish Kings, mid-17th century. Enlarged 1908.

✦✦ **Bernardine church** of the Conversion of St Paul [11], Gothic, 1557–69, altered with stucco work, 1603–7, by *Jacopo Balin(?)*. Facade 1827. Monastery building, second half of 16th century, expanded 17th–18th century.

✦ **Brigittines' convent** (now Ursuline) [12] founded by king Władysław Jagiełło in thanksgiving for his victory over the Teutonic Knights at Grunwald in 1410. Church of Our Lady of Victories 1412–26, with later tower, rebuilt turn of 15th century. Vaulting and gable after 1550. Chancel with Renaissance/Mannerist vault decoration added first half of 17th century. Painting of St Bridget mid-15th century. Monastic wing first half of 17th century.

Czartoryski **palace** [14], first half of 18th century. Lubomirski (later Sanguszko, often called the Radziwiłło **palace** [15], ca. 169 3 by *Tilman van Gameren*, rebuilt in neo-Classical style 1823, by *Jakub Hempel* and *Ignacy Stompf*, and 1829, by *Ferdynand Konotkiewicz*.

✦✦ **Discalced Carmelites' convent** [16] founded by Katarzyna Ligęza. Church of St Joseph, interior with stucco decoration, 1635–44. Belfry 1908. Monastic building contemporary, with incorporated older palace of Rafał Leszczyński, 1630 by *Jacopo Balin*.

✦✦ **Carmelites' church** [17], ca. 1742 by *Paweł Fontana*.

Church of St Nicholas [**18**], late 16th century, vault 1640.

Uniate church [**19**] 1607–33, some alterations 1860s.

Augustinian monastery [**20**] in Kalinowszczyzna. Church of St Agnes, built in stages between 1647 and 1698. Monastery 1667.

Just outside the city, to the south-east lies Majdanek **Concentration-camp**, started autumn 1941. Well-preserved layout, ✦✦ with remnants of watch-towers, fencing, gas-chambers and cremato-ria. Holocaust monument and **museum** of German persecution and the Final Solution. Soon after its liberation by the Red Army in the summer of 1944, it was recycled for use as a concentration-camp for Polish patriots being sent to Siberia, a function it fulfilled until 1946.

LUBOMIERZ   MAP 6 ✦

Benedictine convent founded 1278. Church 1726–30 by *Johann Jakob Scherhofer*. Tower 1554, superstructure 18th century. Painted decoration, 1730 by *Georg Wilhelm Neunhertz*. Monastic building 15th–16th century, rebuilt after 1726, expanded 19th century. Neo-Classical **Town Hall**, after 1802.

LUBORADZ   MAP 6

Country house late 16th century, rebuilt 1681–4; inside, stucco and painted decoration.

LUBORZYCA   MAP 21

Church of the Holy Cross, before 1433. Vaults 15th–16th century.

LUBOSTROŃ   MAP 10 ✦✦✦

Very good Palladian **country house** of Skórzewski family, 1800 by

Stanisław Zawadzki. Ambitious but very successful design, with a wonderful circular hall.

✦✦ LUBSKO   MAP 3
Church, mid-14th century, tower 13th century. Remodelled 1517. Galleries 16th–17th century. Traces of Gothic murals, furniture Renaissance/Mannerist. **Town Hall** 1580 by *Antonio Alberto*.

ŁUKÓW   MAP 25
Bernardine **church** of the Holy Cross and monastery, 1770. **Piarist college** and church, 1733–62 by *Antonio Solari*.

LUSŁAWICE   MAP 22
Neo-Classical **manor house**, early 19th century. Now the residence of the composer Krzysztof Penderecki.

LUSZYN   MAP 17
Parish church, 1595.

✦✦ LWÓWEK ŚLĄSKI   MAP 6
Parish church of the Assumption, two-tower facade and carved portal late Romanesque, 13th century. Main body of church rebuilt 1520 by *Konrad Pflüger*. Galilees with galleries, 1559 by *Johann Lindner*. Font ca. 1560.
Town Hall, 14th century, expanded 15th century. Tower 1504, interiors with fantastic late Gothic rib vaulting, 1524, by *Wendel Roskopf*. Bas-reliefs, sgraffiti and painted decoration Renaissance. Tomb of the dukes of Jawor (formerly in the Franciscan church), mid-14th century. Fine sculpture of a recumbent knight and his lady. Bakers' and cobblers' **stalls** 1494. **Houses** in market square, Renaissance, with portals mostly mid-16th century.
Franciscan church, late 13th century, repeatedly altered. Monastery, 15th–16th century, remodelled 19th century. Town **walls** 14th century; towers adjoining Bolesławiec and Lubin Gates, 13th–14th century. Walls of outer ring early 15th century, with 16th-century rondelles.

MACIEJOWIEC-GÓRA   MAP 6
Renaissance **country house** with arcaded courtyard, after 1600. Sgraffiti 1632.

✦ MAKOWICE   MAP 6
Church, early 16th century, expanded 1598; sgraffiti 1596. Tombstones and epitaphs, 16th–17th centuries.

MAKÓW MAZOWIECKI   MAP 18
Parish church, 16th century.

MAŁA WIEŚ   MAP 18 ✦✦
Beautifully-proportioned neo-Classical **country house** of Walicki
family, 1783–6 by *Hilary Szpilowski*. Very good contemporary
stucco and mural decoration of interior, particularly in dining
room (views of Naples and Warsaw) and the cabinet with
grotesques.

MALBORK (MARIENBURG)   MAP 8 ✦✦✦
Monastery-castle of the Teutonic Order and Grand Master's palace.
Capital of the Teutonic Order state from 1309 until 1457, then a
Polish royal residence, after 1773 a Prussian barracks. One of the
greatest castle-and-town complexes, and the largest brick castle
ever built. Heavily restored from 1817 as a symbol of German might
in the east, first by *Karl Friedrich Schinkel* (1817–42), then
Ferdinand von Quast (1840s) and *Konrad Steinbrecht* (1882–1922),
giving an interesting review of progressive approaches to conservation. Partly destroyed by Russians 1945.

High castle or monastery, fortifications of outer wall and dansker
(latrine tower) 1280. Chapter house, chapel with ornate carved portal, wings and cloister 1344. Middle castle (residence) fortifications
late 13th century. West wing with great refectory 1330-40. Infirmary
and east wing late 14th century. Palace of Grand Master, with two
refectories (summer and winter) with centrally-supported vaulting, 1399 by *Nikolaus Fellenstein*. Forecourt or lower castle , ca.

1310, with arsenal and church of St Lawrence, 1358. Fortifications of whole complex 1330–50. Buttermilk Tower, 1335–40, two-tower bridge gate 1341. Outer wall with semicircular towers 1416–20 by *Nikolaus Fellenstein*. The castle now houses a **museum**, with a gallery of medieval sculpture, arms and armour, and a fascinating collection of amber.

Town **walls** with towers, 1352–83. **Parish church** 1468–1523, vaulting 1538. **Town Hall** 1380, rebuilt 1460.

MAŁUJOWICE (MÖLLWITZ) MAP 11

Church of St James; chancel 1260, nave 1290. Tower superstructure 15th century. Painted decoration 14th–16th century, including some, ca. 1400 from the workshop of Master *Theodoric* of Prague. Richly decorated West door. Site of the Battle of Möllwitz, 4 May 1741, Frederick the Great's first victory over the Austrians.

MARGONIN MAP 9

Parish church, beginning 17th century, redecorated after 1750.

MARKUSZÓW MAP 27

Parish church of St Joseph, 1667–82. Wooden vicarage 18th century. **Church** of the Holy Ghost 1609, by *Piotr Durie*.

MĄTOWY WIELKIE MAP 8

Church, brick with timber parts ca. 1340, tower superstructure, 1741. Painted ceiling after 1741.

✦ MCHY MAP 11

Parish church 1575–1616. Neo-Classical **manor house** ca. 1799.

MELSZTYN MAP 22

Ruins of **castle** of Castellan Spytek Leliwita, later of Jordan family, ca. 1340. Renaissance wing second half of 16th century.

✦ MĘTNO MAP 1

Romanesque stone **church**, third quarter of 13th century.

✦✦ MICHALICE MAP 11

Wooden **parish church** of St Michael, 1614 by Master Carpenter *Miller*. Organ loft 1668, tower 1730. Painted ceiling 1624, wall paintings 1663; furniture second half of 17th century.

✦✦ MIECHÓW MAP 19

Monastery of Canons Regular of the Holy Sepulchre founded 1169.

Church of the Holy Sepulchre and St James the Minor, 1394–1410 (with Romanesque stone parts, ca. 1233), rebuilt 1749–71. Sculpture Rococo, 1765 by *Wojciech Rojowski*. Unusual spire ca. 1820. Murals 1380. Furniture Rococo, second half of 18th century. Good Baroque organ case, last quarter of 18th century. Chapel of the Holy Sepulchre, ca. 1535, supposedly a copy of the Holy Sepulchre in Jerusalem. Monastic building with cloister, Gothic/Renaissance, 1534. House of Generals of the Order, second half of 18th century.

MIEDNIEWICE   MAP 17 ✦
Reformed Franciscans' Monastery. Church 1731–48, by *Jozef Fontana, Tommaso Belotti* and *Mateusz Osiecki*. Monastery 1692–1704, rebuilt 1793 by *Antonio Castiglione*.

MIĘDZYLESIE   MAP 16 ✦
Pilgrimage **chapel** with enclosure 1756.

MIĘDZYLESIE (MITTELWALDE)   MAP 6
Parish church 1640s. Renaissance **castle**, ca. 1580; palace with gate added 1686; a nice example of a house growing organically grander.

MIĘDZYRZECZ   MAP 4
A very old town, supposedly the site of one of the first Benedictine Abbeys in Poland. **Parish church** of St John the Baptist, 14th century; vault and gables ca. 1520, chancel late 16th century. **Protestant church**, neo-Classical, early 1830s, by *Karl Friedrich Schinkel(?)*. Neo-Classical **Synagogue**, mid-19th century (Międzyrzecz was also the seat of the great Hasidic teacher Dab Baer, the 'Maggid of Międzyrzecz'). Ruin of royal **castle**, mid-14th century, expanded after 1520 and 1564. House of Międzyrzecz subprefects, 1719, rebuilt second half of 19th century, now a small regional **museum. Town Hall**, neo-Classical, after 1823, with parts 17th–18th century.

MIĘDZYRZEC PODLASKI   MAP 25
Parish church 1755. Facade neo-Classical, 1818 by *Piotr Aigner*.

MIERONICE WODZISŁAWSKIE   MAP 19 ✦
Charming tiny medieval **parish church**. Chancel second half of 13th century; nave 15th century, murals first half 14th century.

MIKUSZOWICE KRAKOWSKIE   MAP 14 ✦
Wooden **church** of St Barbara, in Gothic tradition, 1690, by Master Carpenter *P. Piotrowski*. Painted decoration 1723. Gothic Madonna, ca. 1420.

MILAKOWO   MAP 15
Site of a medieval town, completely destroyed by the Russians in
1945. **Church**, 1324–50, interior neo-Classical, ca. 1823.

◆◆   MILICZ   MAP 11
Ruins of **castle** of the dukes of Oleśnica, 14th century, expanded
after 1536 and 17th century. Interesting neo-Classical **country
house**, ca. 1800 by *Karl Gottfried Geissler*. Gate 1814, by *Leonard
Schatzel*. Timber **church** (originally Protestant) ca. 1710. Another of
the 'churches of grace' - see JAWOR

MIŁOSŁAW   MAP 9
Mielżyński **country house**, early 19th century. In 19th-century landscape **park**, neo-Gothic hunting lodge in the shape of a castle.

◆   MINOGA   MAP 21
Parish church with two-tower facade, 1736.

MIŃSK MAZOWIECKI   MAP 18
Country house, first half of 17th century, rebuilt in neo-Classical
style second quarter of 19th century.

◆   MIROGONOWICE   MAP 20
Wooden **manor house**, second half of 18th century, wall paintings
ca. 1800. Formal **park** and 19th century manorial farm buildings.

MIRSK   MAP 5
Parish church, Gothic/Renaissance, 1562–7. **Town Hall** 1794–6;
tower Renaissance, 1559.

◆   MISZEWO MUROWANE   MAP 17
Parish church, octagonal, formerly vaulted from central supporting pillar, 1444; rebuilt ca. 1780.

◆   MŁOCHÓW   MAP 18
Fine **country house**, early 19th century, by *Jakub Kubicki*. At nearby
Rozalin, neo-Renaissance **house**, ca. 1850, by *Henryk Marconi*.

MŁODOSZOWICE   MAP 11
Church, 15th century Gothic triptych 1495.

◆   MŁODZAWY   MAP 20
Parish church of the Holy Ghost, 1716–40 by *Kacper Bażanka*.
Belfry 1779.

MNICHÓW   MAP 19 ✦✦
Wooden **parish church** of St Stephen, 1765–70. Bell-tower 1768.
Unusual example of entirely Baroque church in wood.

MODLIN   MAP 18
Fortress with brick-and-earth forts, begun on the orders of
Napoleon, who apparently contributed some ideas (Chasse-loup
Battery, Star Forts), 1806–10, by *Prosper de Chasseloup-Laubat* and
François N.B.Haxo. Expanded after 1815 by *Ludwik Mallet* and ca.
1834 by *Ivan Dehn*. Main Building with two towers, and Napoleon,
Ostrołęka and Zakroczym Gates, 1833–40, by *Jan Jakub Gay(?)*.
Rings of outer forts 1870 and 1910. In use until 1939, when it held out
for three weeks against the Wehrmacht.

MODLISZEWICE   MAP 19
Ruins of fortified **manor house** of Primate Jan Lipski, on island,
1630.

MODLNA   MAP 17 ✦
Renaissance wooden **church**, ca. 1600.

MODLNICA   MAP 21 ✦✦
Parish church, 1553, rebuilt second half of 17th century; ceiling and
wall painting 1562. Kucharski chapel 1622. Pretty neo-Classical
manor house of Konopka family, 1783–7, rebuilt ca. 1820, by Master
Carpenter *Karol Kryszkier*.

MOGIELNICA   MAP 20
Neo-Classical **Town Hall**, 1821 by *Hilary Szpilowski*.

MOGILNO   MAP 10 ✦
Benedictine abbey founded 1065 by Bolesław the Bold. The granite
parts of the walls are from the original Romanesque late 11th-cen-
tury church. Western crypt, 12th century; church vault after 1550.
Two-tower facade 1797.

MOJĘCICE   MAP 6 ✦
Church, 15th century, rebuilt mid-16th century; painted decoration
and sgraffito second half of 16th century.

MOKOBODY   MAP 25 ✦
Neo-Classical **parish church,** founded by Jan Ossoliński, 1798–1819,
by *Jakub Kubicki*.

✦ MOKRSKO MAP 19
Romanesque ashlar **church**, now chancel of parish church, Baroque, 1676. On nearby meadow, ruins of Renaissance **castle** of Piotr Kmita, 1519–26.

✦ MORĄG (MOHRUNGEN) MAP 15
Market town founded 1280 by Teutonic Order. **Parish church**, 1305–12, rebuilt early 16th century. Murals second half of 15th century. **Town Hall** 1444, now **museum** dedicated to the philosopher Johann Gottfried Herder, who was born here in 1744.

✦✦ MORAWICA MAP 21
Church, 1748 by *Francesco Placidi*. **Vicarage**, 1606, built on remains of Tenczyński family medieval manor house.

MORDY MAP 25
Church, 1708, facade 1737. **Manor house** 18th–19th century.

✦ MORYŃ (MOHRIN) MAP 3
Church, Romanesque/Gothic, late 13th century. Tower ca. 1300. One of the best examples of a 13th-century type of village church common to western Pomerania, built of granite ashlar. Rather wonderful in its primitive severity.

✦ MSTÓW MAP 19
Originally a satellite of the **monastery of the Canons Regular** in Wrocław, this became a monastery in its own right in 1220. Church 1718, on foundations of 13th century church. Fortifications with towers and gate, 17th century.

✦ MYŚLENICE MAP 21
Parish church 1465, tower 1543. Baroque alterations 1669 and 1790. Domed Koniecpolski chapel 1644.

MYŚLIBÓRZ MAP 1
Inhabited since the 4th century BC, this was a fortified market town in the middle ages.
Parish church, late 13th century, expanded 1593. **Dominican church** and monastery, 1275, rebuilt ca. 1440. Chapel of St Gertrude, early 15th century. **Town Hall** 1771.

NADARZYN MAP 18
Neo-Classical **parish church**, 1806 by *Jakub Kubicki*.

Parish church 1712. **Country house** second half of 18th century; interior neo-Rococo, second half of 19th century.

Małachowski family **country house**, 1771-3 by *Ferdynand Nax*, rebuilt ca. 1880. **Museum** dedicated to the novelist Bolesław Prus. In small highland-style chalet, 1905, by *J. Koszczyc-Witkiewicz*, where another novelist, Stefan Żeromski, lived and worked, there is a **museum** dedicated to him.

Parish church of SS Peter and Paul, 1405–41, reconstructed 1495. Chapels 15th–16th century, sacristy 1526; spire 1790. Renovated 1869.
Franciscan church first half of 14th century, nave ca. 1420, converted into storehouse 1812. Surviving wing of monastery ca. 1675. **Castle**: north wing ca. 1360, west wing 1530s, superstructure 17th/18th century, and south wing 1771. Gatehouse 1534, expanded 17th and first half of 18th century. Renaissance well-head ca. 1600. Town **walls** with towers second half of 14th century, expanded 15th century. Kraków Gate, second half of 14th century. **Town Hall** tower 1389.

Wooden **parish church** of St Stanisław, Baroque, 1728. Also wooden **Orthodox church**, 18th-19th centuries.

Country house with two curved colonnaded ranges, Baroque, 1773-81, built for Łoś family. Parish church 1790-1804; mausoleum of Puzyna family, 1881.

Manor House, Baroque, 1730; stuccoed interiors.

Kruszyński family **country house** 1804, by *Hilary Szpilowski*, partly remodelled 1868.

Castle of Teutonic Knights, 1380-1400, forecourt ca. 1520.

Remnants of Gothic murals. Town Walls with towers 1380s.

✦✦✦ NIEBORÓW MAP 17

Country house built for Cardinal Michał Radziejowski, 1690-6, by *Tilman van Gameren*. The house later passed to the Ogiński and, in the 18th century, to the Radziwiłł family. It was Princess Helena Radziwiłł who gave Nieborów its present aspect, at the turn of the 18th and 19th centuries. Most of the interiors (with the notable exception of the remarkable baroque tiled staircase) date from this period, as does the good collection of Polish, French and English furniture, most of the objects and the paintings. Among the latter, a

good head by *Ribera* and a lovely protrait of Princess Helena by *Vigée-Lebrun* stick in the mind. Also, in the library, itself one of the most attractive rooms, a pair of fine terrestrial and celestial globes by the Venetian *Vincenzo Coronello*, 1683, which come from Versailles. Group of ancillary buildings adjoining palace by *Szymon Bogumił Zug*, including a brewery, ca. 1774; two orangeries, partly wooden, ca. 1795; coach-houses and stables. Formal **park** with parterres and trimmed espaliers, after 1690, by *Tilman van Gameren*, and first half of 18th century; canal after 1736. Neo-Classical farm-buildings, fourth quarter of 18th century, by *Szymon Bogumił Zug*. See aslo ARKADIA

NIECHANOWO MAP 9
Neo-Classical **country house**, 1783, with some 19th century alterations. Formerly property of Żółtowski family.

✦✦ NIEDZICA MAP 21
A Hungarian marcher post, only incorporated into Poland in 1918.

The castle, belonging originally to the Berzeviczy, then the Horwath and latterly the Salomon family, used to be perched high up on a cliff overlooking the Dunajec river, but a recent dam has turned it into a lakeside fortress. The upper castle of 1330 was expanded ca. 1636. Late Renaissance middle and lower castles of 1601, were rebuilt 1641 and 18th–20th century. In the 16th century a relative of one of the owners of the castle married an Inca noble-woman, and their son fled from Spanish captivity and took refuge at Niedzica. This gave rise to a persistent legend that the treasure of Montezuma is buried here. **Parish church**, originally early 15th cen-tury, rebuilt in Baroque style 18th century and 1912.

NIEDŹWIADNA   MAP 23 ✦

Church of St Stanisław, mid-16th century. Simple and severe rec-tangular Gothic village church.

NIEDŹWIEDŹ   MAP 21 ✦

Parish church of St Wojciech, 1486–93 by Master *Mikołaj* of Lublin. Portico 1798. Good Gothic Madonna, ca. 1420, paintings ca. 1530. Neo-Classical **manor house**, 18th–19th century.

NIEMCZA (NIMBSCH)   MAP 11 ✦

Site of a battle in 1017 when the Poles defeated the Emperor Henry II. **Castle** of the dukes of Brzeg and Legnica, Renaissance, ca. 1585 by *Bernardo Niuron*, rebuilt after 1735, 1830 and later. St Hedwig's **chapel,** turn of the 14th century, remodelled 1714. Town **walls** after 1430.

NIEMODLIN (FALKENBERG)   MAP 11 ✦

Once the capital of a tiny duchy.**Parish church**, chancel early 14th century, nave and tower second half of 15th century, remodelled first half of 18th century. **Castle** begun 1573, expanded ca. 1740 and 1788. Gate second half of 18th century.

NIEPOŁOMICE   MAP 21 ✦✦

Castle built as a hunting lodge for King Zygmunt Augustus, 1550–71, by *Tomasz Grzymała*. The first major Renaissance resi-dence in Poland after the Wawel, and therefore very influential. Originally, there was a second floor and a third level of galleries, ca. 1639, running round all four sides of the courtyard. Fine Renaissance portal 1552.

Parish church of St Mary and the Thousand Martyrs, founded by Kazimierz the Great 1350. Some redecorations 1690, by *Tilman van Gameren*. Frescoes of Umbrian-Sienese type, after 1350 in sacristy.

Good Renaissance Chapel with Mannerist Branicki tomb, 1596, by *Santi Gucci*. Lubomirski Chapel 1640, stucco by *Giovanni Battista Falconi*.

✦ NIESZAWA   MAP 10
Parish church, 1468. Tower 1592. **Town Hall** 1821, expanded 1859.

✦ NIETULISKO   MAP 20
Neo-Classical ironworks of the Bank of Poland, 1834–45 by *Karol Knape*; ruins of **industrial buildings**, with culverts and bridge, and houses for staff.

NIEZDÓW   MAP 27
Neo-Classical Lubomirski family **country house**, ca. 1800, rebuilt 1847. Inside, neo-Classical plasterwork.

✦ NIWISKA (BERGENWALD)   MAP 4
Parish church of St Catherine, 13th/14th centuries. **Country house** 1753, expanded 19th century.

NIWISKI   MAP 25
Church founded by Ossoliński family, Baroque, 1787. Neo-Classical **country house**, second half of the 18th century.

NOWA WIEŚ KRÓLEWSKA   MAP 9
Parish church, late 13th century; superstructure of tower 1908.

✦ NOWE   MAP 8
A small market town purchased from the dukes of Mazovia by the Teutonic Order in 1313, reincorporated into Poland 1466.
Parish church of St Matthew; chancel 1366, nave late 14th century; expanded 1912. Murals 14th–15th century.
Franciscan church (later Bernardine), early 14th century, remodelled 1663 and 1779, reconstructed 1903.

NOWE DWORY (NEUHÖFEN)   MAP 4
Church of St John the Baptist (originally Protestant), timber, 1792, by Master Carpenter *J. Schönecke*; tower 1615.

NOWE MIASTO N/WARTĄ   MAP 9
Parish church of the Holy Trinity, second half of 15th century. Gable and chapel 1593 and 1614. Painted decoration of vaults 1563.

NOWE MIASTO   MAP 18
Parish church 1459, rebuilt mid-17th and 20th century.

NOWE MIASTO LUBAWSKIE   MAP 15 ✦✦
Parish church of St Thomas the Apostle, 1330, nave 1350. Działyński chapel 1651. Murals second half of 14th century and 1642; furniture 14th–18th century. Town **walls** 1340s. Small local **museum** in the Brodnica Gate.

NOWE MIASTO N/PILICĄ   MAP 20 ✦
Lovely little town on what used to be a ford on the Pilica river. Granowski, later Małachowski, **country house**, latterly the property of the Bławdziewicz family, first half of 18th century, altered 1820s. Fine setting and park. Baroque **Capuchin monastery** and church, second half of the 18th century. Inside, paintings by *Franciszek Smuglewicz* and *Szymon Czechowicz*.

NOWOGARD (NEUGARD)   MAP 2
Originally a castle-town belonging to the bishops of Kamien, mostly destroyed in 1945. **Parish church**, Gothic, 16th century.

NOWOGRODZIEC   MAP 6
Magdalenes' convent church, 1788–93, furniture contemporary, tower 1880. **Parish church** of St Nicholas, 17th century. **Town Hall** 1795. **Ruins** of 13th century monastery.

NOWOSIELCE   MAP 29
Wooden **parish church** of St Mary Magdalen, 1595, rebuilt 19th century; painting first quarter of 16th century.

NOWY DWÓR MAZOWIECKI   MAP 18
Good neo-Classical **parish church**, 1792.

NOWY JASIENIEC   MAP 10
Castle built last quarter of the 14th century by the Teutonic Knights, under Polish rule since 1410, property of Kościelecki family from 1466. Rebuilt 15th and 17th centuries.

NOWY KORCZYN   MAP 22 ✦
Burgh founded by Bolesław the Shy in 1258, fortified by Kazimierz the Great in the 14th century. In the mid-15th century it had 30,000 inhabitants, making it one of the largest cities in Europe. It lay astride several trade routes, and its position made it a convenient meeting-place. In 1404 one of the first pre-parliamentary assem-

blies took place here. The Tatar Khan and the Grand Master of the Teutonic Order came here ot do homage to king Kazimierz the Great. **Parish church** of the Holy Trinity, first half of 17th century. Furniture contemporary.

Franciscan monastery founded 1257 by Bolesław the Shy and the Blessed Kinga. Church of St Stanisław, chancel mid-13th century, nave 14th century, with remarkably fine vaulting. Belfry 18th century. Painted decoration of vaults 1761, by *Mikołaj Janowski* and *Mateusz Rejchan*.

Neo-Classical **Synagogue**, end of the 18th century.

✦ NOWY SĄCZ   MAP 22

An old market settlement with town charter from 1292, at the centre of what was a rich area in the Middle Ages. **Collegiate church** of St Margaret, founded by Cardinal Zbigniew Oleśnicki 1446; towers 15th and first half of 16th century; rebuilt 18th–19th century. **Canons' house**, end of 15th–17th century; now **museum** of regional ethnic kit, but also of mainly sacral sculpture from highland churches. **Franciscan church** (now Protestant), built 1297 but completely destroyed by fire 18th century. Lubomirski chapel 1663.

✦ NOWY TARG   MAP 21

Parish church of St Catherine, ca. 1343, nave 1606, tower 1765. Belfry 1701. **Museum** of highland folk-culture.

✦✦✦ NYSA (NEISSE)   MAP 13

From 1201 this was a residence and private town of the bishops of Wrocław.**Parish church** of St James [1], built on the site of an older Romanesque church, completed with chancel and ambulatory with radiating chapels, 1424–30, by Master *Peter of Ząbkowice*. Chapel of the Dead (now baptistery) 1650, Holy Trinity and Blessed Sacrament chapels 1752. Church partially reconstructed after 1945. Fine collection of epitaphs and monuments. Bell-tower 1474–93, by *Nikolaus Hirz*, superstructure 1516. **Hospital church** of St Barbara [2], 14th century, altered in 1544 and 1732. **Palace** of bishops of Wrocław [3]: north-east wing 1624, remaining wings 1729, by *Christoph Tausch, Michael Klein* and *Felix Anton Hammerschmidt*. Inside, early 18th- century stucco. Complex of buildings popularly called **Court of bishops** of Wrocław [4]: main building late 17th century, in ruins. **Museum**, containing mixed collection of archaeological finds as well as furniture, objects and paintings (including one by *Cranach the Elder*), mostly from former German country houses sacked in 1945. **Jesuit college** or 'Carolinum' [5], founded 1622. Church of the Assumption built by Bishop Karol Ferdynand

Vasa, 1688–92 by *Giovanni Battista di Quadro*. College building 1673, in great hall, stuccoes, late 17th century, by *Francesco Cygno*. **Secondary School [6]** 1725, *Christoph Tausch* and *Michael Klein*. **Monastery of the Canons Regular** of the Holy Sepulchre [7], founded 1239, present building 1727, by *Michael Klein*. Church of SS Peter and Paul completed by *Felix Anton Hammerschmidt*, interior with stucco work and painted decoration, 1730 by *Thomas* and *Felix Anton Scheffler*. Monastic building lengthened 19th/20th century. **Weigh-house** in market square [8], 1604. **Houses** in the old town mostly Gothic-Renaissance, 16th century, rebuilt 18th–19th century. Town **walls** founded by Bishop Przecław of Pogorzela, ca. 1350, expanded with addition of rondelles second half of 16th century. Towers 16th and 17th century. Earth-and-masonry bastion fortifications, modernized and expanded 1758 by *Gerhard Kornelius von Wallrave*. **Cemetery church** of the Holy Cross, so-called Jerusalem Church, 1633–9, chapels 1692.

OBJEZIERZE   MAP 9

Neo-Classical **country house** of Węgorzewski family, 1790s. Attic parapet 1841, by *Alexandre de Saint-Omer*. Wings 1906.

OBLĘGOREK MAP 20
Museum dedicated to the life and works of the novelist and Nobel prize winner Henryk Sienkiewicz, in small manor house, part wooden chalet, part Italian villa, offered to him by his grateful readers, in which he spent his holidays 1899-1914.

OBORY MAP 17
Carmelite monastery founded 1605. Church nave 1649, chancel 1694, expanded with addition of chapel, sacristy and tower 1740–9. Monastic building 1741–53, rebuilt 1825.

OBORY MAP 18
Wielopolski family **manor house**, 1681–8, by *Tilman van Gameren*; outbuildings and park 18th century.

✦ OBRA MAP 4
Cistercian abbey founded 1231. Church of St James 1722–57; painted decoration 1754. Furniture Rococo, third quarter of 18th century.

✦ OBRZYCKO MAP 9
Church of SS Peter and Paul, 1714–28 by *Pompeo Ferrari*, one of a group of concentric churches built by this architect in this area. Baroque **Town Hall**, ca. 1650.

ODRZYKOŃ MAP 29
Ruins of 14th–15th-century **castle** , originally belonging to the Kamieniecki family. In 1530 the Middle Castle was acquired by the Boner family, and from then on, the two parts passed to various owners independently of each other. In the 19th century, the 'High Castle' belonged to the Biberstein-Starowiejski family, and the 'Middle Castle' to the Counts Fredro. In his *Revenge*, the dramatist Aleksander Fredro turned the situation into the plot of a comedy.

OGRODZIENIEC MAP 19
Very imposing ruin of **castle**, 1530–45, built as the grandiose seat of the wealthy merchant and banker Seweryn Boner. It was conceived in the Renaissance style, but Boner, whose patents of nobility were very fresh, had it archaized and made to look more 'medieval'.

OJCÓW MAP 21
Ruin of royal **castle**, built 14th century by Kazimierz the Great.

OKSA MAP 19
Calvinist, now **parish church** founded by Andrzej Rey, 1570.

OKUNIEW MAP 18
Neo-Classical **parish church**, 1828–35, by *Jakub Kubicki*.

OŁAWA (OHLAU) MAP 11
Parish church; chancel ca. 1300, nave 1587, by *Bernardo Niuron*.
Tower 16th century. Rebuilt in neo-Gothic style 1886. **Castle** of the
dukes of Brzeg and Legnica, 1359–98, rebuilt 1588 by *Bernardo
Niuron* and 1661 by *Carlo Rossi* and *Luca Giovanni*. Neo-Classical
Town Hall, 1823, by *Karl Friedrich Schinkel*, tower 1637-68.

OLEŚNICA (ÖLS) MAP 11 ✦✦
A settled town since the 11th century, from 1255 the capital of the
dukes of Oleśnica. **Castle** begun 14th century by Duke Konrad,
rebuilt in 16th century as residence for Podiebrad family. West
wing and round tower 1561 and mid-18th century. East wing 1586,
by *Bernardo Niuron*. South wing 1608. Arcaded gallery 1590s, new
palace and east foregate 1563, by *Gasparo Cuneo(?)*. Staircase building and connection of castle with palace and of palace with church
1616. Sgraffiti and sculptural decoration Renaissance and
Mannerist, second half of 16th century, stuccoes early 17th century
and 18th century. Castle church 1469, chapels and sacristy after
1500. Interior redecorated 17th/18th century, chapel of the princes
of Württemberg 1698. Pulpit 1605. Renaissance tombs of Prince Jan
of Podiebrad and Krystyna Szydłowiecka.
Parish church of St Mary and St George ca. 1380. Fortifications early
17th century. Town **walls** 14th century, outer ring first half of 16th
century. Wrocław Gate first half of 14th century, superstructure
16th century.

OLESNO MAP 12 ✦✦
Church of St Anne, wooden, 1518. Adjacent to it, a second church,
on a star-shaped groundplan, 1670, by Master *Maciej Snopek*; triptych early 16th century. A remarkable building.

OLIWA MAP 8 ✦✦✦
Cistercian abbey founded 1188 by Duke Sambor I of Gdańsk.
Romanesque/Early Gothic church, and since 1925 cathedral, of the
Holy Trinity, first half of 13th century, frequently laid waste (twice
by pagan Prussians, three times by Teutonic Knights). Rebuilt by
Grand Master of Teutonic Order, 1350. Vaulting of nave and
transept added 1582, facade refashioned in Rococo style 1771.
Murals in choir 1587. Very important Rococo organ with moving
parts, 1763-88, by *Michael Wulff* and *F.R.Dalitz,* carvings by
Brother Altanus - lots of angels with trumpets. Transept organ ca.

1698. Tombs of Kos family, 1620, by *Willem van den Blocke(?)*. Paintings by *Bartłomiej Strobel*, *Hermann Han* and *Andreas Stech*. Monastery buildings 13th-15th century, refectory with Gothic/Mannerist vault, 1594. Monastery granary 14th century, rebuilt 1933. Abbots' granary 1723. Old **Abbot's palace**, 15th century. Baroque New Palace 1637, rebuilt 1756, now a **museum**. Formal **park** with parterres, espaliers and canals, mid-18th century. Fortifications 14th-15th century; gatehouse 17th century.

✦ OLKUSZ   MAP 21
In the Middle Ages, this was the centre of mining (mainly silver) in the Olkusz hills. **Church** of St Andrew, founded first half of 14th century by Bolesław the Short. With its fine, slender columns, a good example of Kraków-based architecture. A building of noble proportions. Vaulting and St Anne's chapel late 15th century. Loreto chapel 1620. Chancel painting late 14th century and 1592. Very good polyptych 1485, by Masters *Jan Wielki* and *Stanisław Stary*. Gothic sculptures representing Madonna with Child and

Man of Sorrows, ca. 1500.Fine organ, 1617-23, by *Johann Hummel*.

OŁOBOK

MAP 12 ✦✦

Cistercian convent, founded 1213 by Prince Władysław Odonic. Church 15th century, rebuilt 17th century, and second half of 18th century. Rococo furniture, 1795; organ and gallery 1779-95. Romanesque crucifix, 13th century.
Wooden **cemetery church** of St John the Baptist, Gothic, 16th century.

OLSZANY

MAP 6

Parish church, turn of the 13th century, nave vault 1522; tower 17th century.

OLSZÓWKA

MAP 21 ✦

Wooden **parish church** of St John the Baptist, ca. 1732. Painted decoration 1760.

OLSZTYN

MAP 19

Ruin of **castle** founded by Kazimierz the Great, mid-14th century. One of the chain of fortified vantage-points defending Kraków from the west.

OLSZTYN (ALLENSTEIN)

MAP 15 ✦✦✦

Castle of Warmia Chapter, second half of 14th century; crystal vaulting beginning of 16th century. Expanded 1530 and 1758. Note Copernicus' sundial - he was the administrator of the castle between 1516 and 1521, and began work on his great work *de Revolutionibus Orbium Coelestium* here. The castle is now the Mazurian **Museum**. Includes archaeological collections formerly in the Prussian Museum at Koenigsberg, as well as a good though uneven collection of paintings, furniture and objects retrieved from the Russian looting of Junker estates in 1944.
Parish church, now cathedral, of St James, ca. 1440, vaults mid-16th century; tower superstructure 1596, a good example of Teutonic Knights' brick Gothic architecture.
Town **walls** after 1378. Timber **grain-stores**, 17th or 18th century.

OLSZTYNEK

MAP 15

Town **walls** with towers, 14th century. Open-air folk building **museum**, with copies and original samples of regional wooden buildings, 18th-19th century, from Warmia, Masurian region and Lithuania.

Important **collegiate church** of St Martin. A well-preserved
Romanesque stone basilica dating rom the 1140s, with 15th–16th
century additions. Northern tower superstructure, vaults and
gables ca. 1547. Some remodelling 1740. Painted decoration and
furniture second quarter of 18th century. Tomb of Chancellor
Krzysztof Szydłowiecki, 1533 by *Bernardo Zanobi de Gianotis*;
bronze bas-relief around base depicting town of Opatów lamenting
his death, 1536 by *Giovanni Cini*. Tomb-brass of the Chancellor's
daughter Anna 1536, by *Gianotis*; and of his son Zygmunt by *Cini*,
both somewhat restored, but charming nevertheless. Madonna by
Timoteo da Urbino (school of *Lucas Cranach*).
Bernardine monastery founded ca. 1471. Church of the Assumption
1751–65.

Parish church, 1710-6, tower 1760. Painted decoration 1733, by *Josef
Matthäus Lasser*; furniture Rococo, 1772.

Originally a hunting lodge of the princes of Mazovia, then of the
Polish Crown, held as a starosty by the Krasiński family of nearby
Krasne from 1659, and the property of Marshal Bernadotte between
1806 and 1810, when it reverted to the Krasińskis. The main house
no longer exists, but there is a surviving neo-Gothic Romantic '**castle**', built ca. 1828 by *General Wincenty Krasiń*ski (1783–1858). It
now houses a **Museum** of the Romantic Movement in honour of the
general's son, the poet Zygmunt Krasiński (1812–1859).
Parish church founded 1825 by General Krasiński, finished 1885 by
Wincenty Rakiewicz. Tombs of Krasiński family, including that of
Zygmunt and of his mother Maria, nee Radziwiłł, by *Luigi
Pampalloni* 1841. The **cemetery** contains the graves of many of the
general's companions-in-arms from the regiment of Chevau-
Legers of the Imperial Guard (including that of the regimental sur-
geon, Dr François Girardot, later Chopin's physician), many of
whom settled here after 1815. See also KRASNE

Settlement dating from 9th century, capital of the Opolanie. Later a
thriving medieval town on the Kraków-Wrocław road.
Collegiate church, now cathedral, of the Holy Cross [1], first half of
15th century, chapels 15th/16th century, facade 1902. Tombs and
epitaphs 16th–18th century.
Franciscan monastery [3] founded 1241. Church of the Holy Trinity,

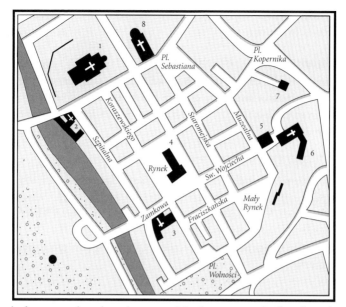

before 1350, chapels and tower 15th/16th century, rebuilt 17th–18th century. Murals in crypt ca. 1350; tombs of the dukes of Opole, second half of 14th century.

Dominican monastery [6] founded before 1295. Choir ca. 1360, nave, northern aisle and tower before 1430, southern aisle ca. 1500; redecorated 18th century and turn of the 19th century.

Jesuit college [5] 1762. Contains local **museum**, a mixed bag. **Hospital chapel** of St Alexis [2], 1420s. Tower of **castle** of the dukes of Opole [7] 14th century. Good set of **houses** in market square, ranging from Gothic-Renaissance, with oriels, through to Baroque. Amusing **Town Hall** [4], a copy of the Palazzo Vecchio in Florence, built 1936. In the suburb of Bierkowice there is an open air **museum** of regional vernacular architecture.

OPOLE LUBELSKIE   MAP 27 ✦✦
Piarist monastery founded 1743 by Tarło family. Church of the Assumption 1650-75, expanded 1757. Furniture and painted decoration Rococo, 1757 by *Antoni Dembicki*. Monastic building before 1740 by *Franciszek Mayer*, expanded second half of 18th century. Belfry 17th century. Belfry gate 1751.

OPORÓW   MAP 17 ✦✦
Delightful moated **castle** of Archbishop Władysław Oporowski, 1434–49. Interior furnished as country residence. Over the road, ruin of interesting neo-Gothic distillery and farm buildings.

Pauline church and remains of monastery, ca. 1450, rebuilt 17th–20th century.

✦ OPOROWO   MAP 11
Timber **Parish church** in Gothic tradition, 1644, tower early 19th century. **Manor house**, ca. 1800, in contemporary park. Its main claim to fame is that the great national poet Adam Mickiewicz stayed here.

✦✦ ORAWKA   MAP 21
Wooden **parish church** of St John the Baptist, late Gothic, ca. 1650, rebuilt with addition of tower 20th century. Chapel 1728. Painted decoration in Renaissance tradition, 1711, by *Father Antoni Tuszyński*. Organ 1674-6.
Woooden **village buildings** typical of the Orawa region, mostly 19th century.

✦ ORCHÓWEK   MAP 28
Augustinian church of St John the Almoner, 1777, by *Paweł Fontana*. Main altar contains a miraculous painting of Our Lady of Consolation, brought here by the Augustinian monks in 1610.

✦✦ ORNETA   MAP 15
Originally a town belonging to the bishops of Warmia, later to the Polish Crown. Spectacular brick Gothic **parish church,** 1370s, with 15th century chapels.
Orthodox church (originally Protestant) in Romantic manner, 1829, by *Karl Friedrich Schinkel(?).*
Town Hall 14th century, with small houses built around it, 17th–18th century.

 OROŃSKO   MAP 20
Manor house in Romantic manner, mid-19th century, by *Franciszek Maria Lanci(?).* Once the home of the painter *Józef Brandt (1841–1915).* **Chapel**, neo-Classical, 1841.

✦ ORTEL KRÓLEWSKI   MAP 26
Wooden **church** (originally Orthodox), 1706, by Master Carpenter *Nazaron.*

✦✦ OSIECZNA   MAP 11
Reformed Franciscans' monastery. Church of St Valentine 1729-33, by *Pompeo Ferrari*, with Rococo interior. Monastic building 1680.

OSIEK   MAP 21 ✦
Wooden **parish church**, early 16th century. **Country house**, early
19th century, rebuilt in Romantic manner.

OSIEK JASIELSKI   MAP 22 ✦
Wooden **parish church** of the Transfiguration, Gothic, 15th century; rebuilt 1640.

OSINY   MAP 27
Tiny wooden **manor house**, second half of the 18th century.

OSMOLIN   MAP 17
Neo-Classical **parish church**, 1791 by *Hilary Szpilowski*.

OŚNO LUBUSKIE (DROSSE)   MAP 3
Parish church, 14th century, tower 15th century. Well preserved
Town **walls** with towers, 14th and 15th centuries.

OSTROŁĘKA   MAP 18
The site of an important battle between the Poles and the Russians
in 1831. General Józef Bem, commanding the Polish artillery, used
his guns to such brilliant effect that what should have been a crushing defeat for the Poles was more of a tactical withdrawal.
Bernardine monastery and Church of St Anthony of Padua
1661–96.

OSTROMECKO   MAP 10
Rococo **country house**, ca. 1730. 'New House' 1849 by *Karl Friedrich
Schinkel (?)*, for Schönborn-Alvensleben family. Park with hunting
lodge and neo-Romanesque mausoleum, 1878.

OSTROPA (STROPPENDORF)   MAP 14
Parish church of St George, with interesting painted wooden nave,
1668. Tower 1641. Baroque furniture, mid-17th century.

OSTRORÓG   MAP 4
Town built 1412 on the private estate of the Ostroróg family.
Parish church, begun 1432, rebuilt 1777.

OSTRÓW LEDNICKI   MAP 9 ✦
Site of fortified seat of the first princes of Poland, on island on
Lednica lake between the two early capitals Poznań and Gniezno.
Ruins of church and adjoining *Palatium*, pre-Romanesque, 10th
century. Not much to see, but quite atmospheric. It was here that

Bolesław the Bold received the Emperor Otto III in the year 1000. According to the chroniclers, the emperor was so impressed by Bolesław and his court that he took his own crown off and placed it on the Polish prince's head, thereby acknowledging his royal status within Christendom. He gave Bolesław the rank of *princeps palatinus*, and head of one of the four 'provinces' of the Empire (Roma, Gallia, Germania, Slavonia). See also GNIEZNO

✦ OSTRÓW LUBELSKI   MAP 28
Parish church, 1755–68.

OSTROWITE   MAP 10
Church ca. 1300, tower and gables, 16th–17th century.

OSTRÓWKI   MAP 25
Wooden **parish church** of St Stanisław, 1743.

OSTRYKÓŁ   MAP 23
Wooden **parish church** of the Holy Cross, 1656–67.

✦ OSTRZESZÓW   MAP 12
Parish church of St Mary; chancel ca. 1337, nave 15th century. Murals 1545 and 1584.
Bernardine monastery and church of St Michael, 1680–1740. Painted decoration 1740, by *Antoni Ignacy Linke*.
Wooden **succursal church** of St Nicholas, 1758. Ruins of **castle** founded by Kazimierz the Great, mid 14th century.

✦✦✦ OŚWIĘCIM (AUSCHWITZ)   MAP 21
Concentration-camp, established in former Polish artillery barracks by the Germans in 1940 for the liquidation of the Polish intelligentsia. Satellite camp (Auschwitz II) at Brzezinka (Birkenau), built in the spring of 1942 for mass-scale implementation of the Final Solution against the Jews. Between 1.1 and 1.5 million people from all over Europe were murdered in these two camps. Auschwitz I contains a **museum**, which is essential for anyone not well versed in the horrors of concentration-camp organisation and life. Auschwitz II is the real thing, with railway track, selection ramp and the whole crazy nightmare of the camp. Not to be missed.
Parish church, 14th-early 15th century, rebuilt in Baroque style before 1681.
Dominican church, first half of 14th century, remodelled, with transposition of nave and chancel, 19th century.

Castle of the dukes of Oświęcim, tower ca. 1300, expanded after 1500.

A dependency of the bishops of Wrocław from ca. 1200.
Parish church of St Nicholas, 1690-3, by *Johann Peter Döbler*. Painted decoration 1694, by *Karl Dänkwart*. Furniture 1693, pictures by *Michael Willman*. **Castle** of the bishops of Wrocław, 15th century, repeatedly destroyed and rebuilt. Wing with tower and staircase for horses, 1638, built for Bishop Karol Ferdynand Vasa; gate and remnants of fortifications 16th century.
Palace of bishops of Wrocław, 1707 by *Michael Klein*, rebuilt 1927. Town **walls**, before 1369, tower of Nysa Gate, called the Sparrow Tower, second half of 14th century, superstructure Renaissance, 1566. **Town Hall** 1538, tower 1618, rebuilt 1827. Sundial 1575.

Lovely Baroque **country house** on island built 1693–1703 for Franciszek Bieliński, Grand Marshal of the Crown, by *Tilman van*

Gameren. Painted decoration of interiors and stucco work contemporary. Expanded mid-18th century by *Jakub Fontana*.

Wooden **church** of St Mary (originally Orthodox), 1653; tower 1783.

Church, 14th century. Ruins of 14th-century **castle**, remodelled late 19th century.

Cistercian convent founded 1242 by Przemysław II and Bolesław the Pious. Church 1720-8, by *Pompeo Ferrari*. Painted decoration 1730, by *Adam Swach*; furniture by *Pompeo Ferrari*. Monastic building ca. 1700, by *Giovanni Catenaci*, and after 1720, by *Pompeo Ferrari*, rebuilt 1773.

Neo-Classical **country house** in landscape park, 1805, by *Karl Friedrich Schinkel*.

◆ OŻARÓW   MAP 12

Characteristic wood and plaster **manor house**, 1757.

OZORKÓW   MAP 17

Weaving town linked to Łódź, with many 19th-century mills and owners' palaces. **Schlösser palace**, second quarter of 19th century. **Scheibler house**, second quarter of 19th century. **Weavers' houses**, some wooden, first half of 19th century.

◆◆ PABIANICE   MAP 19

Parish church, Renaissance, 1584, by Master *Ambrogio*. A somewhat primitive reduced version of Płock cathedral.

Renaissance **manor house** of Kraków chapter, 1571 by *Wawrzyniec Lorek*. Houses a regional **museum**: more African masks than one would expect to find in this part of the world. Several Baroque and neo-Classical **houses**. **Weavers' houses**, some wooden, second quarter of 19th century.

◆ PACZKÓW (PATSCHKAU)   MAP 13

Well preserved Medieval town. Astonishing, if not beautiful, **parish church** of the Virgin Mary, St John the Baptist and St John the Evangelist, 1361–89; vaults 1472 and 1491. Its decorative parapet wall, 1529, gives it a massive cubic aspect. Maltitz chapel 1447 with Renaissance tomb slabs, redecorated 1588. St Roch chapel 1701, with Renaissance altar, 1588.

Impressive town **walls**, ca. 1350, expanded 15th–16th century. Kłodzko Gate, 15th century, superstructure with decorative parapet wall, Renaissance, 1595. Wrocław Gate, 14th century and 1462. Ząbkowice Gate, 15th century, superstructure with decorative parapet wall, Renaissance, late 16th century. **Town Hall** 1822, with Renaissance tower, 1552.

PACZOŁTOWICE   MAP 21

Wooden **church**, wooden, 1520, paintings contemporary.

PAKOŚĆ   MAP 10 ✦

Reformed Franciscans' monastery, founded 1637 by Działyński family. Church 1656, expanded 1764. Paining in main altar 1648 by *Bartłomiej Strobel*. Monastic building before 1680. Calvary 1635.

PAPOWO BISKUPIE   MAP 10

Parish church, 14th century. Ruin of Teutonic Knights' **castle**, ca. 1300, property of Polish Crown from 1466, and of bishops of Chełmża from 1505.

PARADYŻ   MAP 19 ✦

Bernardine monastery and church, 1757, with impressive Rococo interior. A local pilgrimage centre.

PARCICE   MAP 12

Neo-Classical **manor house**, early 19th century.

PARKOWO   MAP 9

Parish church, a Baroque/neo-Classical rotunda, 1780-1802.

PASŁĘK (PREUSSISCH HOLLAND)   MAP 15. ✦✦

Town founded 1297 by Teutonic Order on site of pagan Prussian settlement, and colonized with settlers from Holland.
Parish church of St Bartholomew, late 13th century, expanded second quarter of 14th and 16th century; interior 1860–74.
Protestant **hospital church**, timber, ca. 1590.
Castle of Teutonic Knights, 1318–30, expanded by dukes of Prussia in Renaissance style, 1543, partly in ruins.
Town **walls** 13–14th century, with towers and three gates.
Town Hall, late 14th-15th century.

PASYM   MAP 16

Parish church, originally Gothic, ca. 1400, entirely rebuilt 1765–73.

PATRYKOZY   MAP 25

Neo-Gothic **country house**, 1832-43, by *Wojciech Jaszczołd*. Park with pavilion ca. 1840.

PAWŁOWICE   MAP 11 ✦✦✦

Grand Mielżyński family **country house** late 18th century, by *Karl Gottfried Langhans*. A fine facade, with grandeur added by two sweeping colonnaded wings. Very fine interior decoration by *Jan Chrystian Kamsetzer*, including a Chinese silk boudoir and a stunning ballroom.

PAWŁOWICE WIELKIE MAP 6

Country house, 1585, with original sgraffiti.

PĘCICE MAP 18

Neo-Classical **parish church**, 1825–32, by *Piotr Aigner*. **Country house** 1808–9, by *Fryderyk August Lessel*, in a contemporary landscape **park** by *Jan Christian Schuch*.

✦✦✦ PELPLIN MAP 8

Cistercian abbey founded 1274 by Duke Mszczuj of Pomerania. Conventual church, and from 1824 cathedral, of St Mary, St Bernard, St Benedict and St Stanisław, 1380–1472. Vaulting 15th century, transept vaults and gable 1557, by *Anton Schultes*. Stalls 1463. Paintings by *Hermann Hahn* and *Bartłomiej Strobel*. Fine organ, 1674-80, by *Andrzej Nitrowski*. East wing of monastery 1276, other wings and cloister first half of 14th century, superstructure 1868. A magnificent building, tempering the monumental severity of Cistercian architecture with delicacy and plenty of light. The former monastery houses a **museum** with a valuable collection of sacral art and a good library.

PĘPOWO MAP 11

Parish church, second half of 15th century, vault with Mannerist decoration 1625; aisles, tower and chapel neo-Gothic, 1820s, by *Franciszek Maria Lanci*. Painting, 1641, by *Bartłomiej Strobel*. Baroque Mycielski **country house**, 1760s. Good but quite a dull building.

PETRYKOZY   MAP 19 ✦

Neo-Classical **parish church** of St Dorothy, 1791, by *Jan Chrystian Kamsetzer*. Founded by Stanisław Małachowski, Marshal of the Great Sejm which passed the constitution of 3 May 1791.

PĘZINO (PÄNSIN)   MAP 2 ✦

Monastery-castle begun by Knights Hospitallers of St John of Jerusalem 1383, extended mid-16th century. Renaissance residential wing, ca. 1600; partly rebuilt 1853. Interesting and quite picturesque.

PIASECZNO   MAP 8 ✦✦

Parish church, first half of 14th century, rebuilt and decorated with stucco-work at the bidding of Jan III Sobieski, in Baroque style, by *Bartholomäus Ranisch*; expanded 1759.

PIASECZNO   MAP 18 ✦

Quite fine Gothic **parish church**, ca. 1560, re-Gothicized after 1950. **Town Hall** 1824, by *Kazimierz Najmski*.

PIĄTKOWA   MAP 29

Wooden Orthodox **church**, 1732.

PIEKARY ŚLĄSKIE   MAP 14 ✦

Pilgrimage centre. Neo-Romaneque **parish church** of St Mary, 1842–9. **Indulgence church** of the Transfiguration and numerous neo-Gothic chapels on the hill, 1896. The miraculous painting of the Virgin, probably early 17th century, was so renowed that it was actually sent to Prague at the request of the Emperor Leopold I and carried around the streets to combat a virulent outbreak of the plague. King Jan III Sobieski also stopped here to pray on his way to Vienna in 1683.

PIENIĄŻKOWO   MAP 8

Parish church in Gothic style, 1593.

PIESKOWA SKAŁA   MAP 21 ✦✦

Spectacularly situated **castle**, originally mid-14th century, expanded in Renaissance style 1578 by the Szafraniec family. Arcaded Mannerist courtyard built for the Zebrzydowski family late 16th century. Bastion fortifications with Mannerist gate, 1640s.In the crypt under the chapel, there are tombstones and sarcophagi of the Szafraniec and Sieniawski families, brought from other places. In the castle there is a **museum** of decorative arts and of the 1863 Insurrection, in which the castle played a role.

PIESZYCE   MAP 6
Country house, 1710, with stuccoed interior.

PIETROWICE WIELKIE (GROSS PETERWITZ)   MAP 14
Wooden **pilgrimage church**, 1743.

✦ PILCHOWICE (BILCHENGRÜND)   MAP 14
Baroque **parish church**, 1780, *Christoph Worbs(?)*. Vicarage ca.
1790. Wooden priest's granary, 18th century.

✦✦ PILICA   MAP 19
Parish church; choir and St Anne's chapel, with Rococo murals, ca.
1500. Padniewski chapel, 1601, by *Kacper Fodyga*. St Joseph's
chapel, with stuccoes, ca. 1700. A fine ornate Mannerist/Baroque
interior. Tombstone of Katarzyna Pilecka, 1555, by *Giovanni Maria
Padovano*. Stucco on elevations, ca. 1700. Warszycki **castle**, 1610,
refashioned in neo-Renaissance style 1876; well preserved
fortifications.

✦ PILZNO   MAP 22
Parish church of St John the Baptist. Main body 14th century, aisles
and tower after 1536. **Augustinian monastery** (now Carmelite)
founded 1403 by king Władysław Jagiełło. Church 15th century,
repeatedly rebuilt; tower 1866. Monastic building 1848.

✦✦✦ PINCZÓW   MAP 20
Town founded in 1428 by Cardinal Zbigniew Oleśnicki on his family estate. It later passed to the Gonzaga-Myszkowski, who had the
only marquisate in Poland, based on the entailed estate of Pinczów.
During the Reformation, the Oleśnickis, who were ardent
Calvinists and later Arians, supported a centre of worship and
study at Pinczów. Foreign Protestants came to teach at the academy
established here in 1551, and many Polish Protestants published
their works here. In 1727 the Gonzaga-Myszkowski family died out,
and the estate was inherited by the Wielopolski family, who
assumed the rights and titles associated with Pinczów.
Baroque **country house** of Wielopolski family, ca. 1780 by
Ferdynand F. Nax(?). Formal **park** , 16th–18th century. Tower of
Myszkowski castle late 16th century, by *Santi Gucci*.
Pauline monastery founded 1436 by Cardinal Zbigniew Oleśnicki.
Church of St John the Evangelist, first half of 17th century. Stalls
mid-17th century, other furniture mid-18th century. Rococo organ

176

case 1757-9, by *Wojciech Szyplewski* . Monastic building second quarter of 17th century. Bell-tower 1691.

Reformed **Franciscans' monastery** founded by Myszkowski family. Church with two chapels, Mannerist, ca. 1620, vault decoration second quarter of 17th century; redecorated in Baroque style. Towers lowered and arcaded courtyard added in front of facade, 1688. The monastery building, 1686–1706, now houses a **museum** of the Arian movement.

On the hill above the town, exquisite **chapel** of St Anne, founded by Grand Marshal of the Crown Zygmunt Myszkowski, Mannerist, 1600, workshop of *Santi Gucci.*

Synagogue, 16th or early 17th century, with Mannerist stucco and stone decoration. The so-called Polish Brethren's **printing office**, turn of 16th century.

The local stone quarries, leased by the architect *Santi Gucci*, supplied not only cut stone, but also fully-carved Renaissance and Mannerist architectural elements, which could be assembled elsewhere. An impressive example of artistic entreperneurship.

PIOTRAWIN MAP 27 ♦♦
Parish church and chapel founded 1440 by Cardinal Zbigniew Oleśnicki on site associated with legend about St Stanisław.

This is where the sejms of Wielkopolska met until the end of the 15th century, and where the szlachta continued to meet to elect the judges for the supreme tribunal of Poland (hence the name). By the 18th century, when Polish public life had sunk to its nadir, this involved the principal factions turning up with hundreds of henchmen armed to the teeth and even whole regiments of private troops, which often led to blood-letting on an alarming scale.

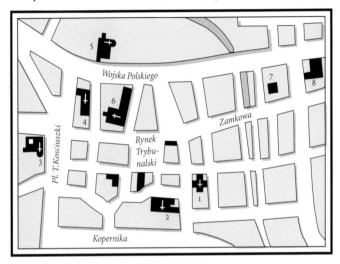

Parish church of St James [**1**], from the turn of the 14th century, vaulting 16th century, two chapels ca. 1674.

Dominican church of St Jacek [**5**], 14th century, redecorated in Renaissance/Mannerist style early 1600s, with addition of St Mary's chapel and stucco decoration. Aisles early 19th century.

Bernardine church of St Mary [**3**], Baroque, 1626–43, rebuilt third quarter of 17th century.

Dominican Nuns' church [**4**], ca. 1630, rebuilt third quarter of 17th century, stucco second quarter of 17th century, tower 1785. **Jesuit Church** [**2**] 1695–1727. Towers and facade 1742. Stucco 1736. Painted decoration 1741, by *Andrzej Ahorn* and 1769 by *Jan Rejsner*.

Piarist church [**6**]. **College** building 1750s, alterations 1803. Royal keep, now regional **museum** [**7**], 1521, by Master *Benedykt*. **Synagogue** [**8**].

✦   PIOTRKOWICE   MAP 20

Bernardine monastery 1652. Church with elliptical Loreto chapel, 1776.

In nearby TARNOSKAŁA, remains of neo-Classical **residence**, end of the 18th century.

PIOTRKOWICE   MAP 11 ✦
Country house, 1693, with stuccoed interiors.

PISARZOWICE   MAP 13
Parish church, late 13th century, chapel ca. 1600. **Country house,**
mid-18th century.

PŁAKOWICE (PLAGWITZ)   MAP 6 ✦
Rather charming Renaissance **country house** of Rampold von
Talkenberg, with arcaded courtyard, 1550.

PŁAWOWICE   MAP 21 ✦
Birthplace of the poet Ludwik Hieronim Morstin (1580–1623).
Country house built for Morstin family, 1805, by *Jakub Kubicki*,
expanded 1886, by *Tadeusz Stryjeński*. Neo-Gothic chapel, 1802.

PŁOCK   MAP 17 ✦✦✦
The capital of the province of Mazovia, an interesting old town in a
superb position on a high escarpment overlooking the Vistula. On
Castle Hill [1], granite traces of fortified palace founded by
Bolesław the Wrymouth, Romanesque, 12th century, on which
Kazimierz the Great built a brick castle in 1353. Most of this was
demolished in the 18th century, leaving only that part of the castle
complex that housed the **Benedictine abbey** (founded 1172), which
became a house of the Order of Missionaries in 1781, and, after
being deconsecrated in 1856, a school. This now houses the
museum, with the usual mixture of local interest, but also a quite
remarkable museum of the Secession and Art Nouveau, including
painting, furniture, sculpture, glass, lamps, jewellery and ornaments. The only other remnants of the old castle are two towers: the
western, "Szlachecka" tower, and a southern tower, its granite
Romanesque base rising into a Gothic brick tower, converted into
the cathedral belfry, mid-16th century by *Gianbattista* of Venice;
spire 1735.
Cathedral of St Mary [2], originally Romanesque, present church
built by Bishop Andrzej Krzycki in Renaissance style, 1532–4, by
Bernardo Zanobi de Gianotis; chancel lengthened 1563 by
Gianbattista. This was the second major Renaissance building in
Poland after the Wawel in Kraków, and is one of the greatest
Renaissance churches north of the Alps. Unfortunately, it was thoroughly restored 1900–3 and painted throughout by *S. Drapiewski*.
The effect is heavy, gloomy and, to my mind, hideous. But the pro-
portions remain. There are also a couple of good Baroque marble
altars, and a superb series of tombs of bishops and canons,

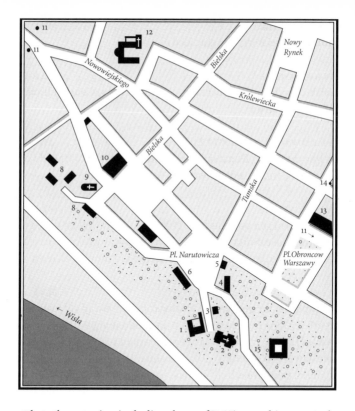

16th–17th centuries, including those of B. Niszczycki, ca. 1560, by *Santi Gucci(?)*; of P. Głogowski, ca. 1580 by *Jan Michałowicz*; and of Stanisław Krasiński, ca. 1617. Also of interest is the 1825 monument to the kings Władysław Herman and Bolesław the Wrymouth, who, according to tradition, were buried here. Also the replica of the famous Płock doors -the originals, made in 1144, are now at Novgorod in Russia. Next to the cathedral there is a diocesan **museum** [3], containing a mixed bag of paintings, sculpture, decorative arts, portraits and Polish sash belts. There is some very good early religious sculpture, some decent paintings and some fine sacral decorative arts. Foreign paintings include works by *Bronzino*, *Bassano* and *Cuyp*.

The **main square**, contains a number of fine buildings, with the Baroque 'Dom pod Trąbami' [4], the neo-Classical guardhouse [5], the courthouse [6]and the series of elegant early 19th century town houses.

Collegiate church of St Michael [7]. Original Gothic church, incorporating fragments of earlier Romanesque structure ca. 1230, turned into Jesuit college 1607, expanded 1773. College rebuilt as school in 1843, by *Antonio Corazzi*. **Granaries** [8], 16th-17th cents.

Parish church of St Bartholomew [**9**], 1356, expanded in 16th century, but in the 17th century a section of the escarpment collapsed, taking half the church down with it. The church was then turned round and remodelled in 1775. The high altar, by *Giovanni Battista Gisleni*, ca. 1632, was transferred from the deconsecrated Benedictine church.

Dominican monastery [**15**], ca. 1230, rebuilt in 19th century with church of St Dominic, ca. 1230-50, interior 18th century.

Reformed Franciscans' monastery and **church,** 1758-71.

Local **government building** [**13**], neo-Classical, 1803 by *David Gilly*. Neo-Classical **Town Hall** [**10**], 1827 by *Jakub Kubicki*, flanked by good Baroque and neo-Classical town houses around **market square**. Prussian **prison**, neo-Classical, ca. 1803 by *David Gilly*; extended in neo-Gothic style, 1846 by *Henryk Marconi*. Circular neo-Classical **tollgates** [**11**], ca. 1825 by *Jakub Kubicki*.

PŁOŃSK   MAP 17

This is where General Władysław Sikorski's 5th Army held off the Bolshevik armies of Marshal Tukhachevsky in August 1920 for long enough to permit Marshal Piłsudski to mount his flanking thrust from the south which saved Warsaw. **Carmelite church** and monastery, founded 1462, redecorated mid-17th century.

PNIEWY   MAP 4

Country house of Szołdrski family, 1739, rebuilt 1872.

PNIÓW   MAP 14

Country house, Baroque, 1770, rebuilt 1840 and 1890.

PODDĘBICE   MAP 12 ✦

Interesting Renaissance **country house** of the Grudziński family, 1617, partly reconstructed mid-20th century.

Parish church of St Catherine, ca. 1610; aisles 1895.

PODOLE   MAP 22 ✦

Wooden **parish church**, turn of the 15th century; polychromy 1542.

PODZAMCZE   MAP 20 ✦

Zamoyski **country house**, built first half of 19th century on site of 17th-century Zbąski castle of Maciejowice. Landscape park with Romantic statues and two pavilions. The house overlooks the battlefield of Maciejowice, where General Tadeusz Kościuszko was wounded and captured by the Russians under General Fersen on 10 October 1794, effectively putting an end to the Insurrection.

POGORZELA   MAP 11
Parish church, first half of 15th century, tower ca. 1600.

✦ POGWIZDÓW   MAP 21
Wooden **parish church**, 15th/16th century. Wooden vicarage 18th
century.

POGWIZDÓW (LANGHELWIGSDORF)   MAP 6
Parish church, ca. 1300, rebuilt 16th and 17th centuries..

POKÓJ (CARLSRÜHE)   MAP 11
Protestant church, Baroque, 1765.

POKRZYWNO   MAP 10
Ruins of Teutonic Knights' **castle**, ca. 1270, ceded to Poland 1454.

POLANKA WIELKA   MAP 21
Wooden **parish church**, first half of the 16th century, rebuilt 1658
and 18th century. Baroque **country house**, 1769, rebuilt ca. 1850.

PONARY   MAP 15
Manor house late 16th century, expanded to mid-19th century.

✦ PONIEC   MAP 11
Parish Church, first half of 15th century; tower, interior and furniture, 4th quarter of 18th century.

✦✦ PONISZOWICE   MAP 14
Wooden **parish church**, late 1400s, chapel ca. 1650; rebuilt ca. 1770.
Furniture mid-17th century. Wooden Belfry 1520.

✦ POPOWICE   MAP 12
Wooden **church**, early 16th century; tower ca. 1700.

✦ POPOWO STARE   MAP 4
Country house, Baroque, 1770–80.

PORĘBA   MAP 14
Palace of the dukes of Pless, 1800, by *Wilhelm Pusch*.

PORĘBA WIELKA   MAP 21
Wooden **church**, early 16th century, tower ca. 1640. **Country house**.
ca.1850, by *Franciszek Maria Lanci*, entirely rebuilt 1958.

PORZECZE MARIAŃSKIE   MAP 18 ✦
Wooden **parish church**, 1776.

POSADA RYBOTYCKA   MAP 29 ✦✦
Unusual two-storey castellated **Orthodox church**,
Gothic/Renaissance, first half of 16th century.

POWRÓŹNIK   MAP 22 ✦✦
Very pretty wooden **Orthodox** (now Catholic) **church** of St James
the Minor, Baroque 1611. Iconostasis and paintings 17th century.
The village is rich in vernacualr architecture.

POZNAŃ   MAP 9 ✦✦✦
Capital of Wielkopolska and a bishopric since 968. Poznań grew in
importance as cities such as Wrocław and Szczecin were lost to
Germany, and by the end of the 18th century it had become the
principal city of western Poland. It was taken over by Prussia in
1793. In the 19th century it was the centre of the Prussian part of
Poland, the Duchy of Posen, and the scene of some of the most

hard-fought if undramatic struggles for the survival of Polishness in the face of German colonisation. In November 1918, the appearance in the city of the pianist and statesman Ignacy Jan Paderewski provoked a rising against the Germans, and Poznań once again became part of Poland. In 1939, after the invasion of Poland, the Germans made Poznań the capital of the new German Province of Warthegau.

The first fortified settlement here was situated on **Ostrów Tumski**, the island lying between two arms of the river Warta [see inset], and ✦✦✦ it is here that the oldest churches are to be found. The **cathedral** of SS Peter and Paul [1] stands on the site of a stone pre-Romanesque church, ca. 970, superseded by a Romanesque basilica 1079 (the remains of both can be seen in the archaeologiacl exhibition under the church floor), and later the present Gothic brick basilica, the

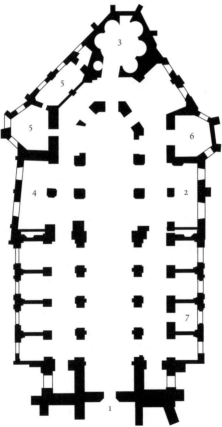

1 - West door, 2 - Szołdrski chapel, 3 - Golden chapel, 4 - Holy Cross or Górka chapel, 5 - Sacristy, 6 - Sacred Heart chapel, 7 - South porch.

main body of which (nave, aisles and two towers) was built 1346–57. The choir, ambulatory and chapels date from 1403–10, and the chapels adjoining the aisle from 1410–28. The whole was remodelled thoroughly in the 18th and 19th centuries, but after extensive damage in 1945, the cathedral was re-Gothicized. Inside, remnants of Renaissance murals, 16th century and, in the Szołdrski chapel, 1616. A remarkable series of Renaissance tomb plates from the workshop of *Peter Vischer*. Epitaphs of Bishop Benedykt Izdbieński, 1560, by *Jan Michałowicz of Urzędów*; of Bishop Adam Konarski, ca. 1576, and of Górka family, 1578, both by *Girolamo Canavesi*; of Bishop Jędrzej Szołdrski, 1652. Triptych 1512; painting by *Krzysztof Boguszewski*, 1628. Pulpit 1720.

Collegiate church of St Mary [**2**] founded by Bishop Andrzej ✦✦
Bniński, on the site of a 10th-century chapel of the first rulers of Poland, brick with ceramic decoration, 1442-8, by *Hans Prusz*, and western gable, by *Wawrzyniec Lorek*.

Psalterists' house [**3**] founded by Bishop Jan Lubrański, 1512. Diocesan **museum**, containing religious painting and sculpture, mostly medieval, with some vestments, textiles and coffin portraits.

College [**4**] founded as embryo university by Bishop Lubrański in 1519. Archbishop's palace [**5**].

Church of St Margaret [**6**], second half of 15th century, with ✦
Romanesque remains, rebuilt 18th century. Adjoining, Oratorian monastery, Baroque, 1771, expanded 20th century.

Church of Knights of St John of Jerusalem in Malta [**8**], ✦
Romanesque, second half of 13th century, expanded 1512. Chapel 1736. This church is all that is left of the Commandery of the Order which founded the first hospital on Polish territory.

Reformed Franciscans' monastery church of St Kazimierz [**7**], ✦✦
1663–75, by *Cristoforo Bonadura* and *Giorgo Catenaci*, redecorated 1796. Monastic building 1704, with some alterations.

In the thirteenth century the growing city spread westwards into what is now the **Old Town**.

Town Hall [**9**], 13th–14th century, expanded 1508 with addition of ✦✦
arcaded galleries. Remodelled, with addition of loggias, decorative parapet wall, outside sgraffiti and stucco, and very fine painted interiors in Renaissance style, 1550s, by *Giovanni Battista di Quadro*. Tower superstructure neo-Classical, 1783, by *Jan Chrystian Kamsetzer*(?). Now houses Historical **Museum** of City of Poznań (which for some reason appears to include Egyptian antiquities and a very good collection of Roman emperors' heads). Neo-Classical **guardhouse** [**10**], 1787 by *Jan Chrystian Kamsetzer(?)*. ✦✦
Houses in old market square, 15th-16th century, standardized by addition of stone arcades, 1535. No. 37, the Red Pharmacy, 1654, by

Tomasso Poncino, facade Baroque, second half of 18th century. No 45 Houses a **museum** of musical instruments. No. 78, the Działyński palace, 1770s, interiors and facade 1780s by *Antoni Hoene*, decoration of facade completed 1815. Renaissance Górka palace, with stone portal, 1548; rebuilt ca. 1600.

♦♦ **Carmelite chapel[11]** 1702. Painted decoration 1735, by *Adam Swach*.

♦♦ **Dominican monastery [12]**, founded 1244. Church of St Dominic 1244–53, rebuilt in Baroque style, 1700–24, by *Giorgo Catenaci*, and 1814. St Jacek's chapel with porch and loggia opening into cloister garden, 1622. Monastery with Gothic cloister, ca. 1500, expanded in Baroque style 17th-early 18th century.

♦ **Dominican convent [13]**; church 1404–30, vault and gable after 1536; partly rebuilt early 1700s. Monastic building with carved beam ceiling, 16th century, rebuilt 19th century.

♦ **Parish church of St Wojciech [14]**, 15th century, expanded first half of 16th century; gables early 17th century. Wooden Belfry 18th century.

♦ **Discalced Carmelites' monastery [15]**, 1635–67 by *Cristoforo Bonadura* and *Giorgio Catenaci*, rebuilt 1830.
Museum of Decorative Arts **[16]**, with furniture, tapestries, textiles, ceramics, glass and oriental arms and armour.

♦ **Franciscan monastery [17]**. Church of St Anthony 1665-1728, by *Jan Koński*. Stucco 17th–18th century; painted decoration ca. 1720, by *Adam Swach*. Rydzyński tomb 1736.

♦♦ **National Museum [18].** Contains Medieval section, with some good stone and wood sculpture, including one ravishing Madonna, as well as some good triptychs and smaller paintings. Fascinating 15th century processional sculpture of Christ on a donkey for use on Palm Sunday. The gallery also contains a good collection of 19th and 20th century Polish painting. But the greatest treat is a quite remarkable collection of Dutch and Flemish masters, and an even more remarkable collection of Spanish and Portuguese painting.
Raczyński Library [19], modelled on the north facade of the Louvre, 1829.
Church of St Martin **[20]**, Gothic; part of vaulting after 1656.

♦ **Carmelite monastery [21]**, founded by Kazimierz the Jagiellon. Church 1470, parts of vaults and gable 1664. Chapel of Our Lady, 1726 by *Pompeo Ferrari*. High altar 1730, by *Pompeo Ferrari*. Monastic building expanded in Baroque style 17th-18th century.
Church of the Holy Cross **[23]**, originally Protestant, ca. 1800 by *Antoni Hoene*.

♦♦ **Bernardine monastery [22]**, second half of 17th century. Church with Mannerist chancel, 1650s by *Cristoforo Bonadura*; nave and

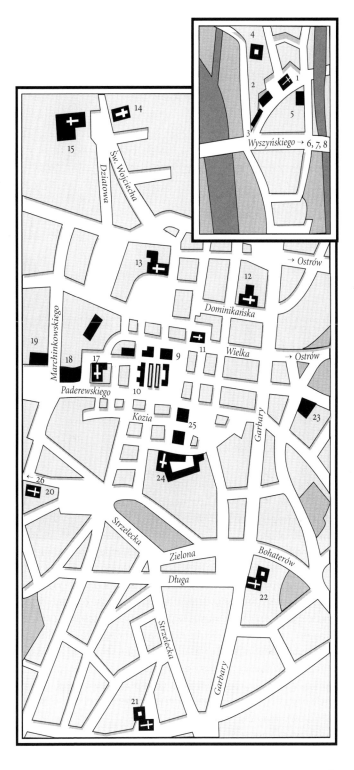

Wyszyńskiego → 6, 7, 8

→ Ostrów

→ Ostrów

Św. Wojciecha

Działowa

Marchinkowskiego

Paderewskiego

Dominikańska

Wielka

Garbary

Kozia

Strzelecka

Zielona

Długa

Strzelecka

Garbary

Bohaterów

← 26

facade ca. 1671, by *Giorgio Catenaci*; facade and towers 1737, by *Jan Steyner*. Loreto chapel, 1668.

♦♦♦ **Jesuit college [24].** Church of St Mary Magdalen, begun 1651 by *Tommaso Poncino*, rebuilt 1686 by *Bartłomiej Wąsowski* and finished 1711 by *Giovanni Catenaci*. Facade with portal 1727–32 by *Pompeo Ferrari*. Stucco by *Giovanni Battista Bianco*; painted decoration by *Karl Dänkwart*. High altar 1727. Pictures 1756, by *Szymon Czechowicz*. This is an extraordinary interior, considering the spatial limitations. The monumental columns create an illusion of depth, and the use of mirrors enhances the available space. It is more of an ante-room to heaven than a place of worship. College building 1733, by *Giovanni Catenaci*. Jesuit school 1685, by *Bartłomiej Wąsowski*.

Parish priest's house [25], 18th century, in corner of building, statue

of Madonna, Gothic, early 16th century.
Neo-romanesque imperial **castle [26]**, 1905–10 by *Francis Schwechten*, a magniificently gloomy Teutonic pile looming over the university quarter.

PRABUTY   MAP 15
Parish church, 1378–1409. Baroque waterworks, 18th century.

PRAKWICE (PRÖKELWITZ)   MAP 15
Manor house, second half of 17th century.

PRANDOCIN   MAP 21 ✦
Parish church of St John the Baptist. Ashlar nave, western apse and tower ca. 1120, chancel expanded 15th century; Gothic murals.

PROCHOWICE   MAP 6
Partly ruined **castle**, ca. 1300; expanded ca. 1540 by *Johann Lindner*. Acquired by the Habsburgs 1675, and subsequently by the Hohenzollerns.

PRÓSZKÓW   MAP 13 ✦✦
Parish church, second half of 17th century; stuccoed and painted interior.
Country house based on a castle of 1563, rebuilt in Baroque style 1677, by *Giovanni Seregno*, and 19th century. Decoration of interiors ca. 1700.

PROSZOWICE   MAP 21
Parish church, 1490s, entirely remodelled 1836.

PRUDNIK (NEUSTADT)   MAP 13 ✦
Town founded 1279 on the Wrocław-Vienna route. **Parish church**, 1738 by *Josef Ignaz Töpper*. Surviving tower of the castle of the dukes of Opole, from the turn of the 13th century. Town **walls** with towers 15th century, one of them housing a **museum**.

PRUSICE (PRAUSNITZ)   MAP 11
Parish church, 15th century; Hatzfeld chapel second half of 17th century. **Town Hall**, second quarter of 16th century.

PRUSY   MAP 11 ✦
Parish church, early 14th century, rebuilt in Renaissance style, with sgraffito decoration, 1612 and 1660.

◆◆ PRZASNYSZ MAP 18
Parish church 16th century. **Bernardine monastery** founded 1585 by
Paweł Kostka (whose brother, Stanisław, was later canonised).
Church, late monumental Gothic with Renaissance details, 1588.
Monastic building 1618.

PRZECŁAW MAP 22
Koniecpolski **country house**, end of 16th century, expanded by Rey
family in neo-Gothic style. Now a hotel.

◆◆ PRZEMĘT MAP 4
Cistercian abbey, founded 1418. Church 1651–90, by *Giorgio
Catenaci*. Gables 1759. Polychromy first half of 18th century.
Furniture late 17th-18th century. Remains of monastery 1758.

PRZEMYKÓW MAP 22
Parish church, 1451-64, aisles late 16th century.

◆◆◆ PRZEMYŚL MAP 29
Important provincial town, astride trading routes from the south
and east, on the border between Poland and the Ruthene lands. The
large number of Renaissance and Baroque town houses testifies to
the town's wealth in the 15–17th centuries. In the 19th century it was
an important Austrian fortress, the plans of which were the crux of
the Colonel Redl affair, which caused a homosexual scandal at the

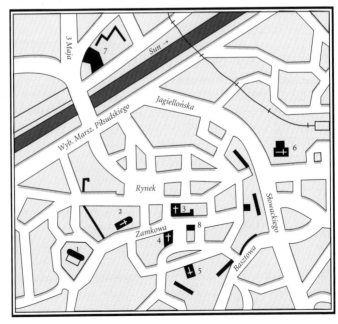

heart of the Imperial family in Vienna. Ringed by 30 miles of defence works and guarded by 1,000 guns, the fortress proved useless against the Russian advance in 1915.

Remains of royal **castle** (on site of 10th–century fort) [1]. Wing with two (of original four) circular angle rondelles, Renaissance, 1511–1553, rebuilt 1612–30, by *Galeazzo Appiani(?)*, remodelled 1762. **Cathedral** of St John the Baptist [2], founded 1375 on the site of a Romanesque stone rotunda dedicated to St Nicholas; built 1460–1571, rebuilt 1744. Octagonal domed Drohojowski chapel, 1578, rebuilt 1720, with painted decoration third quarter of 18th century. Elliptical Fredro chapel, 1724. Sculpture 4th quarter of 15th century, two Renaissance tombs. Bell-tower 1764, superstructure 1907.

Franciscan monastery [3] founded 1235. Church of St Mary Magdalen, 1777, stone sculpture Rococo, 1760 by *Fabian Fesinger*. Painted decoration 1777, by *Stanisław Stroiński*. High altar with sculpture by *Maciej Polejowski*, 1764. Rococo organ 1781-3, with good carvings by *Maciej Polejowski, Piotr Barzycki and Franciszek Duńczewski*. Monastic building after 1780.

Jesuit college [4] designed by *Giaccomo Briano*, 1622. Church, 1627–79 by *Jakub Solari*, rebuilt 1760s and 19th century. College uilding 1687–1720, superstructure 1846. **School**, 1757, houses Diocesan **Museum**, mainly of sacral arts, including fine collection of textiles, mainly vestments, some made out of Ottoman fabrics. **Discalced Carmelites' monastery** [5] founded by Count Michał Krasicki 1627. Church (served as Uniate cathedral 1784–1945), Baroque, 1630; drum and wooden dome, first half of 19th century; rebuilt, with the addition of stucco, 1884. Monastic building with two cloister gardens, expanded 18th century and 19th century. **Reformed Franciscans' monastery** [6] founded 1627. Church, 1645, rebuilt 1909. Monastic building late 17th century.

Bell-tower of Orthodox Church, 1777, rebuilt 1925.

Benedictine convent [7], founded 1616. Church 1777, painted decoration after 1780, by *Stanisław Stroiński*. Church wall with loopholes, second half of 17th century.

City **museum** [8]. The usual jumble of archaeology and local history, including some interesting Orthodox sacral arts and Judaica.Also, a museum of the First World War.

PRZEWORSK   MAP 29 ✦✦

Fortified **monastery of Canons Regular** of the Holy Sepulchre. Church built 1430-73, remodelled 1785, withparts of the vaulting recreated in the late 19th century. Font and painting Gothic, furniture Baroque. Chapel of Holy Sepulchre, 1692, redecorated ca. 1845.

The monastery building dates from the second half of 17th century. Fortified **Bernardine monastery** founded 1476. Church of St Barbara, end of 15th century, tower first half of 16th century, gable of chancel first half of 17th century, vaults second half of 18th century, facade 1902. Monastic building after 1512.

Town **walls**, first half of 16th century. Lubomirski **country house**, neo-Classical, 1823.

PRZEZMARK (PREUSSISCH MARK)   MAP 15
Remains of **castle** of Teutonic Knights, 1331; passed into private ownership 1521 and rebuilt 1585 by *B.Bernwardt*.

PRZYCZYNA GÓRNA   MAP 4
Parish church, mid-14th century, restored 1595 and 1665. Murals first half of 15th century.

✦✦ PRZYDONICA   MAP 22
Wooden **parish church** of Our Lady of the Rosary, 1527. Painted decoration Renaissance, first half of 17th century. Two Gothic triptychs.

PRZYSUCHA   MAP 20
Parish church, 1786. Turrets 1902. **Synagogue,** Baroque, late 18th century.

PSARSKIE   MAP 4
Parish church, Gothic, 1462-1500. Baroque interior from second half of 18th century.

✦✦ PSZCZYNA (PLESS)   MAP 14
Settled since 10th century, a ducal town from the first half of the 14th century. In private hands since 16th century, Promnitz **palace** on site of former ducal castle, 1743–67 by *Christian Jahne*, rebuilt for Hochberg family 1870-4, by *Hippolite Alexandre Destailleur*, creator of the 'Ritz' style and architect of the great Rothschild mansion at Waddesdon in England; interiors contemproary, fully furnished, with collections of miniatures and armour. An astonishing place. Gate 1687, by *Consillo Milius(?)*. "Ludwikówka" **palace**, ca. 1800 by *Wilhelm Pusch*.

PSZENNO   MAP 6
Parish church, late 14th century, southern aisle and eastern gable ca. 1490; rebuilt 1552. Baroque interior, with good tombstones.

Church of St Giles, 14th/15th century, expanded 1910 by *Józef Pius Dziekoński*. An unassuming building, but wonderfully situated and heavily fortified with late 16th–century fortifications.

A trading port from the 13th century, and the home port of the Polish war fleet in the first half of the 17th century. **Parish church**, 14th century, with parts before 1283; chancel vault before 1645. Paintings, school of *Hermann Hahn*, first half of 17th century. Timber **hospital**, ca. 1720.

Czartoryski **country house**, 1722–36, by *Johann Sigismund Deybel* and *Franciszek Mayer*; rebuilt in neo-Classical style, ca. 1800, by *Piotr Aigner* for Prince Adam Czartoryski. Rebuilt 1844 by *Józef Górecki* and 1861 by *Julian Ankiewicz*. Between the 1780s and 1831 Puławy was an important magantial court and the centre of political and cultural activity. Neo-Classical **villa** of Marynka, 1794 by *Piotr Aigner*. Exquisite little residence built for Princess Marya Czartoryska, who after separating from her husband, Prince Ludwig of Württemberg, lived at the side of her parents. **Park**, laid out in 1798 by *Princess Izabela Czartoryska* in collaboration with *John Savage* (who stayed here from 1791 to 1816), *Jean-Pierre Norblin*, *Wojciech Jaszczołd* and *Piotr Aigner*. Neo-Classical Temple of Sybil, 1801, and neo-Gothic cottage, 1800 both by *Piotr Aigner*. These two were erected to house the artistic and historical collections of Princess Izabela Czartoryska, which now form the nucleus of the Czartoryski Museum in Kraków. The famous Leonardo da Vinci hung in the gothic cottage.

Parish church, modelled on Pantheon in Rome, 1800-3 by *Aigner*.

Residence of the bishops of Płock and one of the religious and cultural centres of Mazovia. An important market town, as can be gauged from the remarkable market square, the longest in Europe. The layout of the town suggests a very ancient settlement. It was here that Napoleon announced, on 31 December 1806, that after Marshal Lannes' minor victory over the Russians just outside the town, the campaign of that year was finally over. This came as a great relief to the Old Guard, which had grumbled so much about the weather and the lack of food, that the Emperor called them a bunch of '*grognards*', a name that stuck. On the hill, which was once crowned with a wooden fort, stands the **castle** of the bishops of

Płock ca. 1368, expanded 1522–38, and in neo-Classical style 1786; rebuilt 19th-20th century.

Collegiate church of St Matthew, ca. 1440, expanded 16th century, redecorated 1560, with a remarkable patterned barrel-vault by Master *Gianbattista* of Venice. Domed chapel of Bishop Andrzej Noskowski, Renaissance, 1554, by *Gianbattista*, with contemporary painted decoration and tomb, 1561. Furniture first half of 18th century. Załuski epitaphs 1718–42. Organ 1830. Bell-tower 1507, rebuilt in neo-Classical style 1783.

Just outside the town, **cemetery church** of the Holy Cross founded by Bishop Andrzej Krzycki, 1531. Murals Renaissance, second quarter of 16th century. A lovely building delightfully situated.

Jesuit college, founded 1566 (since 1773 Benedictine). Church of St Joseph 1717. College building expanded 1825.

Reformed Franciscans' church and monastery, 1640, rebuilt 19th century.

Chapel of St Mary Magdalen, 1538, entirely reconstructed ca. 1950.

Town Hall tower, first half of 16th century .

PUŃCÓW   MAP 14
Parish church, nave with central pillar supporting vault, 1518; facade and tower end of 19th century.

✦   PYRZYCE   MAP 1
Parish church of St Maurice, turn of 14th century, parts mid-13th century.

✦   PYZDRY   MAP 9
Franciscan monastery, founded before 1277. Church 14th century; Baroque painted decoration 1733, by *Adam Swach*.

✦   RABKA   MAP 21
Wooden **parish church**, 1606, in the Gothic tradition; restored in the second half of the 18th century.

✦   RACHOWICE   MAP 14
Parish church with a late 15th century chancel, and wooden nave 1668. Tower 1780s. Somewhat rustic contemporary furniture.

RACIĄŻEK   MAP 10
Castle of the bishops of Kuyavia, 1335, expanded several times and, in 1720, remodelled into a Baroque residence, now in ruins.
Parish church founded by Bishop Henryk Rozdrażewski, 1597.

RACIBOROWICE
MAP 21 ✦

Parish church founded by the Kraków prelate and historian Jan Długosz in 1460. The choir is original, the nave was added in 1476. Gothic paintings and sculptures, and Renaissance tomb plaques.

RACIBOROWICE (HARTMANNSDORF)
MAP 6 ✦

Romanesque **parish church**, 2nd quarter of 13th century. Central pillars, nave vaulting and tower 1577. An ornate interior, with furniture from the 16th to the 18th centuries.

RACIBÓRZ (RATIBOR)
MAP 14 ✦✦

A fortified settlement on the Oder river, inhabited since the 9th century, and the capital of a Piast duchy since 1177. **Castle** of the dukes of Racibórz, end of 13th century. Chapel 1287, originally two-storeyed, altered 1519 and 1873. The castle later passed to the Habsburgs, for whom it was expanded in 1603. In the 19th century, all of it except for the chapel and the gate tower was turned into a brewery.

Parish church ca. 1300 and later, pillars and vaults 1592. 'Polish' hapel 1426–46, altered 1770s. Tower 1580. Chapter house 1418, enlarged 1891.

Dominican church, after 1300, interior altered 1637 and 1774. Neo-Romanesque facade 1874. Gaszyński family chapel with rich stucco decoration, 1650.

Dominican nuns' church, 1335. Painted decoration 1635, tomb of the Dukes of Racibórz, ca. 1500. Houses **museum** of local history, with some good Silesian painting and sculpture from the 14th to 18th centuries. Town **walls** ca. 1300. 'Prison' tower with Renaissance superstructure, after 1547. **Courthouse**, 1820s by *Karl Friedrich Schinkel*.

RACIECHOWICE
MAP 21

Wooden **parish church** with Rococo interior, 1720, expanded 1902. Wooden **manor house**, 1760. Grain-store, 1774.

RACŁAWICE
MAP 21 ✦

Wooden **parish church** 1511. Painted decoration 17th century.

RACOT
MAP 9 ✦

Elegant neo-Classical **manor house** built for Prince Antoni Barnaba Jabłonowski ca. 1790, probably by *Dominik Merlini*.

RADECZNICA
MAP 27

Bernardine church 1686–95 by *Jan Michał Link*.

RADKÓW   MAP 6

Parish church (originally Protestant), 1570, rebuilt 1740. Town
Houses 17th–18th cents.

✦   RADLIN   MAP 11

Castle of Opaliński family, late 1500s; acquired by the Sapieha family 1696. **Parish church**, 1688 by *Grzegorz Lendz*. Octagonal
Renaissance sepulchral chapel of Andrzej Opaliński and his wife
with unusual stucco work, 1611.

✦✦ RADOM   MAP 20

An ancient market town astride the junction of roads leading from
Lublin in the east, Kraków and Kielce in the south, Piotrków in the
west, and Warsaw in the north. A royal burgh from the 14th century, and a provincial capital under the Russian partition.

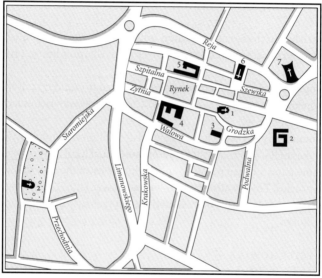

Parish church of St John the Baptist [1], founded by Kazimierz the
Great. Choir, tower and Rosary chapel turn of the 15th century;
main body neo-Gothic, 1909 by *Józef Pius Dziekoński*.
Kochanowski chapel, with Renaissance/Mannerist decoration,
1633. The rectory is a converted part of the former royal castle.
Bernardine monastery [2] founded 1468. Church of St Catherine,
mainly early 16th century, expanded 1912 by *Stefan Szyller*.
Crucifixion group end of 15th century. Kitchen building 16th cen-
tury. **Piarist monastery** [4], 1756 by *Antoni Solari*. Church of St Jan
Kanty entirely rebuilt; front wing of college neo-Classical, 1818.
Town Hall [5] with guardhouse, 1848, by *Henryk Marconi*.

Provincial government building 1827, by *Antonio Corazzi*. **Museum**, with some local historical material and a gallery of Polish painting 18th-20th centuries.

RADOMIERZYCE (RADMERITZ)   MAP 5

Country house on artificial island, ca. 1728 by *Johann Friedrich Kärcher* and *Christoph Beyer*. Formal park with Baroque sculptures.

RADRUŻ   MAP 30

Wooden **Orthodox church**, 1669.

RADZIEJOWICE   MAP 18

Headquarters of the Radziejowski family, which blotted its copybook in 1655, when Vice-Chancellor Hieronim Radziejowski, after a tiff with the king, changed sides and helped the invading Swedish armies ravage the country.

Palace of Cardinal Michał Radziejowski (the traitor's brother), 1684. Rebuilt for Krasiński family in Neo-Classical style. Adjacent Renaissance **manor house**, 1606, similarly transformed into Romantic "Little Castle", 1802 by *Jakub Kubicki*. Romantic landscape park, 1817 by *Antoine d'Alphonse de Saint Omer*. Neo-Classical **parish church**, 1820 by *Jakub Kubicki*.

RADZIKOWICE (STEPHANSDORF)   MAP 13

Parish church, 14th century; rebuilt in Renaissance style ca. 1600, and in Baroque style 1679.

RADZISZÓW   MAP 21

Neo-Classical **manor house,** beginning of 19th century, by *Sebastian Sierakowski*.

RADZYMIN   MAP 18

Mean little market town, birthplace of Isaac Bashevis Singer. The **parish church**, probably by *Jan Chrystian Kamsetzer*, was rebuilt after 1897 by *Konstanty Wojciechowski*. **School**, 1843, by *Antonio Corazzi*.

RADZYŃ CHEŁMIŃSKI (REDEN)   MAP 10 ◆

A good example of a Teutonic Knights' **monastery-castle**, from the first quarter of the 14th century. Only one of the three wings is left standing, with only traces of the others, but an imposing building nevertheless.

Parish church, ca. 1310; nave and tower ca. 1340. Redecorated in

Renaissance style 1580s. Dąbrowski chapel 1587. Painted ceiling 17th century. Pictures 1643, by *Bartłomiej Strobel*. **Cemetery chapel**, founded 1285, 14th century; remodelled 1851.

✦✦ RADZYŃ PODLASKI   MAP 27
Lovely baroque **country house** built for Chancellor Stanisław Szczuka, ca. 1690 by *Augustyn Locci*, and expanded for General Eustachy Potocki 1758, by *Jakub Fontana*. Sculpture and decoration of facades Rococo, by *Johann Redler*. Formal park with parterres, remnants of espaliers and canal, mid-18th century. Orangery 1750s, by *Jakub Fontana*; sculpture and decoration by *Johann Redler*. Very fine Renaissance/Mannerist **parish church,** 1641. Mniszech tomb, early 17th century, probably from the Pinczów workshop.

✦ RAKONIEWICE   MAP 4
A small market town whose population was swelled in the 17th and 18th centuries by Protestant refugees from Austrian-ruled Silesia. Timber **Protestant church**, 1763, tower 1781.

✦ RAKÓW   MAP 20
Small market town, from 1567 the estate of the magnate Jan Sienieński, who became a Calvinist during the Reformation and thereafter member of a sect known as the Arians or Socinians, after their founder, the Sienese nobleman Fausto Sozzini, who took refuge at Raków on the invitation of Sienieński. An academy was founded at Raków in the last decades of the 16th century, and this became the centre of Arian thought, attracting students from all over Europe. It gave rise to the famous Raków Catechism and a whole library of Socianian literature which was disseminated throughout the world. Spinoza, Locke and Voltaire are among those known to have been influenced by these writings. The academy and press were closed down under Catholic pressure by the Senate in 1638. See also LESZNO. **Parish church** of the Holy Trinity, founded by Bishop Jakub Zadzik, 1645.

✦ RASZYN   MAP 18
A village just south of Warsaw on the Kraków road and the scene of a battle in 1809, when Prince Józef Poniatowski, commanding the armies of the Duchy of Warsaw, defeated the Austrians under Archduke Ferdinand. **Parish church**, 1654, rebuilt 1790, by *Szymon Bogumił Zug*. Neo-Classical **Post-Office**, late 18th century, by *Szymon Bogumił Zug*.

RATOWO   MAP 17
Reformed Franciscans' monastery, founded 1685. Church 1736–60.

RAWA MAZOWIECKA   MAP 19
Tower and surviving walls of the **castle** founded by the dukes of
Mazovia ca. 1350. **Jesuit college** founded 1613. Church early 17th
century, facade mid-18th century. College building 17th–18th centuries. Neo-Classical **Town Hall** 1822, by *Bonifacy Witkowski*.

RAWICZ   MAP 11
A town founded for Protestant artisans fleeing from Austrian-ruled
Silesia. Neo-Classical **church** (originally Protestant), 1808 by *Karl
Gottfried Langhans*. **Town Hall**, 1756.

RDZAWA   MAP 21
Wooden **manor house**, Baroque, 18th century.

RESZEL (RÖSSEL)   MAP 16 ✦
Castle of the bishops of Warmia, erected between 1350 and ca. 1450,
rebuilt 1594; south wing reconstructed in 1807 as a **Protestant
church**. **Parish church**, mid-14th century, rebuilt 1475–1503; vaulting 1476, by *N. Schewnemann*. Tower 1837. Remains of **town walls**
and two bridges, 14th–15th centuries.

RODAKI   MAP 21
Wooden **parish church** in late Gothic style, 1601.

ROGALIN   MAP 9 ✦✦
Important Palladian **country house** built for Kazimierz Raczyński,
1768–73 by *Ignaz Graff*; arcades added 1782. Interiors neo-Classical,

by *Domenico Merlini* and *Jan Chrystian Kamsetzer*. Neo-Classical stables and coach-house, 1801. Riding school ca. 1820. Farm labourers' quarters after 1800. Formal and landscape park with numerous pavillions, mainly neo-Classical, including a fine sepulchral chapel, 1820, modelled on the '*Maison Carrée*' at Nîmes, containing sarcophagi of members of the Raczyński family. The family came to prominence at the end of the 18th century and played a very important and creditable part in the struggle against German economic and cultural offensives in the early 19th century in this area of Poland. The Raczyńskis built and endowed a public library in Poznań (see above), and published a large number of manuscripts and primary texts. The last owner of Rogalin, and the last of his line, Count Edward Raczyński, was the Polish Ambassador to the Court of St James in 1939 and signed the treaty that launched the Second World War. He remained in exile, and in 1979 became President of the Polish government in exile. His remains were brought here in great pomp aboard the Polish presidential aeroplane, after his death in 1993, aged 102. The house is furnished with the remains of the original contents, supplemented by overflow from the National Museum in Poznań and more recent acquisitions. There is a fair collection of Italian and Dutch 17th and 18th century furniture, some Polish and French 18th and 19th century furniture, portraits, including works by *Rigaud*, *Silvestre*, *Batoni*, *Bacciarelli*, *Grassi*, *Lampi* and others, two busts by *Canova*, a Ganimede by *Thorwaldsen*, tapestries and objects. There is also a small collection of 19th century painting built up by the Raczyńskis, the only major European artist represented being *Monet*.

ROGOŹNICA   MAP 6
Concentration-camp of Gross-Rosen, established by the Germans in 1941 as a satellite of Sachsenhausen. Some 40,000 people were killed here.

ROGÓW   MAP 14
Parish church, late 13th century, tower and chapel 16th century. Renaissance **country house**, ca. 1600. North wing early 19th century.

ROGOŹNO   MAP 10
Parish church, late 15th century, rebuilt before 1668.

ROKICIE   MAP 17
Late Romanesque **parish church**, ca. 1250.

ROKITNO MAP 18 ✦
Parish church, 1693, by *Tommaso Belotti*; remodelled 1886, by *Konstanty Wojciechowski*.

ROKITNO MAP 4 ✦
Parish church, 1756, by *Karl Martin Frantz*. Painted decoration and furniture contemporary.

ROKOSOWO MAP 11
Bizarre but splendid neo-Gothic **country house**, built 1849–54 by *Friedrich August Stüler* for the Mycielski family; from 1867 the property of a branch of the Czartoryskis.

ROPA MAP 22 ✦
Wooden **parish church**, Baroque, 17th century, tower and portico ca. 1800. Lovely Baroque **manor house** of Siemieński family 1803, with surviving Renaissance parts, 16th century.

RÓWNIA MAP 29 ✦
Wooden **church**, originally Uniate, 1792. Furniture contemporary.

RÓŻANY STOK MAP 24 ✦
Dominican monastery founded by Tyszkiewicz family. Church, second half of the 18th century. Monastery building 1662, expanded after 1759.

ROŻENTAL MAP 15
Wooden **parish church**, 1761, with Rococo interior. Late Gothic sculptures.

ROZKOCHÓW (ROSSWEIDE) MAP 14
Country house, 1734, with 16th-century remnants.

ROŻNÓW MAP 22 ✦
Wooden **parish church**, 1661. Unfinished Renaissance residence of Hetman Jan Tarnowski, 1560s, including Italian-type fortifications, with bastion, curtain and gate. Neo-Classical **manor house**, first quarter of 19th century, with contemporary painted decoration.

ROŻNÓW (ROSEN) MAP 12
Wooden **church**, 1788. Gothic triptych late 15th century.

RUDAWA MAP 21
Parish church with mid-13th-century chancel and 15th/16th century

nave. Tower, part wooden, 1541. Chapel of St Kazimierz ca. 1614.

RUDAWICA   MAP 4
Church, first half of 16th century, parts 14th century.

RUDNO   MAP 21
Impressive ruins of **Tenczyn Castle**, built mid-14th century by
Andrzej Tenczyński. Transformed in Renaissance style 1570 and
1610 by Jan Tenczyński. Devastated by Swedish invaders in 1655.

RUDNO   MAP 18
Country house, early 19th century, by *Hilary Szpilowski*.

RUDOŁTOWICE   MAP 14
Manor house, Baroque, second half of 18th century.

✦✦ RUDY (GROSS RAUDEN)   MAP 14
Cistercian abbey founded 1252. Romanesque church, third quarter
of 13th century. Chapels rebuilt in Baroque style, 1670s. Tower 1724.
Chapel of the Virgin Mary 1726. Facade 1790. Monastery building
1679, by *Melchior Werner*. Abbot's palace, 1730. After the abolition
of the monastery, the whole complex of buildings was turned into a
residence of the Prussian dukes of Ratibor.

RUDZIENKO   MAP 18
Wooden **manor house**, first half of 19th century.

✦   RUDZINIEC (RÜDGERSHAGEN)   MAP 14
Wooden **church** with painted decoration, 1657.

RUNOWO KRAJEŃSKIE   MAP 9
Parish church, 1606.

RUSINÓW   MAP 20
Dembiński family **country house**, late 18th century, by *F. F. Nax*.

RUSSOCICE   MAP 10
Parish **church**, early 16th century; vaults and top of tower 1694.

RYBIENKO   MAP 18
Neo-Classical **country house**, after 1790.

RYBNICA LEŚNA (REIMSWALDAU)   MAP 6
Timber **parish church**, 1608, with contemporary polichromy.

RYCHNOWO (REICHENAU)   MAP 15 ✦
Wooden **church** (originally Protestant), early 18th century. Painted
decoration ca. 1730. Gothic triptych 1517.

RYCHWAŁD   MAP 21
Baroque **parish church**, 1756. Neo-Classical manor house, first half
of 19th century.

RYDZYNA   MAP 11 ✦✦
Magnificent baroque **country house**. Originally a castle, built
1403–22 for Jan of Czernina, transformed into a residence for Rafał
Leszczyński before 1795, by *Giuseppe Simone Belotti*, and remodelled in 1704 by *Pompeo Ferrari*. Rafał's son Stanisław was elected
King of Poland in the same year, with the backing of Charles XII of
Sweden. But when his supporter was defeated at the Battle of
Poltava (1709), Stanisław was ousted by a rival king, Augustus II,
who had the support of Peter the Great of Russia. Stanisław's
daughter was married to the French Dauphin, the future Louis XV,
and, although he was once again elected to the Polish throne in 1733,
he was once more forced to flee by foreign troops, and he ruled as
titular king of Lorraine in France rather than Poland. Rydzyna was
bought in 1736 by Aleksander Sułkowski, a nobleman from a family
that shot to prominence as favourites of the Saxon kings of Poland,
with whom they vied in their taste for Rococo luxury and taurine
excess. The vast house is a fitting reflection of this. It was redecorated in 1746 by *Karl Martin Frantz*, and up to 1786 by *Ignaz Graff*.
Ranges ca. 1770 by *Ignaz Graff*. **Parish church**, 1746 by *Karl Martin
Frantz*. Interior decoration and furniture 1786, by *Ignaz Graff*.
Good tomb slab of Jan of Czernina, ca. 1423. Baroque **Protestant
church**, elliptical, 1783 by *Ignaz Graff*. **Town Hall** 1752.

RYMANÓW   MAP 29
Parish church, 1781. Sienieński tomb ca. 1580.

RYTWIANY   MAP 20 ✦✦
Camaldolite monastery founded 1621 by Jan Tenczyński. Delightful
church with side chapels, 1637. Lavish contemporary stucco work
and furniture, painted decoration and pictures by *Venante da
Subiaco*. Monastery building and Tenczyński's hermitage with
stucco before 1637, by *Giovanni Battista Falconi*.

RYWAŁD   MAP 10
Capuchin monastery founded 1748 by Czapski family. Church
1689-1733.

RZĄŚNIK (SCHÖNWALDAU) MAP 6
Baroque **country house,** 1734, by *Martin Frantz.*

RZEMIEŃ MAP 22
Keep of Tarnowski, later Lubomirski fortified residence, before
1530; redecorated in neo-Gothic style 1857. Earth bastion
Fortifications, ca. 1640.

RZEPIENNIK BISKUPI MAP 22
Church, turn of 15th century, tower later.

◆◆◆ RZESZÓW MAP 29
Once a prosperous and pretty small town, Rzeszów came to resem-
ble more and more a Jewish Shtetl by the end of the 19th century.
The Germans massacred a large proportion of the inhabitants, and
the fighting of 1944 ravaged the town, which was finally blighted by
Stalinist planning.

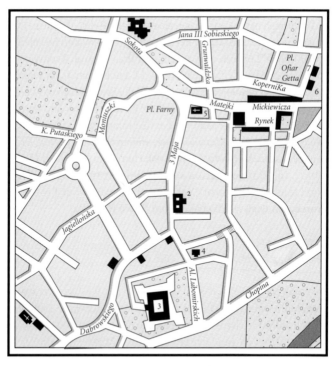

Bernardine monastery [1], founded by Ligęza family after 1610.
Church of the Assumption 1624–9. High altar with alabaster bas-
reliefs, before 1637. Eight statues of members of Ligęza family in
choir, by *Sebastiano Sala(?).* Furniture Baroque and Rococo.
Lovely organ and gallery, ca. 1774, by *Wojciech Szyplewski* and *Otto*

Rieger. Miraculous figure of Our Lady in side chapel decorated with delightful illustrations of the miracles attributed to her. Furniture Baroque and Rococo.

Piarist monastery [2] founded by Lubomirski family. Church of St John the Baptist 1649, with stuccoes by *Giovanni Battista Falconi*. Facade 1707, by *Tilman van Gameren*. Monastic buildings remodelled 1707 by *Gameren*. Painted decoration ca. 1695. At present a **museum** of local history with an undistinguished collection of pictures.

Parish church of St Stanisław and St Wojciech [5], first half of 15th century. Aisles added and church redecorated in Baroque style 1754. Good, but dull, not improved by hideous murals.

Renaissance "**Lesser Synagogue**" [6] in the Old Town, early 17th century, rebuilt ca. 1900 by *Zygmunt Hendel* now a ruin. Baroque "**Great Synagogue**" [7] in the New Town, 1710; rebuilt in 1950s to house city archives.

Remains of Ligęza, later Lubomirski, **castle** [3], including tower ca. 1620 and Italian type bastion fortifications; mostly remodelled 1906. Small Lubomirski **palace** [4], now a theatre, early 18th century by *Tilman van Gameren*; much altered.

RZGÓW   MAP 19

Wooden **parish church**, 16th century. Octagonal chapel 1699. Tower 1790.

SADŁOWO   MAP 17

Baroque **parish church**, 1752. Neo-Classical **country house**, ca. 1800.

SAMBORZEC   MAP 20

Parish church, rebuilt and expanded from late Romanesque core in 1688 and again in 1880..

SAMOTWÓR (ROMBERG)   MAP 11

Interesting Palladian **manor house**, 1787 by *Karl Gottfried Langhans*. Built for Major Gottlieb Albrecht Sauern and his wife, née Marie Clairon d'Haussonville, and betraying strong English influences, particularly in the decoration of the interiors.

SAMSONÓW   MAP 20

Neo-Classical **ironworks**, 1822. Ruins of blast furnace, fuel hoist and factory halls.

Important **church**, 1400; rebuilt in Mannerist, Baroque and neo-Gothic styles. Sancygniowski tomb, tabernacle and font late 16th century, by *Santi Gucci*. Good Rococo organ, late 18th century; plenty of putti. Gate and fragments of fortifications of a late 16th-century **manor house** surrounding the existing house, built 1882 for Deskur family.

Very old city, the capital of one of the principalities into which Poland was divided in the 13th century. It spanned trade routes and prospered from the grain trade down the Vistula, but also stood in the front line of attacks from the east and was several times devastated by the Tatars. Like many such royal towns, it went into decline in the seventeenth century, and never recovered. But it has maintained a number of buildings testifying to its ancient glories, and these are enhanced by its picturesque position on the banks of the Vistula. On one of the hills dominating the city stands the **castle** founded by Kazimierz the Great. Surviving wing with two angle towers, begun ca. 1350, remodelled 1520-6s by, Master *Benedykt,* and in 1597; converted into prison 1825. On the left, looking down on the city, is the **Dominican monastery**, founded 1226 by Bishop Iwo Odrowąż. Church of St James, Romanesque with moulded brick decoration from the second quarter of 13th century, dressed by North Italian masons. Choir, originally mid-13th century, rebuilt with stucco decoration in Renaissance style, 1624–31. Sandomierz Martyrs' chapel, with Mannerist/Baroque stucco decoration, 1642. Paintings in polyptych 1599. Bell-tower turn of the 13th century. Surviving east wing of monastery, mid-13th century, rebuilt 1674.

Church of St Paul 1434. Mannerist stucco decoration, 1642. Some alterations 1745. St Barbara's chapel before 1718. Furniture mid-17th century and first quarter of 18th century. Belfry 1745. Wooden priest's house, 1694, rebuilt 19th century.

On the other hill stands the **cathedral** (until 1818 the collegiate church) of the Nativity of Our Lady, founded by Kazimierz the Great in 1382 on the foundations of an earlier church. Facade and chapter-house 1674. Exterior restored 1895. Bell-tower 1743, spire 1759. Painted decoration of chancel Ruthenian, first half of 15th century. Mansionary chapel Rococo, 1775, by *Bartłomiej Gołębiowski* and *Mateusz Rejchan*. Altars with sculpture 1773, by *Maciej Polejowski*, and 1767, by *Wojciech Rojowski*; silver tabernacle 1639 and 1699. Organ 1698, by *Andrzej Nitrowski*. Epitaphial painting 1520. The inside of the cathedral is decorated, if that is the right word, with a sort of calendar, showing a martyrdom for every day of the year, and, under the organ loft, with paintings illustrating the history of Sandomierz, including Tatar massacres, Swedish rapine and a now rare representation of Christian children being ritually murdered, '*crudelissime jugulati*', by Jews. These extremely unpleasant confections, dating from 1708–37, are of very poor quality, but they do provide an extraordinary insight into how crude late baroque Catholicism could be.

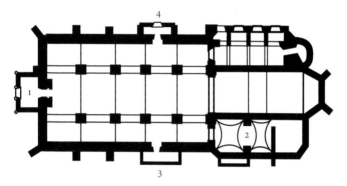

1 - West door, 2 - Mansionary chapel, 3 -Chapel of the Immaculate Conception, 4 - North door.

Długosz House, 1476 by Master *Jan* of Kraków, rebuilt third quarter of 17th century; houses diocesan **museum**, containing a collection of sacral art and very good textiles, including a 'polonaise' Persian rug.

Jesuit college, known also as the '*Gostomianum*', founded 1602 by Henryk Gostomski; originally Renaissance, rebuilt 1826 and later.

Town Hall, Renaissance, after 1550. Tower second quarter of 17th century. Marvellous decorative parapet of moulded brick and terracotta.

Oleśnicki house on Market Square, Baroque, 1770s by *Father Józef Karśnicki*, now city **museum**, of strictly local interest. Baroque **Synagogue**, 1758.

Hospital church of the Holy Ghost, 15th century, rebuilt in Baroque style.

Benedictine convent (now seminary), founded 1613. Church of St Michael 1686-92, by *Jan Michał Link*, altered 1769. Furniture late 17th century. Pulpit 1695, by *Mateusz Roskwitowicz*, illustating the genealogy of the Benedictine Order. Belfry 1749. Chaplain's house 1771, by *Father Józef Karśnicki*. Outdoor pulpit ca. 1770. Monastic building 1637; west wing with pavilions 1672; north wing added 1906. Gate pavilion 1771, by *Father Józef Karśnicki(?)*.

Reformed Franciscans' monastery founded 1679. Church of St Joseph rebuilt 1823. Arcaded courtyard second half of 18th century. **Town walls** with towers, after 1350; altered 16th century. Opatów gate superstructure Renaissance, mid-16th century.

SANNIKI   MAP 17

Undistinguished 19th century **country house**. In 1828 the composer Fryderyk Chopin spent part of the summer here, when the estate belonged to the family of his friend Konstanty Pruszak.

✦   SANOK   MAP 29

Royal **castle**, built 1540, repeatedly rebuilt. The surviving wing now houses a **museum**, containing a collection of icons and Orthodox sacral art, a good collection of 19th- and 20th-century Polish painting, arms and armour, and various odds and ends. **Open-air museum,** with examples of regional wooden buildings, 18th–19th century, including Orthodox churches.

ŚCIBORZYCE MAŁE (STEUBENDORF)   MAP 13

Parish church, Gothic/Renaissance, 1602.

✦   ŚCIBÓRZ   MAP 13

Baroque **manor house**, built 1668 for the Wrocław prelate J.H.Heymann.

ŚCINAWA (STEINAU AM ODER)   MAP 6

Orignally the property of the nuns of Trzebnica, later the capital of a tiny independent principality. The town was almost annihilated in 1945. **Parish church**, before 1491.

ŚCINAWA NYSKA (STEINSDORF)   MAP 13

Church, second quarter of 18th century by *Josef Ignaz Topper*. Its tower, a survival from an older church, dates from 1586.

✦   ŚCINAWKA ŚREDNIA (MITTELSTEINE)   MAP 6

Parish church of St Mary Magdalen, 14th century, rebuilt in Baroque style 18th century. Chapels added 1739. Vicarage 17th century.

✦✦   SEJNY   MAP 24

Magnificent **Dominican monastery,** founded in 16th century by Prince Jan Wiśniowiecki. Church 1610–9, expanded and rococo stucco and furniture added 1760. Organ after 1762. Wolmer family chapel 1830. **Synagogue** ca. 1860. **Talmudic school** ca. 1850.

Lovely wooden **parish church** of St Philip and St James the Apostle in picturesque setting, first half of 16th century.

SEROCK   MAP 18
Interesting parish **church**, Gothic, after 1520. Nice Baroque font.

SICINY (SEITSCH)   MAP 4 ✦✦
Parish church, 1740 by *Martin Frantz*. Contemporary furniture and painted decoration by *Christian Philipp Bentum* and *Ignaz Axter*. **Country house**, mid 18th century.Contemporary painted decoration by *Christian Philipp von Bentum*.

SIECIECHÓW   MAP 20 ✦✦
Benedictine abbey founded first half of 12th century. Church 1739–67. Polychromy 1779, by *Szymon Mańkowski*. Ruin of east wing of monastery, with 12th-century Romanesque traces, rebuilt 1733. Prior's house 1733. Abbot's palace 1800—23.

Estate town belonging to the Czartoryski family, developed by Princess Michał Ogiński, née Aleksandra Czartoryska, to create a remarkable neo-Classical ensemble. During her lifetime, Siedlce was a centre of social and cultural life, and she herself wrote plays for her own court theatre. Czartoryski **residence**, rebuilt for Princess Aleksandra Ogińska in 1782 by *Stanisław Zawadzki*; burnt 1944 but rebuilt 1950. **Chapel**, 1791 by *Zygmunt Vogel* - the only building designed by this well-known Polish watercolourist and decorator.

Parish church of St Stanisław 1748, facade 1793 by *Stanisław Zawadzki*. Priest's House 1774.

Town Hall, with figure of Atlas on top of tower, 1789, by *Stanisław Zawadzki*, now a small local **museum**. Neo-Classical **Post-Office**, first half of 19th century. Prison 1844, by *Henryk Marconi*.

Baroque **parish church**, 1775. Neo-Classical **country house** of Krzycki family, 1775. Interiors 1790, by *Jan Chrystian Kamsetzer*, heavily influenced by English designs, particularly those of Campbell and Kent.

Knight's **keep** dating from beginning of 14th century; superstructure 15th century. Murals with legend of King Arthur and Sir Gawain, ca. 1330.

Mannerist **country house**, 1618, expanded late 18th century; now derelict. Chapel 1615. Gatehouse 1614.

Ironworks dating from 1821–41, now **museum** of industrial history.

Missionaries' monastery founded 1633 by Chancellor Lew Sapieha. Church 1628, facade 1790. Organ ca. 1780, by *Stanisław Kędlarski*. Monastic building 1725.

Wooden **parish church**, founded 1440. Painted decoration Renaissance, 1643–78. Gothic sculpture of Mater Dolorosa ca. 1480.

Baroque wooden **chapel**, 1740. **Manor house** dating from the turn of
the 18th century. Granary ca. 1850. The village is full of highland
vernacular architecture.

Cradle of the Sieniawski family, which produced several statesmen
and one great Hetman of the Crown. His only daughter, the last of
the name, was one of the richest heiresses in Europe after her first
husband, a Dönhoff, died leaving her his fortune. She was assidu-
ously courted and finally in 1731 chose Prince August Czartoryski,
thereby laying the foundations for the financial revival of that family. The Czartoryskis rarely stayed here, and the Baroque
Sieniawski **country house**, dating from the first half of 18th century,
by *Giovanni Spazzio*, rebuilt in 1763 by *Joachim Hempel*, was little
more than a palatial villa set within the formidable bastion fortifications, dating from 1680. The house was remodelled and the two
wings raised in 1881, by *Bolesław Podczaszyński*. It was rebuilt
almost from scratch in the 1980s. The adjoining town, founded by
the Sieniawski family in 1676, suffered badly during the First World
War.
Dominican monastery founded before 1677. Church 1719–49, by
Giovanni Spazzio. Monastic building before 1754. Under the
church there is a sepulchral crypt containing the sarcophagi of
members of the Czartoryski family, including Princess Izabela,
Prince Adam Jerzy, Prince Władysław, and some of their consorts,
including Princess Maria Amparo de Vista Allegre, daughter of
Queen Christina of Spain, and Princess Marguerite d'Orléans,
granddaughter of Louis-Philippe, King of the French.

Reformed Franciscans' church, 1754 by *Antoni Solari.*

A very old town and one of the most important centres of administration in central Poland from the 11th to the 14th centuries. **Parish
church** of All Saints founded by Kazimierz the Great ca. 1370,
rebuilt in the 16th century, redecorated 1682. **Dominican monastery**
(now Ursuline convent) founded 1260. Church, ca. 1300 and ca.
1380, rebuilt in Baroque style early 18th century. Monastic building
ca. 1300, 16th century and 1651. The 15th-century so-called
'Jagiellonian House' contains a **museum** - a mixed bag, with a few
interesting Polish pictures.

♦♦ SIERAKÓW   MAP 4

Bernardine monastery founded 1619 by Opaliński family. Church, 1639 by *Cristoforo Bonadura the elder*, facade 1740 and 1865. Opaliński tombs 1642, by *Sebastiano Sala*, and 1748. Timber **Protestant church**, 1785.

♦ SIERNIKI   MAP 9

Neo-Classical **country house** built 1786, by *Jan Chrystian Kamsetzer*, for Katarzyna Radolińska, née Raczyńska. Stucco and wall decoration contemporary. This Palladian villa-style house was widely copied.

♦ SIERPC   MAP 17

Benedictine convent founded 1620 around an older church, 1483–1513. Monastic building after 1703. **Church** of the Holy Ghost, 1519, with contemporary murals.

♦♦ SIEWIERZ   MAP 19

In the middle ages this town was the capital of a small principality, which was acquired in 1443 by the diocese of Kraków, which owned it until 1790. As the title went with the town, the bishops of Kraków were Princes of Siewierz as well as being princes of the Church. Romanesque **church** of St John the Baptist, second quarter of 12th century, entirely reconstructed 1947–56. **Parish church**, early 16th century, rebuilt first half of 17th century, and, in Baroque style, 1783. Ruins of **castle** built in the second half of 14th century by Prince Jan of Cieszyn.

♦♦ SKALBMIERZ   MAP 21

Delightful little town, which acquired city rights in 1342 and prospered on trade with the Russian lands. It reached its peak in the 15th century, but was devastated by the Swedish wars of the 1650s and the subsequent plague. In August 1944 the inhabitants were summarily massacred by the German army. **Collegiate church** of St John the Baptist, 15th century, with remnants of Romanesque towers, from the turn of the 12th century, partly rebuilt first half of 17th century. Painting of the Adoration of the Magi by *Jacob Jordaens(?)*.

♦♦ SKĘPE-WYMYŚLIN   MAP 17

Local pilgrimage centre with **Bernardine monastery**, 1510, by *Father Bartolomeus*. Church lengthened 1616 and redecorated in Baroque style 1767. Tower 1749. St Anne's chapel 1524. Painted decoration, 1777, by *Father Walenty Żebrowski*. Monastic building expanded

17th–18th century. Arcaded gallery with three towers, 18th century. Zieliński sepulchral chapel, 18th century.

SKIERNIEWICE MAP 17 ✦
Palace of the archbishops of Gniezno 1619, expanded with addition of chapel, 1765 by *Ephraim Schröger*. Neo-Classical gateway ca. 1780, by *Schroger*. **Parish church** with circular nave, 1781, by *Schröger*, founded by Primate Antoni Ostrowski. Good interior and furniture designed by *Schröger*. Fine **railway station** by *Adam Idzkowski*, 1846.

SKOMLIN MAP 12
Wooden **parish church**, 1740. Rococo painted decoration 1776, by *K.Więckowski*.

SKOTNIKI MAP 19 ✦
Wooden **parish church**, 1528; rebuilt 1768. Inside, a good medieval painting of St Anne and a contemporary *santa conversazione*.

SKOTNIKI MAP 20
Baroque timber **manor house** of Bogorya Skotnicki family, late 18th century. **Parish church** founded by Archbishop Jarosław Skotnicki in 1347, altered ca. 1770.

SKRZATUSZ (SCHRÖTZ) MAP 9
Parish church, 1694. Decoration, furniture and sculpture 1690s.

SKRZYDLNA MAP 21 ✦
Baroque wooden **parish church**, 16th century, nave 1787. Tower 1838. Funeral monument to the founder, Prokop Pieniążek, who died in 1587.

SKRZYNNO MAP 20 ✦
Parish church, 1638. Sculpture of Madonna ca. 1420. Dutch painting of Madonna ca. 1500.

SKRZYSZÓW MAP 22 ✦
Wooden **parish church**, 1517 by Master *Jan of Czchów*, expanded 19th century.

ŚLADKÓW DUŻY MAP 20
Country house, late 18th century by *Ferdynand F. Nax*.

SŁAWKÓW   MAP 21
Parish church ca. 1250, nave second half of 15th century. Baroque
priest's house, late 18th century. Baroque wooden **inn**, turn of the
18th century. Wooden **houses**, 18th-19th century.

SŁAWNO   MAP 7
Parish church, 1320s. **Town walls** before 1400. Słupsk and Koszalin
Gates 1450s. Modernist **church**, 1925; with Gothic 16th-century trip-
tych inside.

ŚLEDZIEJOWICE   MAP 21
Neo-Classical wooden **manor house**, 1823.

✦   SŁOBITY (SCHLOBITTEN)   MAP 15
Derelict Mannerist **country house** of von Dohna family, ca. 1622,
rebuilt in Baroque style, with addition of colonnades and outbuildings, in 1723 by *Joachim Ludwig Schültheis von Unfried*. Sculpture
1708, by *Jan Blommendael*. Baroque farm buildings, 18th century.

SŁOŃSK (SONNENBURG)   MAP 3
Church, 1475. Tower 1603. Rebuilt in neo-Gothic style 1818, by *Karl
Friedrich Schinkel*. Altar Mannerist. Remains of 14th-century **castle**
of the Knights Hospitallers of St John of Jerusalem, rebuilt in
Baroque style 1627, by *Peter Post* of The Hague and *Cornelis
Ryckwaerdt*, and again in the 1870s.

SŁOPANOWO   MAP 9
Wooden **church**, 1695. Painted decoration contemporary.

✦   SŁUBICE   MAP 17
Neo-Classical **country house**, ca. 1790 by *Hilary Szpilowski*. Temple
in park ca. 1820, by *Alexandre d'Alfonse de Saint Omer*.

✦   SŁUPCA   MAP 10
Town established in 1290 by the bishops Poznań. **Parish church** of
St Lawrence, mid-15th century, vaults 16th century. Wooden suc-
cursal **church** of the Assumption and St Leonard, 16th century,
chapels 1730, tower 1765. Polychromy first half of 18th century.
Gothic painting of St Leonard.

SŁUPIA STARA   MAP 20
In ancient times the centre of iron-smelting on a large scale. **Court**
of the abbots of Święty Krzyż, 1782.

SŁUPSK (STOLP) MAP 7

A 10th-century fortified settlement that became the headquarters of the princes of Pomerania in the Middle Ages. **Church** of St Mary, second half of 14th century, with later alterations. **Dominican church** of St Jacek, 15th century. **Town walls** with towers, after 1400. Mill Gate, ca. 1400. New Gate, part of residence of princes of Pomerania, ca. 1500, now houses small local **museum** with good tapestries, paintings and armour. Castle mill ca. 1310.

SŁUŻEWO MAP 10

Parish church, 1560. Interior 1899.

SMARDZEWICE MAP 19

Franciscan church 1683–99. Monastic building 1746.

ŚMICZ MAP 13 ✦

Parish church, 1750 by *Josef Ignaz Topper*. Painted decoration ca. 1770, by *Franz Sebastini*, furniture contemporary.

ŚMIEŁÓW MAP 9 ✦✦

Attractive **country house** built for General Augustyn Gorzeński in 1797 by *Stanisław Zawadzki*. A blueprint for the east-European neo-Classical country house. Painted decoration ca. 1800, by *Antoni* and *Franciszek Smuglewicz*. Fascinating group of Romantic farm buildings built to resemble Gothic village, contemporary, also by *Zawadzki*. The Romantic poet Adam Mickiewicz stayed at the house in 1831 when it was the property of the Gorzeński family. It now houses a small **museum** dedicated to his memory. The house later passed to the Chełkowski family.

SMOLAJNY MAP 15

Residence of Bishop Adam Grabowski, 1746; gate with tower 1765.

SOBIBÓR MAP 28

Concentration-camp set up by the Germans in 1942, where some 250,000 people were killed. It was closed down after a revolt by the prisoners in October 1943, when some prisoners managed to escape. **Museum.**

SOBIESZÓW (HERMSDORF) MAP 6 ✦

Castle of the dukes of Świdnica and Jawor, later of Schaffgotsch family, 1353. Chapel 1393. Two lower courtyards with tower added first half of 16th century. Ringed by wall with rondelles, ca. 1560 and lower fortifications, 1648.

✦ SOBOTA MAP 17
Parish church, 1518, with Renaissance gables, mid-16th century
Renaissance Sobocki tombs, mid-16th century. **Country house** in
the form of a small **castle**, second half of the 19th century.

✦ SOBÓTKA MAP 11
Parish church, early 15th century, rebuilt in Baroque style 1739.
Under the floor are the remnants of a Romanesque stone basilica,
first half of 13th century. **Church** of St Anne, 1516, rebuilt in Baroque
style, ca. 1700. On the hill overlooking the town is a 19th-century
neo-Renaissance **residence** built on the foundations of an unfinished 12th-century Augustinian monastery.

SOKOLNIKI MAP 12
Manor house, mid-18th century.

✦ SOŚNICA MAP 11
Parish church with central pillar supporting vaults, 1504. Chapel
and replica of *Scala Santa* in the church of St John Lateran in Rome,
1776.

SPYTKOWICE MAP 21
Parish church, 1645, tower after 1664. Palace of bishops of Kraków
1630, by *Marcin Szyszkowski*, on the foundations of a 16th-century
castle.

SREBRNA GÓRA MAP 9
Neo-Classical **manor house** with stucco and pictorial decoration,
ca. 1799, belonging to the Radzymiński family.

SREBRNA GÓRA (SILBERBERG) MAP 6
Medieval silver mining centre. **Fortress** built 1765-77, by *L. von
Regeler* for Frederick II of Prussia.

ŚREM MAP 9
Parish church of the Assumption, end of 14th century, tower and
chapel 16th century. **Franciscan monastery** and Church of the
Nativity of Our Lady, late 17th-early 18th century. **Church** of the
Holy Ghost, end of 16th century, with neo-Gothic additions ca.
1840.

✦ ŚRODA WIELKOPOLSKA MAP 9
A thriving market town from the 13th century, named after the day
(środa: wednesday) on which it was licensed to hold its market.

Collegiate church of St Mary, 1428, expanded at the turn of the 15th century. Mannerist chapel with tomb of Jeremi Gostomski, Palatine of Poznań, 1598–1602. Early Renaissance tomb with effigy of Jan Pampowski, 1510.

ŚRODA ŚLĄSKA (NEUMARKT) MAP 6

Romanesque **parish church** of St Andrew, ca. 1200, rebuilt 1270s. Chancel 1388. Facade 1828. Belfry first half of 15th century. **Franciscan monastery church** of the Holy Cross, second half of 14th century, interior remodelled 1675. Monastic building 1722.
Town walls mid-14th century. **Town Hall**, 15th century, rebuilt 1593 and later.
Small city **museum.** In 1988 an important archaeological find was made here, comprising a crown and jewels probably belonging to the princes of Silesia or the kings of Bohemia, from ca. 1350.

STANIĄTKI MAP 21 ◆◆

Benedictine convent, founded 1228. Church of St Mary and St Wojciech second half of 13th century; oratory 1712. Painted decoration Rococo, 1760 by *Andrzej Radwański*. Monastic building 1650.

STARA KAMIENICA (ALT KAMNITZ) MAP 6

Parish church, later Protestant; nave 15th century, chancel 1624.

STARA WIEŚ MAP 29 ◆

Pauline monastery and church (Jesuit since 1821) 1728–62; monastic building rebuilt 1886.

STARA WIEŚ MAP 25 ◆

Country house of the Radziwiłł family, 1650s, rebuilt for the Galitzine family in neo-Gothic style 1843. Interiors 1862, by *Bolesław Podczaszyński*.

STARE BIELSKO MAP 14

Parish church, second half of 14th century, tower 15th century; rebuilt 19th century. Painted decoration fourth quarter of 14th century and 16th century. Triptych early 16th century.
Neo-Romanesque **Protestant church**, 1827. Tower 1853.

STARE BOGACZOWICE (ALTREICHENAU) MAP 6

Cistercian (now Ursuline) **church** 1689, by *Martin Urban*, rebuilt 1826. Furniture 17th-18th century.

STARE CHĘCINY   MAP 19

Church with free-standing twin towers, 1680s by *Tilman van Gameren(?)*.

STARE DRAWSKO (ALT DRAHEIM)   MAP 2

Village belonging to the Knights Templar from 1288, and subsequently to the Hospitallers. Ruins of Hospitallers' **castle**, ca. 1350.

♦♦♦ STARGARD SZCZECIŃSKI   MAP 1

A trading town from the 12th century, and later a member of the Hanseatic League.

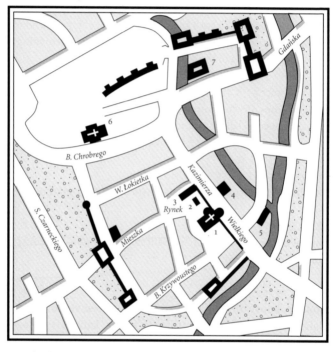

Parish church of St Mary [1], late 13th century, expanded ca. 1400 by *Heinrich Brunsberg*, vault mid-17th century. A good example of a type of pseudo-cathedral, a parish church built on a cathedral layout by a rich and aspiring trading town. **Church** of St John [6], ca. 1408 and 1464, rebuilt 19th century. Organist's house, 15th–16th century. **Town walls** 1298, rebuilt 16th century. Gates 16th century. **Town Hall** [3] 1638. Gothic town **house** [4] with richly decorated gable, 16th century. Guardhouse and wigh-house [2]. Granary [7].

STAROGARD GDAŃSKI   MAP 8

Parish church, first half of 14th century, expanded 14th–15th centuries. **Town walls**, 14th-15th century.

STAROŹREBY   MAP 17
Baroque **manor house**, turn of the 18th century. Neo-Gothic gateway and pavilion, first half of 19th century.

STARY SĄCZ   MAP 22 ✦✦
Parish church of St Elizabeth, 14th-15th century, rebuilt after 1644.
Poor Clares' convent founded in 1280 by the Blessed Kinga, wife of Bolesław the Shy. Church of the Holy Trinity completed 1330, redecorated in Baroque style. Pulpit 1671 and stucco altars 1696, by *Baldassare Fontana*. Blessed Kinga's chapel, originally Gothic, rebuilt second half of 17th century. Furniture 17th-18th century. Good picture of the Sorrowing Christ, 1470. Monastic building with cloister, Renaissance, 1605 by *Jan de Simon*.
Medieval fortifications; with superstructure, round tower and entrance clock tower 1605, by *Jan de Simon*.

STARY ZAMEK (ALTENBURG)   MAP 11
Romanesque **parish church**, third quarter of 13th century.

STASZÓW   MAP 20
Parish church, first half of 15th century, redecorated with Renaissance/Mannerist stucco-work, 1625. Tenczyński chapel 1613–25. **Town Hall**, 1738.

STAWISKI   MAP 23
Reformed Franciscans' monastery founded 1697 by Fortunat Zamoyski. Church 1790. Monastic building after 1697.

STEGNA (STEEGEN)   MAP 15
Baroque timber **church** (originally Protestant), 1683.

STERDYŃ   MAP 25 ✦✦
Extraordinary **country house**, ca. 1750, belonging to Ossoliński family, rebuilt, with addition of two wings, in an unusually bold neo-Classical style, 1806 by *Jakub Kubicki*. Latterly the property of the Krasiński family. Virtually in ruins.
Good baroque **parish church** founded by Chancellor Jerzy Ossoliński 1783, with Rococo stucco-work.

STĘŻYCA   MAP 27
Parish church of St Martin, 1434, expanded 1520 in Renaissance style, partly reconstructed.

✦✦ STOCZEK (SPRINGBORN) MAP 16

Bernardine (now Marist) **monastery** and pilgrimage complex. Church founded by Bishop Marcin Szyszkowski in 1641. Chancel and tower 1711, by *Josef Herbst(?)*. Arcaded gallery with four chapels, 1711. Monastic building 1666, expanded 1717.

STOLEC (STOLZ) MAP 6

Romanesque **parish church**, second half of 13th century, remodelled 16th and 18th century. Inside, a goood late Gothic triptych. Baroque **country house** and three outbuildings, second half of 18th century.

STOŁPIE MAP 28

Keep of fortified seat of the dukes of Włodzimierz, 13th century.

STOPNICA MAP 20

Parish church of SS Peter and Paul, founded by king Kazimierz the Great in 1362. Heavily reconstructed after war damage.

ST·RABLA MAP 25

Manor house of Starzeński family, 18th century, rebuilt 1840. Wooden storehouse, ca. 1792.

STRONIA (STRÖNN) MAP 11

Romanesque rotunda **parish church**, second half of 13th century, tower later.

STROŃSKO MAP 12

Romanesque **parish church** of St Ursula and the Eleven Thousand Virgins, second quarter of 13th century, expanded 1726. Tower 20th century. Romanesque stone tympanum.

STRÓŻA MAP 27

Baroque votive **chapel** on triangular plan, 1767.

STRYSZÓW MAP 21

Manor house, 17th century; expanded 1741.

✦✦✦ STRZEGOM (STREIGAU) MAP 6

Inhabited since Roman times, this town became an important weaving centre in the Middle Ages.
Church of the Knights Hospitallers of St John of Jerusalem. Magnificent Gothic nave, second half of 14th century by Master *Jakob*; vaulting fourth quarter of 15th century. Completed ca. 1520.

Architectural sculpture, including three portals with tympana, second half of 14th century and ca. 1400. Tabernacle, first half of 15th century. Chapel of St Anthony adjoining town gate, ca. 1520.
Town walls late 13th or early 14th century, outer ring mid-15th century. **Town Hall** first half of 16th century.
Synagogue (now church of St Barbara) end of 14th century, expanded ca. 1500.

STRZELCE OPOLSKIE (GROSS STREHLITZ)   MAP 14 ✦
Wooden **cemetery church** 1690, by Master Carpenter *Jan Brychczy*. **Town walls**, 15th century, with late 17th-century bell-tower. Wooden granary, 18th century.

STRZELCE ŚWIDNICKIE (STREHLITZ)   MAP 6 ✦
Parish church, early 14th century. Well-preserved murals ca. 1360.

STRZELIN (STREHLEN)   MAP 11
Church of St Gothard, Romanesque 12th century rotunda turned into tower of church, 14th and 15th centuries.

STRZELNIKI   MAP 11
Church, ca. 1300, tower superstructure 1688. Murals early 15th century.

STRZELNO   MAP 10 ✦✦✦
Premonstratensian convent. Romanesque church of the Holy Trinity and St Mary, after 1175. Columns between nave and aisles with remarkable figure bas-reliefs. Unusual centrally-supported chapel of St Barbara. North portal with carved tympanum ca. 1230.

Facade and chapels on south side ca. 1750.
Romanesque **church** of St Procopius, ca. 1160, superstructure turn of 15th century.

✦ STRZESZÓW   MAP 11
Church of St Jadwiga, 14th century, remodelled ca. 1500. Interesting Renaissance painted ceiling.

STRZYŻÓW   MAP 28
Late 18th-century **country house**, rebuilt in neo-Classical style after 1836. Octagonal pavilions, 18th century.

STUDNISKA (SCHÖNBRUNN)   MAP 5
Romanesque **church**, second quarter of 13th century, annexes later.

✦✦ STUDZIANNA-POŚWIĘTNE   MAP 19
Oratorian monastery, first quarter of 18th century. Painted decoration of church 1726, by *Adam Swach*, and late 18th century. Symmetrical bell-towers and gate, mid-18th century.

STUDZIENIEC   MAP 9
Timber **manor house**, first half of 18th century.

STUDZIENIEC   MAP 17
Neo-Classical **country house** with colonnades, turn of the 18th century by *Hilary Szpilowski*.

STUDZIENIEC (STREIDELSDORF)   MAP 4
Church ca. 1480. Painted wooden choir vault ca. 1550. **Country house**, 1786 with some reworking in 1855.

✦✦ SUCHA   MAP 21
Castle of Komorowski family. Expanded from Renaissance manor house, ca. 1554, by addition of residential wings and arcaded galleries in Mannerist style, 1614. Alterations in Baroque style ca. 1708. The castle passed to the Wielopolski family, and its last owners were the Tarnowskis.
Church 1614, in Gothic tradition.
Monastery of Canons Regular, 1630. Bell-tower 1818. Baroque wooden **inn**, end of 18th century.

SULECHÓW (ZÜLLICHAU)   MAP 4
Parish church, with 14th century chancel; nave and aisles 1499. Vault, tower and gable 1562. **Castle**, 16th century, altered 1750 and

expanded in neo-Classical style 1750 and ca. 1850. Krosno Gate 1704.

SULEJÓW-PODKLASZTORZE   MAP 19 ✦✦✦

Important **Cistercian abbey** founded in 1176 by king Kazimierz the Just, with monks from Morimond in Burgundy. Romanesque stone ashlar basilica of St Thomas, completed 1232. Fine west portal and rose window. Furniture Baroque and Rococo. East wing of monastery with chapter house, Romanesque. Cloister early 15th century. Fortified group of 15th-18th-century farm buildings making up the south wing. Moorish Tower, 15th century, other towers 16th century. Arsenal, turn of 16th century.

SULISŁAWICE   MAP 20

Church with Romanesque nave, ca. 1250, east end ca. 1600. Furniture Baroque.

SULMIERZYCE   MAP 11

Wooden **Town Hall**, 1743, and a number of 18th and 19th century wooden houses.

SUPRAŚL   MAP 26 ✦✦

Important religious centre of the Orthodox faith since the 17th century, and also the seat of an Uniate bishopric. **Basilian Friars' monastery**, founded 1498, with Orthodox church of the Annunciation, 1511; heavily reconstructed after war damage. Archimandrite's palace, 1635, with stuccoed interiors, second half of 17th century. Monastery buildings, late 17th century and 1764. Tower Gate, ca. 1750.

SURCHÓW   MAP 28

Neo-Classical **country house**, 1819. Painted decoration 1820, by *Mikołaj Monti*.

SUSZ   MAP 15

Parish church, ca. 1315, repeatedly rebuilt. Furniture early 17th century.

ŚWIĄTKOWICE   MAP 12

Wooden **manor house**, Baroque, late 18th century.

ŚWIDNICA (SCHWEIDNITZ)   MAP 6 ✦✦✦

Old trading settlement originating in the 6th century, that once rivalled Wrocław. It dealt in livestock and grain from Poland, wood and furs from Lithuania, cloth from Flanders, and wine from Hungary. It became the capital of a Piast principality in 1291, and the last Piast Princess of Świdnica married the Emperor Charles in 1353.

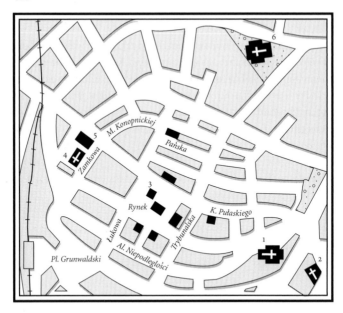

Parish church of St Stanisław and St Wojciech [**1**]: three-apse chancel with crypt 1353; nave with chapels second half of 14th century, by Master *Jakob* (aisle vaults 1385). Sculptural decoration 14th–15th century. Nave vault 1535. Spire of tower 1613. Painted decoration 1739, by *Johann Georg Etgens*. Furniture, sculpture and paintings early 1700s. Polyptych 1492.

Commandery and **church of the Knights of the Holy Cross** [**2**], 1720, altered 1868. **Ursuline convent** [**4**] and church of St Joseph 1772. Convent school 1734 and 1763. **Jesuit college** [**5**], 1667, with church of St Barbara, 1501, converted into warehouse 1818.

Timber **Protestant church** [**6**], 1658 by *Albrecht von Säbisch*. Painted decoration and furniture late 17th to early 18th century. The largest and best preserved of the 'churches of grace' - see also Jawor and Milicz.

Town Hall [**3**], originally 14th century, expanded early 16th century, remodelled 1726 in Baroque style, and 19th century. Tower 1555, spire 1765. Now a **museum**. **Palace** of the abbots of Lubiąż 1725, by *Felix Anton Hammerschmidt*.

Castle of Kietlicz family, mid-16th century, rebuilt ca. 1602 and 19th century. **Church** 14th–15th century, with good Gothic and Renaissance furniture and important sculptures.

ŚWIDNIK   MAP 22
Baroque wooden **manor house**, 1752.

ŚWIDWIN   MAP 2
Castle of the Wedel family, begun before 1317; passed to the Knights Hospitallers of St John in 1540 and abandoned by them in 1808.

ŚWIEBODZIN   MAP 4 ✦
Parish church of St Michael, end of 15th century, expanded 1541, altered 17th century. Neo-Gothic facade, 1857. Gothic triptych 1556.

ŚWIECIE   MAP 10
Beside the present town, on the meadows along the Vistula, the remains of this historic and once-important town, enclosed in the remnants of town walls. **Parish church**, early 15th century, main body and tower Renaissance, 1566. **Bernardine monastery** and Church 1720, expanded 1741. **Castle** of Teutonic Knights 1338, rebuilt as Polish royal castle 1540s.

ŚWIERZAWA   MAP 6
Parish church 1382, main body first half of 15th century. Romanesque **cemetery church**, second quarter of 13th century, remodelled with addition of tower after 1500.

ŚWIERZNO   MAP 1 ✦
Wooden **manor house** belonging to Flemming family, 1718–28 by Master *J.A.Hase*. Painted decoration of ballroom 1728.

ŚWIĘTA ANNA   MAP 19 ✦
Bernardine monastery (now Dominican convent). Church begun 1609. Stucco work in St Anne's chapel 17th-18th century. Painted decoration Baroque, furniture Baroque and Rococo, sculpture of St Anne ca. 1500.

ŚWIĘTA LIPKA   MAP 16 ✦✦
Jesuit monastery and major pilgrimage complex around the trunk of the lime tree in which Our Lady is supposed to have appeared. Probably a clever adaption of pagan tree cults. The original carved Madonna was chopped up by the Prussian successors of the Teutonic Knights and replaced in the 17th century by the painting, brought by Polish Jesuits. Church 1680s, by *George Ertly* of Wilno.

Painted decoration 1737, by *Matthias Meyer*. Furniture 17th–18th century. Splendid Baroque organ, 1721-51, by *J. Mosengel* and *C. Pencker*. Important treasury. Arcaded gallery with four chapels 1707. Sculptures 1748, by *Christoph Perwanger*. Monastery 1697.

✦✦ ŚWIĘTY KRZYŻ   MAP 20
Benedictine abbey on Łysa Góra (the Bald Hill), founded first half of 12th century by king Bolesław the Wrymouth, allegedly on the site of an old pagan temple and ritual circle. Church 1789, on Romanesque remains; interior ca. 1800. Monastery with cloister, mid-15th century, remodelled with addition of two wings, ca. 1643. Oleśnicki chapel with Mannerist tomb and altar 1620. Painted decoration 1782, by *M. Rejchan*. Gate late 18th century. The monastery contains a small historical **museum**. A very picturesque place, but quite eery when the light fades.

✦ ŚWINY   MAP 6
Picturesque ruin of Świnka family **castle**. The family lived here from the 13th century right up to 1713. Square keep 14th century, expanded and altered 15th and 16th century. Lower castle, including palace with two round towers, 1620s. Fortifications with rondelles. The castle was sacked by theRussians in 1764. Church ca. 1330, with good, mostly Renaissance, Świnka family tombs.

SYCÓW (GROSS WARTENBERG)   MAP 11
Protestant church 1789, by *Karl Gottfried Langhans*.

✦✦ SZADEK   MAP 12
Parish church, before 1335 and 15th century. Vaulting 1551. Murals 1451, by Master *Jan* of Wrocław, and 16th century. Altars early 17th century. Bell-tower, 14th-15th century.

✦✦ SZALOWA   MAP 22
Wooden **parish church**, 1739. Painted decoration, ornamental sculpture and furniture second half of 18th century.

✦✦ SZAMOTUŁY   MAP 9
Collegiate church of St Stanisław, 1542, incorporating walls of earlier church. Altars Mannerist, paintings and crucifix Gothic. Renaissance brass of Andrzej of Szamotuły from the *Vischer* workshop in Nuremberg, 1511. Tomb of Jakub Rokossowski ca. 1580, by *Girolamo Canavesi(?)*.
Reformed Franciscans' monastery church, pre-1682. **Keep** of Górka family castle, ca. 1518; now a **museum**.

SZANIEC   MAP 20
Parish church of St Mary, 1499, founded by Krzesław of Kurozwęki,
Bishop of Kuyavia.

SZCZAWIN   MAP 18
Country house, ca. 1827 by *Adam Idźkowski*.

SZCZAWIN KOŚCIELNY   MAP 17
Reformed Franciscans' church 1661, rebuilt in neo-Classical style
1787, by *Hilary Szpilowski*.

SZCZEBRZESZYN   MAP 27 ✦
A medieval town astride the Kiev-Kraków trade route, the property
of the Zamoyski family from the 16th to the 19th centuries.
Parish church of St Nicholas, 1620, altered later.
Franciscan monastery and church 1638.
Synagogue with Renaissance/Mannerist decoration, second quar-
ter of 17th century.
Secondary **school** and four teachers' houses, 1822.

SZCZECIN (STETTIN)   MAP 1 ✦✦
Though wealthy and powerful in early times, when it was the chief
seaport for the Pomeranian Slav principalities and briefly as a
Hanseatic port , this city at the month of the river Oder had a somewhat lacklustre existence in the late middle ages and suffered from a
succession of German and Swedish masters. It did not come into its
own again until the late 19th century, when it flourished as an opu-
lent German port. One can still see evidence of this through the
destruction of 1945 and the blight of communist planning and dere-
liction.
Castle of the dukes of Pomerania [1], on the site of an ancient fortified centre. South wing with two towers rebuilt from Gothic main
residential building 1503–38. East wing Renaissance, 1569. Two
wings and chapel added 1577, by *Wilhelm Zacharias*. Fifth wing
Mannerist, 1619. Whole castle altered in 1736 and 1874 with addition
of south-eastern tower, northern loggia and superstructure of
northern wing. Partly reconstructed after extensive war damage.
Town Hall [4] 13th century, altered and expanded, with ceramic
decoration, mid-15th century, workshop of *Heinrich Brunsberg*;
remodelled 17th century.
Franciscan (now Pallotine) **church** of St John [5]. Choir with
ceramic decoration before 1300, main body 14th century. **Church** of
St James [6]. Chancel 1387, body proper with ceramic decoration
turn of 14th century, by *Heinrich Brunsberg*. Tower completed

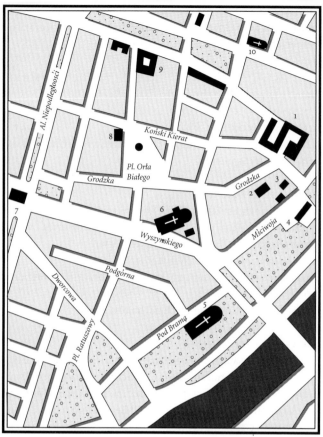

1504. Heavily reconstructed after war damage. Parish hall, 14th–15th century.

Palace of the Estates' Diet [**9**] 1727, by *Gerhard Kornelius von Wallrawe*, expanded 1885. Houses National **Museum**, with a very fine collection of Pomeranian medieval painting and sculpture, and a good gallery of Polish painting from the 18th-20th centuries. Town **gates** with sculptural decoration by *Gerhard Kornelius von Wallrawe*. Nakło Gate [**7**], 1728.

Church of SS Peter and Paul [**10**], with butressed interior and coloured ceramic decoration 1470s, lengthened 16th century. Painted ceiling 1703. Loitz family **house** [**2**] 1547 (they owned a trading fleet and were the bankers of the Jagiellon dynasty). Houses and granaries [**3, 8**], 15th–19th century.

✦ SZCZEKOCINY   MAP 19

Lovely baroque **country house** built for Urszula Dembińska née Morstin ca. 1780, by *Ferdynand Nax*, with neo-Classical curved colonnades, outbuildings and pavilions, first half of the 19th century. The last owner was Jan Ciechanowski, Poland's wartime ambassador in Washington.

Parish church, second half of 17th century, facade 1782, by *Ferdynand Nax*.

SZCZEPANKOWO   MAP 25

Parish church of St Wojciech, 1547, originally an outlying priory of the Benedictine abbey at Płock.

SZCZEPANÓW   MAP 22

Parish church founded by Jan Długosz in 1470. New church built on 1914, by *Jan Sas-Zubrzycki*. **Cemetery church** of St Stanisław, 1781.

SZCZEPANÓW   MAP 6

Parish church, 1571. Tombs 16th-17th century.

SZCZUCZYN   MAP 23 ✦

Piarist monastery founded by Vice-Chancellor Stanisław Szczuka 1711, by *Tilman van Gameren(?)* and *Józef Piola*.

SZCZYRZYC   MAP 21 ✦

Cistercian abbey founded 1245. Church of the Assumption 1620, still in Gothic tradition; altered 19th century. Monastic building 16th–19th century. Granary with gate 17th century. **Museum** of sacral art, arms and armour, textiles and painting.

SZESTNO (SEEHESTEN/SCHESTEN)   MAP 16

Protestant church (originally Catholic), 1401 and 1620. Ruin of **castle** of Teutonic Knights, 1367.

SZEWNA   MAP 20 ✦

Parish church of St Nicholas 1777, by *Father Józef Karśnicki*; interior Rococo. Priests's and curate's houses 1788, also by *Karśnicki*.

SZPROTAWA (SPROTTAU)   MAP 4 ✦

Mentioned in the year 1000 as the place where king Bolesław the Brave met the Emperor Otto III.

Parish church, 14th century, expanded 1424. Vaulting mid-16th century, chapels redecorated 17th century. Furniture second half of 17th-first half of 18th century. **Town Hall**; east tower 1586, west tower 1732. Expanded 1862.

SZREŃSK   MAP 17

Parish church, 1531.

SZTUM (STÜHM) MAP 8

Teutonic Knights' **castle**, 1326, altered 1414; reverted to the Polish Crown 1468. Some 19th-century rebuilding.

SZTUTOWO (STUTHOF) MAP 15

First German **concentration-camp** in Poland, established on 2 September 1939 to exterminate the articulate Polish population of Pomerania. Some 85,000 people were murdered here. Original camp accommodation, gas-chambers, crematoria, **museum**.

✦ SZTYNORT (STEINORT) MAP 16

Country house of the Lehndorff family, c 1700, wings 1829; rebuilt in neo-Gothic style mid-19th century. Park with neo-Classical pavilion and tea-house 1816, and neo-Gothic chapel 1826.

✦✦ SZYDŁÓW MAP 20

Castle founded by Kazimierz the Great, second half of 14th century. 'Lesser Treasury' (now Regional **Museum**) adapted from 1528 tower. Gatehouse early 17th century. **Parish hurch** of St Stanisław, founded 1355, enlarged mid-16th century. **Church** of All Saints, 14th–15th century. **Synagogue**, with Renaissance/Mannerist decoration, 16th–17th century. Well-preserved **town walls** mid-14th century. Kraków Gate expanded early 16th century.

✦✦✦ SZYDŁOWIEC MAP 20

Delightful little town, with moated **castle**, begun ca. 1450, originally the cradle of the Szydłowiecki family, which passed to the Radziwiłł family by marriage. Most of the present castle dates from 1526, with remodelling from the 1620s. Gate tower and domed chapel with stucco, 1627. **Parish church** of St Zygmunt founded by Szydłowiecki family, 1490. Altars Mannerist, 1627, sculpture and painted polyptych Gothic, early 16th century. Tomb of Treasurer Mikołaj Szydłowiecki Renaissance. Radziwiłł tomb neo-Classical, 1795, by *Jakub Monaldi*.**Town Hall** 1626, by Master Masons *Kacper* and *Wojciech Fodyga*. **Jewish cemetery** with 18th–19th-century tombstones.

SZYDŁOWIEC MAP 11

Succursal **church** 1617, by *Antonio Rusco*. Carved furniture contemporary, by *Hermann Fischer*.

SZYMBARK (SCHÖNBERG) MAP 15

Bishop's **castle** with 12 towers, ca. 1386, expanded 17th century; partly in ruins.

SZYMBARK   MAP 15

Fortified Renaissance **manor mouse** of Fładysz family, mid-16th century, remodelled 17th century.

SZYNWAŁD   MAP 8

Parish church, 14th century, expanded with addition of nave, tower and Kostka family chapel 1594.

TARCZEK   MAP 20

Romanesque **parish church**, early 13th century. Renaissance triptych, ca. 1540.

TARŁÓW   MAP 20 ✦✦

Parish church of the Holy Trinty with two symmetrical domed chapels, 1655. The inside is decorated with elaborate stucco-work round a cycle depicting the life of Our Lady and a fascinating Dance of Death.

TARNOBRZEG   MAP 20 ✦

Dominican church, 1693, by *Jan Michał Link*. Tower and aisles 1904. Silver tabernacle in high altar 1767. Just outside the town, in what is now the suburb of Dzików, is a **country house**, built in the 18th century for Jan Tarnowski, rebuilt in neo-Gothic style in 1830 by *Franciszek Maria Lanci*. Tarnowski was an important collector, and in the 19th century Dzikow was home to, among others, *Rembrandt's* 'Polish Rider', now in the Frick Collection, and *Canova's* 'Perseus', now in the Metropolitan Museum in New York.

TARNOGÓRA   MAP 28

Country house of the Tarnowski family, 1830s.

TARNOGRÓD   MAP 27 ✦✦

Parish church, ca. 1770, by *Bernard Meretyn(?)*. High altar (formerly in collegiate church in Zamość), mid-17th century, with paintings, 1604, by *Domenico Tintoretto*.

TARNÓW   MAP 22 ✦✦

Cathedral [1] (formerly collegiate church) of the Nativity of Our Lady, ca. 1400, expanded and modified up to the 19th century. Contains very fine Renaissance tombs of the Tarnowski family by *Giovanni-Maria Padovano* and others, and Ostrogski tombs, 1620, by *Willem van den Blocke(?)* and *Johann Pfister*. Good Gothic stalls. **Canons' houses** in cathedral square, first half of 16th century. **Mikołajowski house [2]**, 1524, now diocesan **museum**. Very good

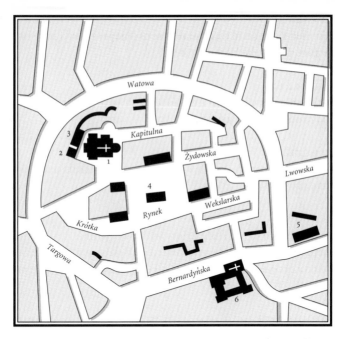

collection of Gothic painting and sculpture, also exceptional holdings of textiles from all over Europe and the East, 14th to 19th centuries.

Bernardine church [5] 1468, rebuilt first quarter of 19th century, now a **museum**.

Bernardine convent [6] (now Bernardine monastery). Church of the Raising of the Cross 1776; monastic building, ca. 1680.

Canons' Houses [3].

Gothic **Town Hall** [4], 15th-16th century, expanded in Renaissance style mid-16th century by *Giovanni-Maria Padovano(?)*. Now houses the City **Museum**, with a good collection of Polish painting, including Sarmatian portraits and works by *Norblin*, *Orłowski*, *Vogel*, *Suchodolski*, *Brandt*, etc. Also a collection of Italian, German and Dutch old masters, and of Italian drawings, including works by *Canaletto* and *Guardi*. The collection includes architectural drawings, glass, ceramics from all over the world, clocks, good arms and armour, and textiles. **Jewish cemetery** with many fine carved tombstones.

Town walls, 14th century, modernized with addition of outer ring 1513–45.

Houses in market square 16th-18th century.

Wooden succursal **church** of Our Lady in Burek, before 1458. Tower 20th century.

TARNOWO PAŁUCKIE   MAP 9 ✦
Wooden **parish church**, 1639, with contemporary polychromy.
Elegant Baroque organ, ca. 1700.

TCZEW (DIRSCHAU)   MAP 8
Parish church, first half of 14th century, expanded with addition of
chapels 15th century. Tower second half of 14th century. **Dominican
monastery** founded 1289. Church, first half of 14th century, rebuilt
15th–16th centuries.

TĘGOBORZE   MAP 22
Neo-Classical **manor house**, early 19th century. Wooden **parish
church**, 1753, expanded 19th century.

TŁOKOWO   MAP 16
Brick **church**, ca. 1500, with wooden tower, 18th century.

TOMASZÓW LUBELSKI   MAP 28 ✦✦
Town founded in 1590 by Chancellor and Hetman Jan Zamoyski,
remaining in the family's possession until 1866.
Wooden **parish church**, Baroque, 1727.

Neo-Classical **Protestant church**, 1823. **Parish church** of St Anthony 1860s, by *Henryk Marconi*. **Weavers' houses**, some wooden, mid-19th century.

◆   TOMICE   MAP 9

The cradle of the Tomicki family and birthplace of Piotr Tomicki (1464–1535), Bishop of Kraków, Chancellor of Poland, statesman and poet. **Parish church** 1463, redecorated in Baroque style 1770. Tomb of Mikołaj Tomicki, 1524.

◆◆◆ TORUŃ (THORN)   MAP 10

Originally an inland port on the Vistula and a member of the Hanseatic League from 1280. A sort of up-river outpost of Gdańsk, where ships were loaded for as far afield as Flanders, this attractive town was both rich and strategically important. The Teutonic Knights, who founded it in 1233 on land leased from the dukes of Mazovia, lost it to Poland in 1466 (Toruń had led the rising against them in 1454), and it remained an object of German envy until Frederick Wilhelm II of Prussia finally managed to get hold of it in 1792. Toruń is notorious amongst other things for being the birthplace of the great astronomer Mikołaj Kopernik, alias Nicolas Copernicus, on 19 February 1473.

Franciscan church of St Mary [1], mid-13th century, expanded 1350s. Good example of a 'hall' church (one in which the two aisles are the same height as the nave), a form much favoured by the burghers of northern towns, producing a lofty but austere effect. Roofs and gables of main body restored 1798. Mortuary chapel of Princess Anna Vasa with her figural tomb, 1636. Murals late 14th century. Stalls, first half of 15th century. Organ 1575-1609, by *Lorenz Weisloch* and *Johann Hellwig*. Gothic crucifix first quarter of 16th century. Enclosure of churchyard and gatekeeper's house late 14th century, arcaded gallery added early 17th century.

Town Hall [2] 1393, by Master *Andreas*, expanded by integration of cloth hall and tower, 1259. Bakers' stalls, ca. 1274, and city scales, ca. 1280. Mannerist upper storey, gables and angle turrets 1603, by *Anthonis van Opbergen*. Interiors redecorated 1737. Tower superstructure 1385 and 1430. Houses regional **museum**. Strong on Medieval painting and sculpture from Prussia, Pomerania and Silesia. Contains the only contemporary portrait of Copernicus, also Sarmatian portraits, Polish painting 16th to 20th centuries, clocks, furniture, glass, textiles, decorative arts, arms and armour.

Jesuit church of the Holy Cross [3] (originally Protestant) 1756, designed by *Andreas Adam Bähr*, Baroque facade by *Ephraim*

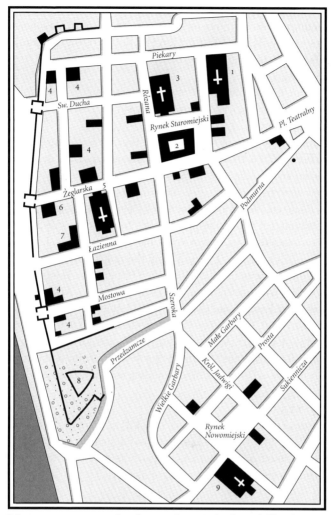

Schröger, tower 1899. Good organ by *Friedrich Rudolf Dalitz* and *Jan Jangenhann*.

Church of St John the Baptist and St John the Evangelist [**5**], second half of 13th century, lengthened ca. 1370. Sacristy 1320. Chapels 1349–1407. Tower 1433, by *Hans Gotland*. Superstructure of nave and aisles 1473, by Master *Prokop*. Galilee 1484, by *Hans Brand(?)*. Spectacular late 13th–14th century murals. High altar 1506. Good Gothic sculpture, including early 14th-century crucifix and Mater Dolorosa, and early 1400s Moses. Brass of von Soest family, made in Bruges, ca. 1360. The bell in the church tower is popularly known as Boża Trąba, God's Horn. It was in this church that Copernicus was baptised.

Church of St James [**9**], built by Teutonic Order 1309. Impressive soaring nave. Chapels 1359–1424. Crown of tower after 1455. Good Gothic murals. Furniture 14th-18th century. Statue of Madonna ca. 1380. Crucifixion ca. 1400. Good Gothic paintings, including Madonna, 1392, and the Way of the Cross, late 15th century. Organ 1611, by *Johann Hellwig*.

Fragments of **castle** [8] of Teutonic Knights, built in the 1250s and demolished in 1454 by the townspeople in their revolt against the rule of the order.

Palace of the bishops of Kuyavia [6], 1693. The city also contains many brick merchants' **houses** of Hanseatic type, with decorative gables and facades, and stone Renaissance or Mannerist portals, dating from the end of 13th century to the mid-16th century, some of them remodelled in later centuries. Of particular note, in the Old Town market square, the 'Star House' (no. 35), with a fine Baroque stucco facade, 1697. Also in Kopernika street, the house known as Copernicus' (no.17) dating from the 1480s, now a branch of regional **museum**, with exhibition on Copernicus. Jesuit College [7]. **City walls**, with towers, 13–14th centuries. **Arsenal** 1824. **Reformed Franciscans' church** and monastery in Podgórze, 1644. Granaries [4]. Fortifications following the Dutch system, after 1629 and 1658; modernized, with addition of outer forts, 1871. On the opposite bank of the Vistula, facing the town, ruins of the Polish royal **castle** of Dybów, 1425; surrounding walls and gate 1462.

♦♦ TOSZEK (TOST)   MAP 14
Castle of the Piast dukes of Racibórz and Opole, mid-15th century. Expanded for Colonna family 1650–66, by *Giovanni Seregno*. **Parish church** of St Catherine, ca. 1450, remodelled 1715, tower 1860. **Cemetery church** of St Barbara, 1750. **Town Hall** 1836.

TRĘBKI   MAP 17
Neo-Classical **parish church** with octagonal nave, 1802, by *Hilary Szpilowski*.

TREBLINKA   MAP 25
German **concentration-camp** in which some 800,00 people were exterminated. Started mid-1941. Razed to the ground by the Germans in 1944. It was here that most of the inhabitants of the Warsaw Ghetto were brought when this was being liquidated in 1942–3, including Janusz Korczak. There is a mausoleum and a symbolic cemetery.

TRÓJCA   MAP 5
Romanesque **parish church**, mid-13th century, rebuilt 1512.

TROPIE MAP 22 ✦
Parish church, legendarily associated with St Świerad. Chancel ca. 1260, nave 1347, expanded in Renaissance style before 1611 and 1634.

TRUTNOWY (TRUTENAU) MAP 8 ✦
Timber **house**, 1720–6.

TRUTOWO MAP 10
Carmelite monastery founded 1717. Church before 1732, tower 1753. Painted decoration and Rococo interior 1738. Monastic building 1740s.

TRYBSZ MAP 21
Wooden Gothic **church** 1567. Painted decoration 1647.

TRZCIŃSKO-ZDRÓJ MAP 1
Parish church of St Mary, before 1281, expanded 14th and 15th century. **Town walls**, 14th century, with 15th-century gates. **Town Hall** 13th century, expanded second half of 16th century, rebuilt ca. 1700.

TRZEBIATÓW (TREPTOW) MAP 2
Parish church of St Mary, first half of 14th century, ambulatory of chancel 15th century, tower superstructure 1773. **Chapel** of St Gertrude, 15th century. **Town walls**, late 13th century.

TRZEBINY MAP 4
Baroque **country house** of Gurowski family, ca. 1690 by *Giovanni Catenaci(?)*, altered 1870.

TRZEBNICA MAP 11 ✦✦
Cistercian convent, founded 1203 for nuns from Bamberg by Henry the Bearded, Duke of Silesia, and his wife Jadwiga, who was later canonized. Romanesque church of St Bartholomew, basilica with transept and crypt under chancel, 1219. St Jadwiga's chapel, in so-called 'doctrinaire Gothic' style, 1269. Externally reclad in Baroque style second half of 17th-early 18th century. Tower 1785. Portal with carved tympanon of David playing the harp to Bathsheba 1240, and another late 13th century. Furniture 1747–89, paintings by *Christian Philipp v. Bentum*, sculpture by *Franz Josef Mangoldt*. St Jadwiga's tomb 1680. Monastic building with two cloister gardens 1726.

TRZEMESZNO MAP 9 ✦✦
Benedictine church, later of Canons Regular; Romanesque basilica with crypt, ca. 1145, rebuilt 13th century. Remodelled and expanded

1791. **Hospital** of St Lazarus with chapel, second half of 18th century. **Almshouse** 1775.

TUCHOLA ŻARSKA   MAP 3
Baroque **manor house**, 1741, rebuilt ca. 1800.

✦   TUCHÓW   MAP 22
Baroque **parish church** of St James, 1794. Furniture Rococo. **Redemptorist church** (originally Benedictine), 1682, expanded 19th century. Inside, miraculous 16th-century picture of the Virgin.

TUCZNO   MAP 2
Parish church 1522, altered 1580s. **Castle** of Wedel family (who later changed their name to Tuczyński), begun 1338 and remodelled entirely into a Baroque palace in the 17th and 18th centuries.

TULCE   MAP 9
Romanesque **parish phurch**, first half of 13th century, expanded, with addition of Baroque facade, 1784.

TULIGŁOWY   MAP 22
Monastery of Canons Regular of the Holy Sepulchre founded 1446. Present building 1770.

TUŁOWICE   MAP 17
Neo-Classical **manor house**, ca. 1800. Virtually destroyed after the war, the house was painstakingly restored by the painter Andrzej Novak-Zempliński and is a delightful example of this small kind of country residence.

TURAWA   MAP 12
Baroque **country house,** 1730. Chapel 1751. Outbuilding ca. 1760.

TUREK   MAP 12
Neo-Classical **weavers' houses**, after 1826. **Parish church**, 1904–13, with murals, stained glass and other decorative elements 1930s, by *Józef Mehoffer*.
Protestant church 1849, by *Henryk Marconi*.

TUREW   MAP 9
Baroque **country house** of Chłapowski family, ca. 1749. One of its owners, Baron Dezydery Chłapowski, a Napoleonic general, turned it into a model estate on English lines in the 1820s.

Parish church, ca. 1530, expanded 1623 with addition of nave and two symmetrical domed chapels. Stucco-work by *Jan Jaroszewicz(?)*, and *Jan Wolff*.

Parish church, 1786. Miraculous Madonna.

Parish church founded by Hetman Jan Klemens Branicki (see Białystok), 1745, expanded 1750s by *Jan Henryk Klemm*. Paintings by *Szymon Czechowicz*. Priest's house, mid-18th century.

A settlement on the old Mazovian border with Lithuania, the home of the Gasztołd family. In 1542 it passed into the hands of king Zygmunt Augustus, who built a strong **castle** in which he stored part of his treasure. The ruins of this can be seen on the meadow outside the town, and a legend persists that the treasure is still there. The town and surrounding land was granted to Hetman Stefan Czarniecki in 1661, and soon passed to the Branicki family. Tykocin was also an important centre of Jewish life in Poland.

Missionaries' monastery founded by Hetman Jan Klemens Branicki (see Białystok). Church of the Holy Trinity 1749. Painted decoration by *Franciszek Eckstein*. Furniture contemporary. Paintings by *Szymon Czechowicz*, Branicki portraits by *Sylwester Mirys*. Substantial Rococo organ, 1749-50, by *Jan Chryzostom Redler*. Monastic building 1750 and later.

Synagogue 1642, rebuilt mid-18th century, now a **museum**.

Hospice for old soldiers 1638.

Benedictine abbey, one of the first in Poland, founded in 1044 by king Kazimierz the Restorer, built on a spectacular defensive position overhanging the Vistula. The place soon became a site of national piety. The present church of SS Peter and Paul and St John the Evangelist dates from the first half of 15th century, on the foundations of a Romanesque basilica. It was remodelled in Baroque style 1622. Rear elevation late 18th century. Furniture mid-18th century, by *Francesco Placidi* and others. Monastic building, originally Romanesque, rebuilt with addition of cloister in Gothic style, 15th century. Wing of second cloister garden and library 1622. Murals 15th and 16th century.

Abbot's house, 15th century, rebuilt 1578. Fortifications early 17th century. Formal park with terraces and Rococo gate, 18th century.

✦ UCHANIE   MAP 28
Parish church of the Assumtion founded by Treasurer Mikołaj
Daniłowicz, ca. 1625, by *Jan Jaroszewicz(?)*, and *Jan Wolff*.
Uchański family tombs ca. 1600.

✦✦ UJAZD   MAP 20
One of the most spectacular ruins going. Mannerist **castle** of
Krzyżtopór, built for Krzysztof Ossoliński 1644, by *Lorenzo Senes*.

Palace with elliptical inner courtyard opening into forecourt
flanked by wings, inside pentagonal bastion fortress, with tower
gate in front. It was heavy with symbolism, having 4 bastions (sea-
sons), 12 great chambers (months), 52 rooms (weeks), 365 windows
- all in order to stress the alleged great age and permanence of the
family. The castle was totally gutted by the Swedish army in 1655,
eleven years after its completion, and this brief life and early demise
only helped to fuel the fantastic tales of its erstwhile grandeur and
luxury. It was said that even the mangers in the stables were of
Carara marble, and that the ceiling of one of the rooms was the bot-
tom of a huge fish-tank.

ULAN   MAP 25
Baroque **parish church**, 1771.

ULESIE   MAP 6
Church, late 15th century, surrounded by fortified graveyard.

ULUCZ   MAP 29 ✦
Wooden **Orthodox church**, early 1500s. Painted decoration
16th–17th century.

UNIEJÓW   MAP 12 ✦
Well-preserverd **castle** built by Archbishop Jarosław Skotnicki,
mid-14th century, expanded 1534, 1645, and ca. 1848. **Collegiate
church**, 1365, expanded second quarter of 15th century and later.

USTIANOWA   MAP 29
Wooden **Uniate** (now Catholic) **church**, 1791. Furniture contemporary.

WABCZ   MAP 10
Parish church, turn of the 13th century, tower mid-14th century.

WĄCHOCK   MAP 20 ✦✦
Cistercian abbey, one of the first in Poland, founded in 1179 by
Bishop Gedeon of Kraków for monks from Morimond in
Burgundy. Romanesque church of St Florian, first half of 13th century. Furniture Baroque and Rococo. Perfect Romanesque chapter
house and Gothic refectory, mid-13th century. Rest of monastery
refurbished early 16th century and expanded in Baroque style.
Cloister, elevations and tower, 1643. Abbot's palace early 16th century. Fortified gateway, first half of 17th century.

WADOWICE   MAP 21
Birth-place of Karol Wojtyła, later Pope John Paul II. **Manor house**
of Mikołaj Komorowski, early 19th century.

WĄDROŻE WIELKIE (GROSS WANDRISS)   MAP 6 ✦
A pilgrimage centre built around the cult of a 14th-century carved
Madonna. **Parish church**, Romanesque, second quarter of 13th cen-
tury. Tower 19th century. Churchyard wall early 17th century.

WĄGROWIEC   MAP 9
Birthplace of Jakub Wujek, born 1541, one of the early translators of
the Bible into Polish. **Parish church**, second half of 16th century.
Painted decoration Renaissance, 1587, furniture Mannerist and
Baroque. **Cistercian abbey church**, second half of 18th century.

WAŁBRZYCH (WALDENBURG)   MAP 6
Protestant church 1788, by *Karl Gottfried Langhans*. **Villa** by *L.
Niederacker*, 1803.

Spare and elegant neo-Classical **country house**, 1783 by *Hilary Szpilowski*, the seat of the Walewski family. In the rainy October of 1806, the vanguard of the French army occupied Łowicz, and its commander, Marshal Davout, installed himself at Walewice with his staff. One morning as the young lady of the house surveyed the sea of mud she would have to cross from the estate office to the main house, a dashing young cavalry officer swept her up in his arms and carried her accross. He was Charles de Flahaut, natural son of Talleyrand, and he would later introduce her to his Emperor. She became Napoleon's most notorious mistress and the mother of one of his sons.

Parish church with pilgrimage complex, built 1681-1706 by Daniel Paschius von Osterberg. Expanded 1715–20, by *K.Dientzenhofer*. Osterberg wanted to recreate Jerusalem, and renamed all the hills and rivers on his estate accordingly. Calvary chapels 17th-19th centuries.

Church of Franciscan monastery founded 1629. Chancel 1696, nave and facade 1746. **Town Hall** 1821, by *Hilary Szpilowski*.
At nearby Winiary, neo-Classical **manor house**, early 19th century, housing Kazimierz Pułaski **museum**, devoted to the part played by Poles in the American War of Independence.

Warsaw is not like other capitals - it did not grow organically as the centre of a state, it was selected late in the day, for geographical reasons. A small but prosperous and well-fortified trading town perched on an escarpment overlooking the Vistula on the Mazovian border with the Grand Duchy of Lithuania, Warsaw was suddenly propelled to fame in 1595, when it was decreed to be the new capital of the Polish-Lithuanian Commonwealth (the old capital, Kraków, was too distant from Lithuania). The existing castle was rapidly expanded to accommodate the king and the Sejm, which began to meet here from 1569. A mercantile walled city sprang up, and a number of magnates' palaces were built in the immediate vicinity. Just outside, in what is now the district of Wola, a space was cleared for elections of Kings of Poland. The city suffered terrible devastation in 1656 at the hands of the Swedes, but when it was rebuilt in the second half of the 17th century, it was no less haphazardly than before, with large stretches of waste ground and huddles of mean housing separating the magnificent palaces of the grandees and the outlying churches. As one German traveller noted, Warsaw gave the impression of a room filled with fine furniture, but all standing in the wrong place. In the mid-18th century, the city, with no more than about 30,000 inhabitants, was still a sleepy place that sporadically came to life when the king arrived to hold a session of the Sejm. But the accession of king Stanisław Augustus in 1764 changed that. He not only lived there all the time, but he exerted huge efforts on bringing the city up to date and developing it. By the 1790s it had got into its stride, and with 120,000 inhabitants it was the tenth largest city in Europe. It enjoyed an artistic and social life to match this importance, and attracted visitors from all over Europe.

The disappearance of independent Poland from the map did not have as drastic consequences for Warsaw as one might have suspected. The period between the Congress of Vienna (1815) and the outbreak of the 1830 Insurrection, when Poland was a semi-autonomous kingdom with the Tsar of Russia being simultaneously king of Poland, saw a marked increase in material wealth, and the appearance of many fine new buildings in the neo-Classical manner. The continuing periods of repression during the nineteenth century did little to stem the natural vitality of the Varsavians, and by the last decades of the century the city had become an elegant European metropolis, with electric lighting and one of the most modern hotels in the world, the Bristol.

The recovery of national independence in 1918 inaugurated a period of great development for Warsaw, which now became the capital of a large European country. The need for national institutions, for administrative and other public buildings, and a highly progressive assisted public housing scheme all contributed to a vigorous growth of the city, in an inspired modernist style. The other arts, freed from the necessity of having to struggle for liberation, launched into various avenues of extreme avant-garde.

The Second World War brought tragedy and a certain historic consecration. Its agony began on 1 September 1939, when the Germans applied their technique of indiscriminate bombing of civilians. The years of occupation saw mass deportation and the annihilation of the city's Jewish population, the Ghetto Uprising of 1943, and finally the Warsaw Uprising of 1 August 1944. The human tally was some 800,000 people, well over half the city's pre-war population. When the city was 'liberated' by the Red Army on 17 January 1945, there was hardly anything to liberate, as the city had been bombed, then fought over hand-to-hand and crushingly shelled, and, finally, dynamited street by street. The destruction is almost unbelievable, and it is highly recommended to go to the City of Warsaw Museum in the Old Market Square to see the film made from German newsreels, in order to appreciate fully what happened.

The post-war period brought mixed blessings to the capital. On the one hand, great swathes of the devastated old city were rebuilt exactly as they had been at the end of the eighteenth century, while damaged buildings such as Łazienki were lovingly and lavishly restored to their former glory. On the other hand the absurd planning or lack of planning of the Communist authorities has left great gaps and canyons running through the middle of the city, destroying its cohesion and spreading the inhabitants over a huge area. The city is, quite simply, a terrible mess.

The greatest triumph of hope over experience, and one of the most successful, as well as the most moving, achievements of the post-war years has been the rebuilding of the **Royal Castle [1]**, which was literally obliterated by the Germans. This had started as a small defensive outpost which grew into a periodic residence of the dukes of Mazovia. In the last quarter of the 15th century, Duke Janusz the Elder built a Great Hall, followed by a Lesser Hall, remains of which can be seen in the present castle courtyard. In 1525 the dukes of Mazovia died out and the province reverted to the Polish Crown. After the Union of Lublin (1569), by which Poland and the Grand Duchy of Lithuania were joined constitutionally, Warsaw was chosen as the meeting-place for the new combined parliament, the Sejm. The castle was enlarged, to accommodate a chamber for the Sejm on the ground floor and the Senate on the first, where an apartment was also fitted out for the king. The necessity of annual

attendance at the Sejm impelled king Zygmunt III to rebuild the castle throughly in the years 1589–1619. The result, a pentagon around a courtyard, with a central tower over the entrance, was the work of *Giovanni Trevano*, with *Giaccomo Rotonda*, *Matteo Castelli* and *Paolo del Corta*. In the second quarter of the following century king Władysław IV added a tower and a gate, using the architect *Giovanni Battista Ghisleni*. He also redecorated the interiors, introducing a theatre and a marble chamber. The castle was thoroughly sacked by the Swedes in 1655, and although the Sejm resumed its sessions there in 1658, it remained in poor condition for the remainder of the century. There were many plans to rebuild the castle, but they came to nothing. King Jan III lived mostly at Wilanów, and his successors Augustus II and Augustus III lived in the Saxony Palace, which they had built for themselves. In 1741 the facade on the Vistula was remodelled, by *Gaetano Chiaveri* and *Antonio Solari*, with sculptures by *Jan Jerzy Plersch*. The Senate chamber was rebuilt 1740-2, by *Zacharias Longuelune*. With the accession of Stanisław II Augustus in 1764 the castle truly became the centre of political and artistic life, and its development reflected this. The king had immensely grandiose plans for rebuilding the castle, most of which remained on paper. But he gradually worked his way through the interiors, stamping his refined taste on the building. He started in the south wing, with the great stairway and the Horse Guards antechamber, 1767 by *Jakub Fontana*. Then came the marble chamber, rebuilt in 1771 by *Fontana*, with sculptures by *Andre Le Brun* and paintings by *Marcello Bacciarelli*. The next wave of redecorating began in 1774, under the direction of *Domenico Merlini*, beginning with the senators' antechamber, with the unique collection of 22 views of Warsaw by *Bernardo Belotto*; including the chapel, the audience room, the bedchamber and private rooms. There followed the magnificent great assembly room, 1777–81 by *Merlini* and *Jan Chrystian Kamsetzer*; the library, 1779–84; the throne room and knights' chamber, 1781-6, with paintings by *Bacciarelli* and *Jan Bogumil Plersch* and sculpture by *Le Brun* and *Giaccomo Monaldi*. In the throne room, the great assembly room and the audience chamber, there are very fine torchères and candelabra by *Jean-Louis Prieur* and *Philippe Caffiéri*. The rooms contain Polish, French and English furniture, and the remnants of the king's collection of Old Masters. After the third partition of Poland (1795), the castle ceased to fulfill any function until 1807, when it became the residence of Frederick Augustus, Duke of Warsaw. It is at this time that the monumental terraces on the escarpment overlooking the Vistula were built, by *Jakub Kubicki*. *Kubicki* was also responsible for some alterations to the Sejm chamber, which was the only part of the castle with a real function between 1815 and 1831. After the defeat of the Polish rising of 1830-1, the castle was stipped of its furniture and collections, and even whole rooms, such as the marble chamber, were removed to Russia. When Poland regained her independence in 1918, the castle was restored as the presidential residence, while the Sejm was moved to a new building in the city centre. Part of the looted contents were returned by Soviet Russia after her defeat by Poland in 1920. In 1939 the castle suffered bomb damage, and on 17 September the roofs and top storey were consumed by fire. It suffered badly from the fighting during the Warsaw Uprising of August-September 1944, and the remaining ruin was methodically dynamited by the Germans during the autumn of that year. After the war, the intention of rebuilding the castle was frustrated by the sheer scale of the project as well as lack of funds, and the site remained a flat paved terrace overlooking the river. In 1971 a rebuilding committee was formed with government support, and by 1974 the bare carcase had been completed. In 1981 the first rooms were opened to the public. The work continues, with minor details being finished off every year, and every year sees a few more elements of the original contents or suitable replacements gradually filling out the interiors -in 1994 alone these included the canopy of the throne room and a couple of dozen Old Master pictures from king Stanisław Augustus' collection, including a couple by *Rembrandt*. Walking around this strikingly beautiful and important interior, it is almost impossible to believe that none of it existed between 1944 and the 1970s.

Old Town:

Column of King Zygmunt III, 1644, by *Costantino Tencalla*, with statue by *Clemente Molli*. One of the very few attractive monuments in Warsaw.

Cathedral [2] (until 1798 collegiate church) of St John, originally a ✦✦ Gothic hall church of Pomeranian type, late 14th century, remodelled several times and finally reconstructed 1947–56 by *Jan Zachwatowicz* to resemble its original aspect. Surviving elements include: tomb of the last dukes of Mazovia, 1528, by *Bernardo Zanobi de Gianotis*; brass of Canon Stanisław Strzelica, 1535; monument to Stanisław Małachowski, 1831, after *Bertel Thorwaldsen*; a crucifix made in Wrocław early 16th century. In crypt, tombs of bishops of Warsaw, dukes of Mazovia, the novelist Henryk Sienkiewicz, the pianist and statesman Ignacy Jan Paderewski, of the first President of the Second Republic, Gabriel Narutowicz, Cardinal StefanWyszyński, symbol of Polish spiritual resistance to communism, and also the sarcophagus containing the remains of Stanisław Augustus, the last king of Poland, finally laid to rest on 14 February 1995, after a long odyssey beginning in St Petersburg in 1798.

Next door, **Jesuit college church** [3] founded 1598 by Zygmunt III, ✦ started 1608, aisle after 1622. Gothic crucifix from Lübeck 1383.

Augustinian monastery [4], founded 1353. Church of St Martin, 18th ✦

century, with earlier parts. Facade 1744. Belfry 1672.

Old Market Square, with burghers' houses of Hanseatic type, 15th-16th century, modified 17th-18th century, all rebuilt after 1945, but with many original fragments reincorporated. **Museum** of the City

✦ of Warsaw **[5]**, of quite specialised interest, but worth visiting for some of the pictures and objects of applied art, and most of all for the twenty-minute film of the destruction of the city by the Germans. Adam Mickiewicz **Museum** (No 18), dedicated to the national poet's life and work, and that of other Warsaw writers, most notably the poet Julian Tuwim. **Town walls** with towers, second half of 14th century. Barbican in front of New Town gate, 1548 by *Gianbattista* of Venice.

New Town:

✦ **Pauline monastery** and Church of the Holy Ghost [6], 1713 by *Józef Piola*. Paintings by *Michael Willmann*, second half of 17th century, taken from the Cistercian church in Lubiąż.

✦ **Dominican church** [7] 1638, by *Giovanni Italiano*. Domed Kotowski chapel 1694, by *Tilman van Gameren*. Bell-tower 1753. Monastic building 1640s.

✦✦ **Church** and convent **of the Sisters of the Blessed Sacrament** [8], founded by Queen Maria Kazimiera, wife of Jan III Sobieski, 1692, by *Tilman van Gameren*. Tomb of Caroline de Bouillon 1746, by *L. Mattielli*. Monastic building 1688, by *Gameren*. South wing ca. 1740, by *Antonio Solari*.

At the northernmost end of the New Town, in a secluded spot, the

✦✦ **parish church** of St Mary [9] 1497, expanded mid-16th century. Bell-tower, mid-16th century.

Sapieha palace [10] 1744, by *Johann Sigismund Deybel*, adapted 1818 as barracks, and 1826, by *Wilhelm Henryk Minter*.

Franciscan monastery [11] founded by Jan III Sobieski. Church of St Francis 1696, by *Giovanni Battista Ceroni*. Lower chapel, first half of 18th century by *Joachim Daniel Jauch*. Facade 1733, by *Jakub Fontana*, with neo-Classical crowning, 1788, by *Jozef Boretti*. Monastic building 1727.

The 17th and 18th century city outside the walls:

Raczyński palace [12], 1786 by *Jan Chrystian Kamsetzer*. Now houses the principal historical archive, Archiwum FłówneAkt Dawnych.

Piarist college church [13] of the Blessed Virgin Mary Queen of Poland, now garrison church, first half of 18th century by *Józef Fontana*; converted into Orthodox church in 19th century, rebuilt as Catholic church 1920s by *Oskar Sosnowski*.

Krasiński palace [14] 1680s, by *Tilman van Gameren*, sculpture of ✦✦
elevation and interiors by *Andreas Schlüter*. In 1765, the building

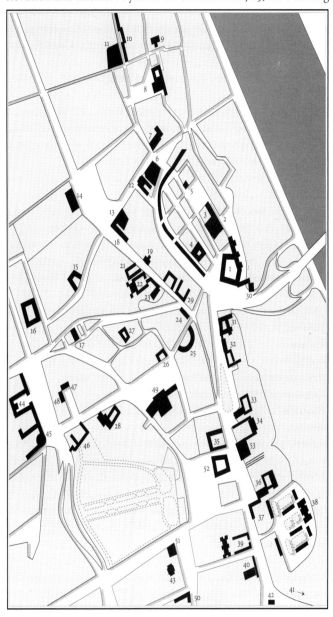

was purchased by the state to house various administrative bodies,
and became known as 'the Palace of the Commonwealth'. Interiors
restyled 1767, by *Jakub Fontana* and 1783, by *Domenico Merlini*.
Now a department of the National Library.
"Four Winds" palace [15], rebuilt for the Warsaw banker Piotr

Fergusson Tepper 1769–80, by *Szymon Bogumił Zug*.

Royal Arsenal [**16**], founded by Władysław IV 1638, expanded and redpeatedly remodelled. Houses Archaeological **Museum**, with strong holdings of Polish material from Paleolithic times, with interesting material from the Bronze and Iron Ages, and the early medieval period.

Przebendowski (later Radziwiłł) **palace** [**17**], 1728, by *Johann Sigismund Deybel*.

Collegium Nobilium [**18**], 1743, by *Jakub Fontana*. The first secular public school in Poland, founded by the Piarist priest Stanisław Konarski in 1740. Redecorated in neo-Classical style 1785, by *Stanisław Kostka Potocki* and *Stanisław Zawadzki*.

Basilian monastery [**19**] with octagonal Baroque church built into its centre, 1784, by *Domenico Merlini*.

Opposite, **Borch Palace** [**21**] (now seat of the Archbishop of Warsaw), ca. 1780, by *Domenico Merlini*, and 19th century.

Palace of General Ludwik Pac [**22**], 1824 by *Henryk Marconi*. Bas-reliefs in the gateway by *Ludwik Kauffmann*. Interesting Mauresque and neo-Gothic interiors, 1820s.

Capuchin monastery and church [**23**], founded by Jan III, 1683,by *Tilman van Gameren*. King's chapel 1736, by *Joachim Daniel Jauch*, restored 1828, by *Henryk Marconi*.

Palace of the bishops of Kraków [**24**], rebuilt by Bishop Kajetan Sołtyk 1762.

✦ **Primate's palace** [**25**], with portico and curved wings, 1777-83, by *Ephraim Schröger* and *Szymon Bogumił Zug*.

Blank's (originally Szaniawski) **palace** [**26**], 1764 by *Szymon Bogumił Zug*. Interiors ca. 1777.

Załuski palace [**27**](now Society of Authors), the first public reference library on the European mainland, founded 1747, when the brothers Andrzej and Józef Załuski pooled their valuable collections and donated the 180,000 books and 10,000 manuscripts to the nation. The library was looted by the Russians in 1795. The building was remodelled in neo-Classical style 1823. Bas-reliefs of Polish kings 19th-20th century.

Reformed Franciscans' church [**28**], 1678. St Mary's chapel 1781. Arcaded gallery in front of church 18th century. Monastic building 1672. **Palace** of Hetman Jan Klemens Branicki [**29**], 1744, by *Johann Sigismund Deybel*.

The Royal Road:

✦✦ Lubomirski or **"Tin-roofed" palace** [**30**] ca. 1720. Now a part of the Royal Castle.

✦✦ Bernardine monastery **church** of St Anne [**31**], original Gothic church second half of 15th century, expanded 1518, remodelled in Baroque style 1667. Facade 1788, by *Stanisław Kostka Potocki* and *Piotr Aigner*. Painted decoration Rococo, 1753 by Father *Walenty Żebrowski*. Furniture mid-18th century. Very fine Rococo organ and gallery, 1701-7 and 1750-3, by monastic brothers *Antoni of Płogów, Klemens of Sierpc*, and *Paschalis Scholtz*. Belfry 1578, rebuilt in neo-Classical style 1821, by *Piotr Aigner*. Monastic building 1518–33, rebuilt 1818, by *Piotr Aigner*. Shrine to the Blessed Virgin, by *Giuseppe Simone Belotti*, 1683.

Warsaw Benevolent Society [32] (originally Discalced Carmelites' convent), 1663, by *Giovanni Battista Ghisleni*. Chapel of St Teresa and monastic buildings rebuilt from Kazanowski palace 1643. West wing 1819 by *Antonio Corazzi*.

Monument to the poet Adam Mickiewicz, with statue by *Cyprian Godebski*, 1898; another of the few passable monuments in Warsaw.

Carmelite church of the Assumption and St Joseph [33], 1661-82, by ✦✦ *Giuseppe Simone Belotti*; facade 1761, by *Ephraim Schröger*; a very early example of neo-Classicism in Poland. Inside, painting of the Marriage of Our Lady, ca. 1750 by *Jan Jerzy Plersch*. High altar 1697, by *Tilman van Gameren*, furniture 18th century.

 Koniecpolski later **Radziwiłł palace** [34], now Presidium of Council ✦ of Ministers and Presidential Residence (it was in this building that on the eve the reformers plotted the coup by which the famous constitution of 3 May 1791 was passed, also where the Warsaw Pact was signed). Present neo-Classical building 1819 by *Piotr Aigner*. In front of it, equestrian **statue** of Prince Józef Poniatowski, nephew of the last king of Poland and Marshal of France, by *Bertel Thorwaldsen*, 1826, another of the very few decent monuments in Warsaw.

Opposite, **Czartoryski** (Originally Dönhoff, later Potocki) **palace** ✦✦ [35], now Ministry of Culture and Art, ca. 1730, by *Johann Sigismund Deybel*. Portico and interiors late 18th century, by *Jan Chrystian Kamsetzer*. Corps-de-garde building 1763, by *Ephraim Schröger*.

Convent of the nuns of the Visitation [36], founded 1654 by Queen ✦✦ Ludwika Maria Gonzaga, wife of Władysław IV and subsequently of Jan Kazimierz. One of the finest Baroque churches in Warsaw, 1727–34, by *Karol Bay*, facade as well as decoration of interior and furniture in Rococo style, completed 1754–62, by *Ephraim Schröger*. Sculpture, high altar and pulpit 1757 by *Jan Jerzy Plersch*. French ebony and silver tabernacle mid-17th century. Monastic building 1674–87.

Tyszkiewicz (later Potocki) **palace** [37], 1786 by *Stanisław Zawadzki*, rebuilt 1786–92 by *Jan Chrystian Kamsetzer*. Interesting severe entrance hall and staircase. The building now houses the important holdings of prints and drawings, including the collection of king Stanisław Augustus, of the University Library, not on public view, but available for study. **Kazimierzowski palace [38]**, originally built by Władysław IV, 1634, rebuilt for king Jan Kazimierz 1660, expanded for Sułkowski family in Baroque style 1732, by *Karl Friedrich von Poppelmann* and *Joachim Daniel Jauch*. Rebuilt to accomodate Warsaw University, in neo-Classical style, 1817, by *Hilary Szpilowski*. Portico 1824, by *Wacław Ritschel*. Two outbuildings 1815–20, by *Jakub Kubicki*, and two wings 1824, by *Piotr Aigner* and *Michał Kado*. The composer Fryderyk Chopin lived in the left-hand wing as a boy, when his father taught at the university.

✦   **Czapski** (later Krasiński, then Raczyński) **palace [39]**, built for Cardinal Michał Radziejowski 1691–1705, by *Tilman van Gameren*, remodelled 1713–18, by *Karol Bay* and *Augustyn Locci*. Two neo-Classical ranges ca. 1792, by *Jan Chrystian Kamsetzer*, and 1852 by *Henryk Marconi*. The Chopin family moved to an apartment on the second floor of the corner wing, and the young composer lived here during his adolescence.

✦✦   **Missionaries' church** of the Holy Cross **[40]**, founded by Cardinal Michal Radziejowski, 1682–96, by *Giuseppe Simone Belotti*. Facade 1730 and 1754, by *Joachim Daniel Jauch* and *Jakub Fontana*. Pulpit 1696, by *M. Treter*. Tomb of Cardinal Radziejowski 1722. Urn containing Chopin's heart.

✦✦   **Ostrogski palace [41]**, one of the pavilions of a Baroque palatial scheme never carried out, with terrace on a semi-fortified platform, 1681, by *Tilman van Gameren*. Now seat of Chopin Society, housing a small **museum** dedicated to the composer.

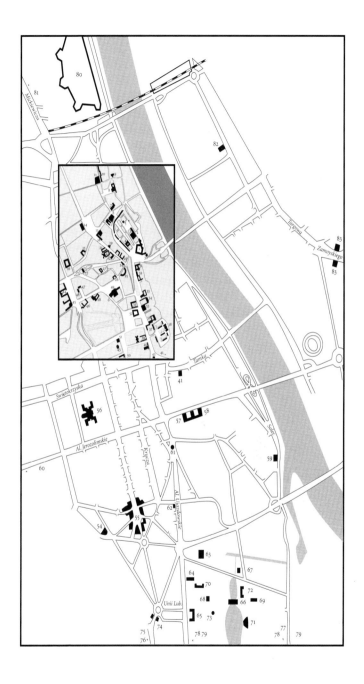

Neo-Classical Warsaw:

Staszic palace [42] (Warsaw Scientific Society), 1821, by *Antonio Corazzi*. In front of it, **statue** of Copernicus, 1830, by *Bertel Thorvaldsen*, 1830, the fourth and last of the acceptable monuments in Warsaw.

✦✦ **Lutheran church** [43] 1777, by *Szymon Bogumił Zug*; a severe neo-Classical rotunda clearly influenced by *Claude Nicolas Ledoux*. Victory Square, whose name has changed more than any others, used to be dominated by a huge Orthodox Cathedral built by the Russians to annoy. It was later the scene of emotive events, when Pope John Paul II first came to Poland-it was here that a great cross was nightly destroyed by the police and daily restored by the faith-full and is now one of the ugliest windswept places in the capital.

The **Saxony Gardens**, originally the grounds of a great residence built by Augustus II and Augustus III, 1715, by *Johann Christoph Naumann*, enlarged 1733 by *Matthaus Daniel von Poppelmann*. Adapted into landscape park 1816, by *John Savage*. Water tower 1854, by *Henryk Marconi*. Nothing remains of the residence, which was totally devastated in 1944, except for two arches of the colonnade, now the Tomb of the Unknown Soldier. At the far end of the gardens, a spectacular range of neo-Classical architecture, including:

✦✦ **Revenue and Treasury Commission Building** [44] (now Town Hall of the City of Warsaw), 1824, by *Antonio Corazzi*; **Stock Exchange** and **Bank of Poland** [45], 1830 by *Antonio Corazzi* and *Jan Jakub Gay*.

✦ "Blue" palace [46] built for Count Stanisław Zamoyski in neo-Classical style, 1815, by *Fryderyk Albert Lessel*. A fashionable salon at the beginning of the 19th century, in which the young Chopin performed. Library pavilion after 1868, by *Julian Ankiewicz*. In 1811 the library was opened to the public. **Mniszech palace** [47] (later Merchants' Club, now Belgian Embassy), 1829, by *Adolf Schuch*. Next door, **Bank** building [48], good Art Nouveau, 1904–6, by *Gustav Landau*.

✦✦ **Grand Theatre** [49] (opera house), 1833, by *Antonio Corazzi* in collaboration with *Adolf Schuch* and *Aleksander Kozubowski*. Balcony on columns at entrance 1893. Rear of building enlarged in 1950s. Right wing houses Polish Theatre **Museum**. When it was built, it was one of the greatest buildings in the city, echoing the importance attached to opera as a form of national self-assertion at the time.

Later 19th-century buildings of note:
Land Credit Society building [50], neo-Renaissance, 1854, by

Henryk Marconi. Now houses Ethnographical **Museum**, with the best collection in Poland of folk costumes and arts. Also surprisingly rich holdings of African, South American and Pacific material.
Zachęta Art Gallery [51], 1898-1903, by *Stefan Szyller*. **Europejski Hotel** [52], 1856, by *Henryk Marconi*.
Bristol Hotel [53] 1899-1901, by *Władysław Marconi*.
Polytechnic [54] main building, with spectacular great hall in exuberant neo-Renaissance style, 1900, by *Stefan Szyller*. **Cooperative Banks Building**, proto-modernist, 1912-17, by *Jan Heurich jr.* ✦

Twentieth-century Modernism:
National Museum [57], built 1926–38, by *Tadeusz Tolwiński*. ✦✦✦
The origins of the collections go back to the last king of Poland, Stanisław Augustus, who was an outstanding collector as well as patron of the arts, and who intended to build a *Muzeum Polonicum* to house his acquisitions. Nothing came of these plans, though a number of his paintings form the nucleus of the collection.
The holdings are very uneven, based partly on surviving pre-war contents, private collections confiscated or left after 1945, and more recent acquisitions. The museum has suffered from chronic underfunding and other difficulties, and is not able to exhibit more than a small part of its collection.
Antiquities: as well as a number of private collections (those of Stanisław Kostka Potocki, Izabela Działyńska, Elżbieta Lubomirska) and some objects from the museums in Wrocław and Szczecin, the collections include a deposit from the Louvre and a number of objects from Polish digs conducted in the 1930s and 1950s. Apart from Egyptian and Coptic objects, there are some important Greek pieces, outstanding Etruscan vases and fine Byzantine frescoes.
Foreign Painting: North European, including works by *Cranach*, *Jost van Cleve*, *Momper*, *Breughel*, *Savery*, *Jordaens*, *Fabritius*, *Terborch*. Italian, including works by *Pinturicchio*, *Gentile Bellini*, *Botticelli*, *Cima da Conegliano*, *Guercino*, *Preti*, *Giordano*, *Tiepolo*, *Belotto*. French, including works by *Philippe de Champaigne*, *Vouet*, *Greuze*, *Hubert Robert*, *Nattier*, *Courbet* and *David*.
Medieval Art: gallery of painting and sculpture, with many tryptichs from Pomerania and Silesia. Figure of 'Beautiful Madonna' from Wrocław and magnificent Madonna with Saints from Wróblewo.
Polish painting: an important collection, from the 16th to 20th centuries. Most important is the holding of 19th-century Polish painting, well worth closer acquaintance, with all the major artists well represented.

The museum also has a good collection of sculpture, both Polish and foreign, miniatures, a small but delightful gallery of Polish decorative arts, and some far eastern collections, mainly of ceramics. There is also a large collection of drawings and prints, of medals and coins, and textiles.

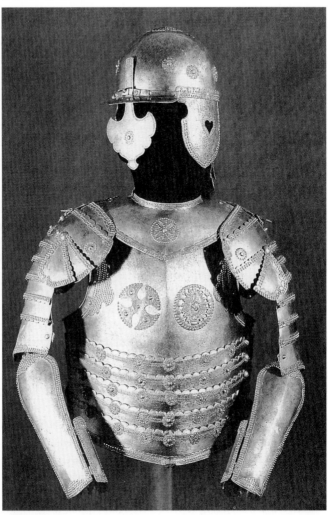

✦✦✦ **Polish Army Museum [58]**, housed in a wing of the National Museum. Collection includes arms and armour, acoutrements, graphic materials and mementoes of military figures, covering the whole history of Poland, right up to the Second World War. Among the highlights are 17th-century arms and armour, saddlery and acoutrements of the winged cavalry (husaria), and good uniforms from the period of the Kościuszko Insurrection of 1794 and the Napoleonic Wars.

The **Sejm**, 1925-8, by *Kazimierz Skórzewicz*. An elegant and functional if uninsipired building.

Ministry of Education Building on Aleja Szucha, 1927-30, by Zdzisław Maczewski. This fine building became the Gestapo headquarters during the war. There is now a **museum** of martyrology in the basements where so many were tortured.

The Ghetto:

In 1940 the Germans began hoarding all the Jews of the capital into the Muranów district, which they turned into a Ghetto. From here they were taken by train to their deaths in Treblinka or other camps. On 19th April 1943 the Jews began to resist openly, and their rising lasted until 3rd May, when German troops overan the whole area. Their struggle is commenmated by the **Ghetto Uprising Memorial**, built in 1948 by *Natan Rappaport* and *Leon Marek Suzin* with materials brought to Warsaw by Hitler for a victory monument. A **Path of Rememberance** marks the death-march from the Ghetto to the place where the people were entrained for Treblinka. Nearby stand the ruins of the Pawiak prison, where some 35,000 Poles and Jews were killed, now a **museum**.

Stalinist city centre:

MDM [55], the 'Central Residential Quarter' on Constitution Square, 1949–52, by *Stanisław Jankowski*, *Jan Knothe* and others. A terrific ensemble of gigantic and massive architecture, sumptuously clad in granite, with outsize bas-reliefs of heroic workers and breeders. As with all Stalinist architecture, a certain prissiness and a lack of proportion ruin the effect. "Mais c'est Place Vendôme!" General De Gaulle is said to have exclaimed when he saw it, presumably in one of his infrequent bouts of humour.

The **Joseph Stalin Palace of Culture** [56], 1952–5, after the design by *Lev Rudniev*, a 'gift' to Warsaw from the Soviet Union. This 234-metre high monstrosity, housing offices, theatres, cinemas, scientific insitutes, and now a casino as well, was executed throughout in the finest materials, including marble, crystal, mahogany and lashings of gold leaf.

The '**White House**', 1948-51, formerly the headquarters of the Polish United Workers' Party, now the Warsaw Stock Exchange.

Other Museums:

Archdiocesan Museum [59], located in small building adjacent to the church of the Holy Trinity on Powiśle. A good collection of mainly sacral art, including pictures, textiles and metalwork.

Railway Museum [60], located in former Warsaw Main Station, with a large collection of engines and rolling-stock.

Marie Curie Museum, ul Freta 16, in the house where she was born.
Museum of Hunting, located in a pavilion in Lazienki Park.

Ujazdow and Łazienki:

✦ **Parish church** of St Alexander [61], a neo-Classical rotunda dating
from 1818–25, by *Piotr Aigner*. Sculpture of Christ in sepulchre,
17–18th century, workshop of *Bernini*. At this church begin the
Aleje Ujazdowskie, originally a Calvary way, laid out 1731 by *Johann
Sigismund Deybel*. Lining it on one side, a number of fine 19th-cen-
tury villas, including Ślesiński villa [62], second quarter of 19th century, by *Antonio Corazzi*, and Sobański villa, 1876, by *Leandro
Marconi*.

✦ **Ujazdów castle** [63], originally a small summer retreat of the dukes
of Mazovia, embellished in the 1520s with Italian gardens laid out
for queen Bona Sforza, wife of Zygmunt I. In the early 1600s,
Giovanni Trevano built for King Zygmunt III a substantial residence on a square castle plan, with four towers and a loggia on the
Vistula side. This was devastated by the Swedes in 1655, and rebuilt
in the 1660s for its new owner, Prince Stanisław Herakliusz
Lubomirski, by *Tilman van Gameren*. In 1766 the castle was
acquired by king Stanisław Augustus, who commissioned a number of projects for its complete rebuilding as his Versailles or
Caserta, but he ran out of funds, and after a fire he donated the gutted shell to the state, which turned it into barracks. Devastated
again in 1944, the castle has been essentially rebuilt in its original
early 1600s shape, but it remains in a raw state, and now houses the
Museum of Contemporary Art.
Astronomical Observatory [64] 1824, by *Piotr Aigner* and *Michal
Kado*.

Belvedere Palace [65], rebuilt 1822 by *Jakub Kubicki* as the residence of Grand Duke Constantine, Tsar Alexander's and later Nicholas I's lieutenant in the Kingdom of Poland. Between 1919 and 1939 it was the presidential residence.

Ujazdów Gardens, former game park of Ujazdów castle, 17th century, cut across for Augustus II by canal and radial avenues, 1728, by *Burchard Christoph von Münnich*. Redesigned for Stanisław Augustus 1774–80, by *Agricola* and *Schulz*, as formal and landscape park surrounding

Łazienki Palace [66]. This is one of the most beautiful buildings in ✦✦✦ Europe, a perfect jewel of a small residence. Originally a bathhouse of Grand Marshal of the Crown Stanisław Herakliusz Lubomirski, 1683-90, by *Tilman van Gameren*, rebuilt for Stanisław Augustus 1775–88, by *Domenico Merlini*. Interiors 1788 and northern elevation 1793–5, by *Jan Chrystian Kamsetzer*, except for one original baroque bath-chamber. Furnished with some good Polish and French furniture, pictures (mainly portraits, by Bacciarelli and others, and old masters) and sculpture from the collection of the last king. Hermitage [67] 1690, by *Tilman van Gameren*, rebuilt 1778 by *Merlini*.

The **White House [68]** 1777, by *Merlini*, with painted decoration by ✦✦ *J.B.Plersch*, a perfect example of a small 'casino' designed to accomodate the king's principal mistress while he was in residence at Łazienki. Louis XVIII of France lived here as an exile from 1801 to 1804.

Myślewicki palace [69] 1778, by *Merlini*. Painted decoration by ✦ *Plersch*. In the days of the last king, his favourite nephew, Prince Jozef Poniatowski, lived here.

Old **orangery [70]**, with collection of sculpture, and **theatre** 1788, by *Merlini*, with decoration by *Plersch*. The only surviving 18th-century court theatre in Europe, still fully equipped with stage machinery.

Island theatre [71], 1790, by *Kamsetzer*. Stage with artificial ruins on island, and amphitheatre on opposite bank. Old guardhouse [72] 1794, by *Kamsetzer*. New guardhouse 1830, by *Jakub Kubicki*. Temple of Diana [73] and Egyptian bridge, ca. 1820 by *Kubicki*.

Mokotów:
Originally an escarpment made fashionable by Princess Elżbieta Lubomirska under the name of 'Mon Coteau' from which it derives its present name. At the end of the 18th century it was dotted with villas and "casini" in which the Warsaw aristocracy played.
Mokotów **toll-gates [74]**, 1818, by *Jakub Kubicki*.
Villa of Princess Elżbieta Lubomirska [75](now Warsaw Music ✦✦

Society) 1773, by *Ephraim Schröger*, rebuilt for Anna Dunin-Wąsowicz in neo-Gothic style, 1825, by *Henryk Marconi(?)*. Landscape park ca. 1775, with Romantic pavilions, 1786, by *Szymon Bogumił Zug*.

✦ Palladian **villa** known as "Królikarnia" [76], built 1789 by *Domenico Merlini* for the theatrical entrepreneur and royal pimp Carlo Thomatis.

Czerniaków:

Bernardine monastery [77], founded by Grand Marshal of the Crown Stanisław Herakliusz Lubomirski, 1694, by *Tilman van Gameren*. Stucco and pictorial decoration and reliquary of St Boniface contemporary. Flemish triptych 16th century.

✦✦✦ **Wilanów** [78]:Originally 'Villanuova', a country retreat built for Jan III Sobieski, ca. 1680, by *Augustyn Locci*. Sculptural decoration by *Andreas Schlüter* and others, pictorial decoration by *Michelangelo Palloni* and *Jerzy Eleuter Siemiginowski*. Wings by *Giovanni Spazzio* added 1725 for new Sieniawski owners, south wing altered 1730 by *Johann Sigismund Deybel*. In 1759, Wilanów passed by marriage to Prince August Czartoryski, who gave it to his

daughter Elżbieta, who had married Prince Stanisław Lubomirski. She added the guardhouse, 1776, by *Szymon Bogumił Zug*. It then passed to the husband of one of her daughters, Stanisław Kostka Potocki, patron of the arts and Minister of Education in the 1820s. The north wing was altered 1848, by *Franciszek Maria Lanci*. In the late 19th century the house passed to the Branicki family, and is now a **museum**. The interiors are furnished with the original contents, most of which survived the war. This includes good Italian,

French and Polish furniture, old master pictures and family portraits (including the magnificent equestrian portrait of Stanisław Kostka Potocki by *Jaques Louis David*), and objects.

Formal park 1682, with parterres, terraces, espaliers and canal, redesigned with addition of landscape parts and Romantic "Grove" at Morysinek, 1799–1821, by *Stanisław Kostka Potocki, Piotr Aigner* and *Wojciech Jaszczołd*. Neo-Classical villa with angle rotunda, 1811 by *Potocki* and *Aigner*. Farm buildings in Romantic manner, early 19th century, by *Potocki, Aigner* and *Jaszczołd*. Riding school 1848, by *Lanci*. Now a **museum** of poster art.

Natolin [79], a lovely neo-Classical villa built for Elżbieta Lubomirska 1782, by *Szymon Bogumił Zug*, altered 1808 by *Stanisław Kostka Potocki* and *Piotr Aigner*. Painted decoration by *Vincenzo Brenna*, stuccoes by *Fryderyk Baumann*. Interiors partly redone in Romantic manner 1845. Landscape park, 18th-19th century, with Doric temple 1834, by *Henryk Marconi*. Farm buildings, 1st half of 19th century, by *Aigner* and *Marconi*. Now the seat of the Warsaw branch of the College d'Europe.

Northern districts:

Warsaw Citadel [80], earth and brick bastion fortress with ✦ caponiers and batteries, 1834, by *Ivan Dehn*. Built after the 1830–1 insurrection as a warning to the Poles not to try to cause trouble again. Four outer forts 1849–65. Bielany, Powązki and Execution Gates by *Andrzej Goloński(?)*. In Pavilion X, small **museum** dedicated to insurgents and revolutionaries imprisoned there before execution.

Camaldolite monastery in Bielany **[81]**, founded 1639 by ✦ Władysław IV. Church with Baroque chancel 1669, and octagonal nave flanked by chapels 1758. Portraits of kings second half of 17th century. Note 14 monks' hermitages.

Praga:

Loreto chapel [82] (relict of Bernardine monastery founded by ✦ Władysław IV), 1645, by *Costantino Tencalla(?)*.
River **toll-house**, 1808. Grochów **toll-gates [83]** 1816, by *Jakub Kubicki*. Neo-Gothic **church** of St Florian, 1888 by *Józef Pius Dziekoński*.

WARTA   MAP 12 ✦✦
Bernardine monastery founded 1467, altered 1721. Church of the Assumption, rebuilt 1764. St Anne's chapel 1612. Painted decoration Rococo, third quarter of 18th century, by *Father Walenty Żebrowski*. Painting by *Tommaso Dolabella*. Tomb of the Blessed

Raphael of Proszowice 1640. Gothic murals in monastery building first half of 16th century.

WĄWELNO   MAP 9
Parish church 1767, by *David Fetzel*.

♦♦ WĘGRÓW   MAP 25
Collegiate church of the Virgin Mary and the Apostles Peter, Paul and Andrew. Original Gothic church burnt by Swedes under Charles XII in 1703. Present splendid building commissioned by Count Jan Bonawentura Krasiński and built 1703–7 by *Carlo Cerone*. Painted decoration 1708, by *Michelangelo Palloni*. Twin bell-towers 1706, by *Tilman van Gameren*. **Reformed Franciscans' monastery** founded 1669 by Krasiński, built 1693, by *Tilman van Gameren*. Church of St Peter of Alcantara and St Anthony of Padua 1710. Paintings by *Michelangelo Palloni*, furniture early 18th century, epitaph in memory of Jan Bonawentura Krasiński 1703 (metal parts by *Andreas Mackensen*). Typical Mazovian market-place, with interesting Baroque **inn**, mid-18th century.

♦ WEJHEROWO   MAP 8
Reformed Franciscans' church founded by Jakub Weyher, 1648. Calvary with 26 chapels, 1655, remodelled 18th and 19th centuries.

♦ WEŁNA   MAP 9
Wooden **church**, 1727. Furniture and painted decoration 1727, by *Adam Swach*.

WIĄZOWNA   MAP 18
Neo-Classical **parish church**, 1788.

♦ WIDAWA   MAP 12
Bernardine monastery, 1638. Painted decoration in church after 1750, furniture early 18th century.

♦♦ WIĘCŁAWICE   MAP 21
Wooden **parish church** of St James the Minor, 1748. Gothic triptych and figure of Madonna.

WIELEŃ   MAP 4
Parish church, 1632. Painted decoration contemporary. On the opposite bank of the river Noteć, at Wieleń Północny, **country house** of Sapieha family, mid-18th century, remodelled after 1784 and 1920. Burnt 1945 but restored.

WIELGOMŁYNY   MAP 19 ✦✦

Pauline monastery, ca. 1466, remodelled 17th-18th century. Chapels 1717 and 1726. Furniture 18th century. Heavily restored. Brass of three knights of the Koniecpolski family, ca. 1475; an outstanding piece, probably made in Kraków. Some 15th-century furniture.

WIELICZKA   MAP 21 ✦✦✦

Unique **salt mine**, worked since 11th century. Every time a pocket of salt was worked out, the miners would carve the remaining rock-salt 'lining' into the interior of a chapel. Hence numerous underground **chapels**. Most notable are St Anthony's chapel 1675, by miner *Kuczkiewicz*, and Holy Cross chapel, 17th century. Small **museum** of mining and the history of Wieliczka. Splendid miniature train built for the Emporor Franz Josef when he visited the mine.

WIELUŃ   MAP 12 ✦✦

Augustinian monastery, founded 1217. Church of Corpus Christi ca. 1350, altered 1497 and 1677. Monastery building 18th century. **Pauline monastery** (now Bernardine convent) founded 1393 by Władysław, Duke of Opole. Altered and rebuilt several times. **Reformed Franciscans' church** of the Annunciation, 1629, facade mid-18th century. **Piarist church**, 1740. Kraków **gate** ca. 1350, superstructure 16th century.

WIERUSZYCE   MAP 21

Gothic/Renaissance **manor house**, 1531.

WIERZBICA GÓRNA   MAP 12

Protestant church, timber, 1722. Baroque **manor house**, 1791, with murals.

WIERZBIE   MAP 12

Wooden Gothic **church**, 16th and 18th century.

WIERZBIĘCICE (OPPERSDORF)   MAP 13

Romanesque **church**, mid-13th century, repeatedly rebuilt. Tower 1576.

WIERZBNA (WURBEN)   MAP 6

Romanesque **parish church**, ca. 1230, rebuilt 15th century, expanded first half of 18th century.

✦ WIGRY   MAP 23

Camaldolite monastery founded by Władysław IV. Church 1704–45, by *Pietro Putini*.

✦ WILCZA   MAP 14

Wooden **parish church**, mid-18th century, by Master Carpenter *J.Sedlaczek*.

✦ WILCZKÓW (HERDHAUSEN)   MAP 11

Parish church, 15th century, with important furniture. Churchyard wall with loopholes, first half of 17th century.

✦ WILKANÓW (WOLFELSDORF)   MAP 6

Country house, 1686, by *Andrea Carove*, partly rebuilt 18th century. Stables before 1736.

✦ WILKOWO POLSKIE   MAP 4

Parish church, ca. 1540. Gothic sculptures. Defensive bell-tower, second half of the 15th century.

✦✦ WIŚLICA   MAP 20

Collegiate church of the Navity of St Mary, founded by Kazimierz the Great in 1350. The best example of south-Polish double-nave 'hall' church. Murals Ruthenian-Byzantine, 1397. Carved memorial tablet 1464, altar fronts and sculpture Gothic. Bell-tower founded by Jan Długosz ca. 1465. Canon's house 1460.

✦✦ WIŚNICZ NOWY   MAP 22

Parish church founded by Prince Stanisław Lubomirski 1621, by *Mattia Trapola*. Furniture 17th century. Fortified **Discalced Carmelites' monastery** also founded by Lubomirski, 1634, also by *Trapola*. Church and underground burial chapel, with stuccoes by *Giovanni Battista Falconi*. Burnt 1942.

Castle, built in 15th century for Kmita family, rebuilt for Stanisław Lubomirski 1621, by *Trapola*, as a classic 'palazzo-in-fortezza'. Grand interiors, with mid-17th-century stucco work by *Giovanni Battista Falconi*. Bastion Fortifications of new Italian type 1621, by *Trapola*. Marvellous Mannerist gate 1621.

Town Hall ca. 1620, by *Trapola*, superstructure 19th century.**Jewish cemetery** with 17th–19th-century tombstones.'Korzynówka' **manor house**, 19th century. Private **museum** um in memory of the painter Jan Mateyko, who used to stay here.

WITKOWICE   MAP 22
Neo-Classical **manor house**, early 19th century, by *Jakub Kubicki.*

WITÓW   MAP 22 ✦✦
Premonstratensian abbey founded 1185. Church, originally erected
before 1240, present structure 1784. Stuccoes 1750, by *Feliks
Urbański.* Organ after 1758. Gate tower 1470, raised early 19th century.

WIZNA   MAP 25
A fortified settlement recorded in the 11th century. **Parish church** of
St John the Baptist, 1526; virtually destroyed in 1944, reconstructed
1951–8.

WŁOCŁAWEK   MAP 10 ✦✦
Important regional centre from medieval times.
Cathedral of the Assumption [1] 1340, expanded 15th century,
restored 1893 by *Konstanty Wojciechowski.* Chapter house ca. 1530.
St Mary's chapel founded by Bishop Jan Tarnowski, 1611, by *Samuel
Świątkowicz.* Stained glass ca. 1360. Painting of Assumption before
1475, by Master *Franciszek* of Sieradz. Tomb of Bishop Piotr of
Bnin, 1493, by *Veit Stoss.* Renaissance bronze chandelier, 1563.

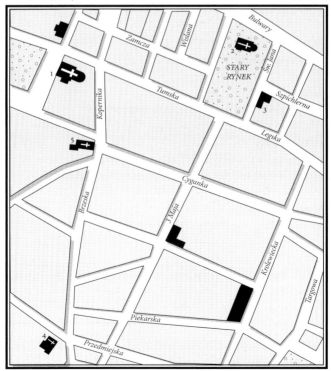

Parish church of St John [2], Gothic, 1538. Renaissance chapel of the Five Wounds of Christ, 1565.

Church of St Vitalis [5], 1330. Triptych mid-15th century.

Reformed Franciscans' church and monastery [4] 1644, towers 1761. Museum [3].

◆◆ WŁODAWA   MAP 28

Market town and important centre of Jewish life from the seventeenth century onwards. **Pauline church** of St Louis, founded 1741 by Pociej family. Present ellyptical church ca. 1780, by *Paweł Fontana*. Furniture, sculpture and painted decoration contemporary, by *Marceli Dobrzeniewski*. Monastic building 1717, by *Józef Piola*.

Fine **Synagogue,** 1767, now a **Museum**.

WŁODZICE WIELKIE (GROSS WALDITS)   MAP 6

Gothic **parish church**, first half of 16th century.

◆ WŁOSZAKOWICE   MAP 4

Parish church on cruciform plan, ca. 1640, workshop of *Cristoforo Bonadura(?)*. **Country house** built for Sułkowski family, on triangular plan, 1751, by *Karl Martin Frantz(?)*. Reworked in 19th century. The composer Karol Kurpiński was born here in 1749.

WŁOŚCIEJEWKI   MAP 11

Parish church, early 16th century.

WODZIERADY   MAP 12

Baroque wooden **manor house**, early 19th century.

WODZISŁAW   MAP 19

Synagogue, converted in 17th century from a Calvinist meeting house of the second half of the 16th century. Now a ruin.

WOJCIECHÓW   MAP 27

Tower-dwelling, beginning of 16th century.

WOJKOWICE KOŚCIELNE   MAP 19

Parish church, originally Romanesque after 1200, repeatedly expanded to 1750.

◆ WOJNICZ   MAP 22

Parish church, 15th century, altered ca. 1754 and 20th century Painted decoration Rococo, 1767, by *Jan Neydorfer*.

WOJNOWICE (WÖHNWITZ)   MAP 11 ✦
Country house in the form of a small castle, surrounded by water, built 1513 for a rich banker of Wrocław in the Gothic style to suggest noble origins. A charming place.

WOJSŁAWICE   MAP 28
Parish church 1690, by *Jan Michal Link*.

WOLA GUŁOWSKA   MAP 27
It was here, on 5 October 1939 that the last battle was fought by regular Polish troops under General Franciszek Kleeberg against the invading Germans. **Carmelite monastery** 1633. Church after 1680.

WOLA RADZISZOWSKA   MAP 21
Wooden **church**, 16th century, spire 19th century. Late Gothic and Renaissance furniture.

WOLBÓRZ   MAP 19 ✦
Very grand summer **palace** of the bishops of Kuyavia, 1626, rebuilt 1773 by *Francesco Placidi*. Ranges and pavilions 1773.

WOŁÓW (WÖHLAU)   MAP 11 ✦
Residence of the dukes of Oleśnica, registered as a town in 1285. **Castle** of the dukes of Oleśnica, mid-14th century, expanded 16th century, rebuilt 18th-20th century. **Parish church** of St Lawrence 1391, vaults after 1465, interior redecorated 1711. **Carmelite monastery**, 1712. Church 1781. **Town Hall** with tower, second half of 15th century, expanded 18th century, remodelled 1820.

WOLSZTYN   MAP 4 ✦
Parish church 1767. Painted decoration 1778. Neo-Classical **country house** 1845.

WOŹNIKI   MAP 14
Reformed Franciscans' church, 1723 by *Giovanni Catenaci*, badly damaged 1945, reconstructed 1978.

WOŻUCZYN   MAP 28
Parish church 1742. **Guardhouse** of vanished residence of Wilhelm Mier (descended from Scottish Muirs), second half of 18th century.

An ancient settlement and capital of the Slav tribe known as the Slęzanie/Slesanii, who gave their name to the province of Silesia. Wrocław became a bishopric within the Polish province of the Church in the year 1000. In 1138 Silesia was one of the five duchies into which Poland was split, to accomodate the sons of king Bolesław the Wrymouth. In the following century, Silesia itself fragmented further into four duchies, and while they continued to be ruled by Polish Piast princes, its formal links with the Polish state grew progressively weaker. In the 15th century, Silesia was lumped into the kingdom of Bohemia, then ruled by a Polish Jagiellon prince. It was still part of the Polish world, and in 1475 the first printed work in Polish appeared here. But in 1520 the city left the Polish political orbit for four centuries, although Polish continued to be the language of the street in Habsburg and later in Prussian and German Breslau.

In 1945 the German army defended the city with determination, only surrendering on 6th May, after Berlin had fallen. The resulting damage was devastating. The city and the whole of Silesia was sliced off Germany in accordance with the Yalta settlement of 1945 and awarded to Poland. A large proportion of the population and the movable heritage of Lwów, the city Poland lost in the east to the Soviet Union, was moved, lock stock and barrel, to the bombed-out ruins of Wrocław, abandoned by the fleeing German inhabitants.

Ostrów Tumski:

✦✦✦ **Cathedral** of St John the Baptist [1], on the site of an earlier Romanesque cathedral. Choir and amublatory 1244, nave and aisles 1302–76.

St Mary's chapel, founded by Bishop Przecław of Pogorzela, 1361, by Master *Peszko*. North tower 1419, superstructure of south tower 1574. South side chapel before 1400, north chapel before 1520. Western galilee 1468, incorporating 12th-century Romanesque columns. Sacristy portal 1517. Murals 15th century. Stalls 1665, pulpit 1723, by *Johann Adam Karinger*, with bas-reliefs by *Jan Jerzy Urbański*. Tomb of Bishop Przecław of Pogorzela ca. 1376, workshop of *Peter Parler*. Bronze tomb of Henryk, Duke of Legnica ca. 1400. Tomb of Johann Roth 1496, by *Peter Vischer*. St Elizabeth's chapel, with sculptural and pictorial decoration, 1679–82, by *Giacomo Scianzi*. Bust of Cardinal Friedrich of Hesse ca. 1668, school of *Bernini*; tomb of same 1683, by *Domenico Guidi*. Altar with sculpture by *Ercole Ferrata*, 1683. Elector's chapel, with altar and epitaph in memory of Bishop Franz Ludwig von Neuburg, 1716–24, by *Johann Bernhard Fischer von Erlach*; stucco by *Santino*

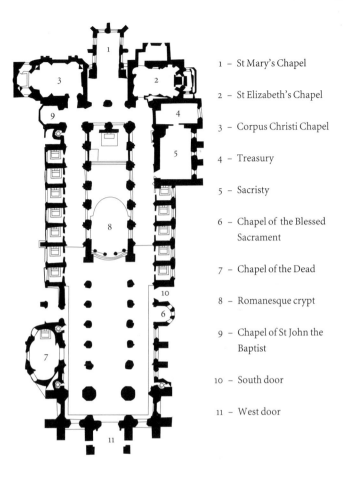

1 – St Mary's Chapel

2 – St Elizabeth's Chapel

3 – Corpus Christi Chapel

4 – Treasury

5 – Sacristy

6 – Chapel of the Blessed
Sacrament

7 – Chapel of the Dead

8 – Romanesque crypt

9 – Chapel of St John the
Baptist

10 – South door

11 – West door

Bussi; dome painted by *Carlo Innocenzo Carlone*; sculpture by *Ferdinand Maxmilian Brokoff*; paintings by *Jan Frans de Backer*. Chapel of the Blessed Sacrament ca. 1675. Chapel of the Dead 1750. **Bishop's palace** [2] 1790s, by *Karl Gottfried Langhans* and *Karl* ✦ *Gottfried Geissler*. **Provost's house** (present Bishop's Palace) 1794, ✦ *Karl Gottfried Geissler*. **Canons' houses**, mostly with Baroque ✦ facades, mainly 16th-17th centuries. **Chapter-house** 1519, portal ✦✦ 1527, now archdiocesan **museum**. Good collection of medieval painting and sculpture, textiles, and gold and silverware, including some very fine pieces.

Romanesque **church** of St Giles [3], first half of 13th century.

Two-tier **collegiate church** of the Holy Cross [4] (with lower church ✦✦ of St Bartholomew), founded by Prince Henry IV. East end 1280, by Master Mason *Wieland*, completed mid-14th century. Aisle vaults 1371, by Master Mason *Günter*. Sculptural decoration late 14th cen-

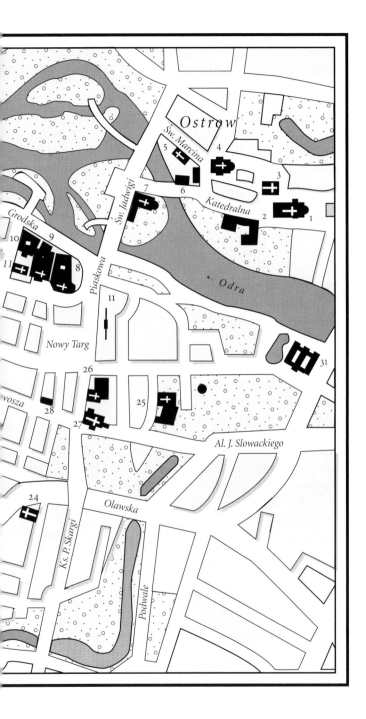

tury. Triptychs, paintings and sculpture Gothic. Tomb of Canon S. Sauer 1533.

Orphanage with decorative facade, 1710, by *Johann Blasius Peintner*.

Church of SS Peter and Paul [**6**], 15th century.

Piasek:

♦♦ **Augustinian monastery** [**7**], founded 1134. Church of St Mary, 1375 by master mason *Peszko* and others, aisle vaults 1395. Side chapels added late 14th-15th century and one, Baroque, 1666. In the south aisle there is a small but good Romanesque stone tympanum from the mid-12th century, immortalising the foundation. Monastic building (now university library) with decorative facade and stuccoed interior 1730, east wing 1789, by *Karl Gottfried Geissler*.

Church of St Anne 1386. Portal, end of 15th century.

Old and New Town:

♦♦ **Church** of St Vincent [**8**] (originally Franciscan church of St James, since 1530 Premonstratensian church) founded by Henry the Pious 1256, rebuilt 14th century. Domed Hochberg chapel, on plan composed of intersecting ovals, 1723 by *Christoph Hackner*.

♦ **Premonstratensian monastery** 1699, by *Hans Frohlich*.

Poor Clares' convent [**9**] (now Ursulines) 1701, by *Johann Georg Knoll*. Church of St Clare 1257.

St Matthew's **church** of the Knights Hospitallers of the Holy Cross [**11**], mid-13th century; polygonal arms of transept and chancel 14th

♦ century; tower completed 1487. **Monastery** of the Knights Hospitallers of the Holy Cross, founded before 1254, present building 1675–1715, designed by *Jean-Baptiste Mathieu(?)*. Houses **Ossolineum** [**10**] (Ossoliński Foundation, founded 1817 by Józef Maksymilian Ossoliński in Lwów, moved to Wrocław after 1945), a collection of some 30,000 prints, 9,000 Polish and 1,000 foreign drawings, also miniatures, old photographs, coins, medals and seals.

Jesuit church [**12**] 1698, built by *Matthäus Biener*. Painted decoration 1706, by *Johann Michał Rottmayer*. Baroque furniture 1730, by *Christoph Tausch*, with sculpture by *Johann Albrecht Siegwitz*

♦♦ and others. **Jesuit college** (now university, founded in 1726 by the Emperor Leopold I), in the form of a long palace with decorated pilastered facades and rich main portal. Inside, decorated staircase and pharmacy with painted decoration by *Felix Anton Scheffler*. Auditorium or '*Aula Leopoldiana*' with frescoes by *Johann Christoph Handke*, sculpture by *Johann Albrecht Siegwitz* and *Franz Josef Mangold*, 1734; a very important Baroque interior.

Jesuit boarding school of St Joseph (now Polish Academy of Sciences), 1755.

Parish church of St Elizabeth [**14**], first half of 14th century. Tower ✦✦
completed 1458, spire 1535. Polygonal Dumlosy chapel 1405. Stone
tabernacle 1455, by *Iodokus Tauchen*, Baroque furniture, organ 1751,
by *Michael Engler* and *Johann Albrecht Siegwitz*. Several hundred
tombs and epitaphs in honour of burghers and civic officials.
Gate 1728, by *Christoph Hackner*.

City Arsenal [**15**] 1578, rebuilt mid-18th century. ✦

Parish church of St Barbara [**16**], 14th century; expanded with addition of towers, ca. 1400. Chancel with sacristy, second half of 15th
century. Stone sculpture of St Barbara ca. 1500.

Reformed Franciscans' church [**17**] (later Sisters of St Elizabeth), ✦
1692.

Church of Divine Providence [**18**] (formerly Calvinist), 1750 by
Johann Baumann.

Spatgen palace [**19**], later royal palace, ca. 1715 expanded 1763, by
Johann Baumann. Facade 1797, by *Karl Gottfried Langhans* and
Karl Gottfried Geissler, wings 1868. South front 1846 by *Friedrich
August Stüller*. Now Archaeological **Museum**.

Stock Exchange [**21**]1826, by *Karl Friedrich Langhans*. ✦

Town Hall [**30**], second half of 13th century, rebuilt and expanded ✦✦
1504, by *Hans Berthold, Bricius Gauschke, Paul Preusse* and others.
An important building, with good interiors and a collection of pictures and silver.

Market Square, with merchants' and burghers' houses, incorporating Gothic elements, 14th–15th century, with gables and mostly
baroque facades.

Parish church of St Mary Magdalen [**29**](since 1525 Protestant ✦✦
church), late 13th-mid–14th century. Chancel 1371, by Master
Mason *Peszko*, vaults of two central bays ca. 1470. Side chapels ca.
1400. Sacristy expanded and heightened ca. 1470. Towers completed 1481. On south side, carved Romanesque stone portal, late
12th century, moved 1546 from Benedictine church in Olbin on the
outskirts of the city. Mannerist portal 1578.

Neo-Classical **Hatzfeld palace** [**28**], 1774, by *Karl Gottfried
Langhans*.

Pachaly palace [**20**] (now university library), 1679, rebuilt 1785 by
Karl Gottfried Langhans, expanded in neo-Classical style 1810 by
Langhans.

Dominican convent [**26**] with church of St Catherine, 1378 and second half of 15th century. Main portal 1740.

Dominican monastery [**27**] founded 1241 by Dominicans from
Kraków. Church of St Wojciech 1260. Church raised and vaulted

1492. Chancel ca. 1300, tower finished 1359. Chapel of the Blessed Czesław, with pictorial decoration and furniture by *Georg Leonhard Weber* and others, 1730.

Bernardine church [25] 1502, altered 1704. Monastic building 15th–16th century, now **museum** of architecture.

Church of St Christopher [24], early 15th century. Tower 1461 and 1575. Annexes 1610.

✦✦ **Augustinian church** of St Dorothy and St Stanisław [22], founded 1351 by Charles IV. Chancel 1381, body proper ca. 1400, by Master Mason *Peter*. Gable mid-15th century. Baroque portals early 18th century. Baroque furniture from end of 17th and first half of 18th centuries. Tomb of H.F. von Spatgen Rococo, 1753 by *Franz Josef Mangold*.

✦✦ **Church of the Knights Hospitallers** of St John of Jerusalem [23] (Corpus Christi) begun ca. 1350, gable ca. 1450.

Town walls 13th–15th century.

✦✦ **National Museum** [31], with a very good collection of Medieval painting and sculpture, some old masters, porcelain and glass, and plenty of eastern textiles, from the Lwów collections.

Office building, 1910, by *Hans Poelzig*.

✦ 'Jahrhunderthalle', 1912–13, by *Max Berg*, a spectacular early use of concrete, to create one of the first great modern stadiums, built to commemorate Germany's great "Patoriotic War" against Napoleon in 1813.

Market house, 1927, by *E. Mendelsohn*.

Suburbs:
Church of the 11,000 Virgins (now St Joseph's), 1823, by *Karl Friedrich Langhans*. **Hospital church** of St Lazarus, second half of

✦ 14th century. **Monastery** and church **of the Hospitallers of St John of God** 1724, by *Johann Blasius Peintner*. Monastic building (now hospital) expanded 1736 and second half of 19th century.

In suburb of MUCHOBOR WIELKI: **parish church** with vault supported on single spiral pillar, ca. 1500, expanded 1914.

WRONKI   MAP 4
Dominican church, after 1650, by *Cristoforo Bonadura(?)*.

✦✦ WSCHOWA (FRAUSTADT)   MAP 4
Important market town in the late middle ages, with a licence to mint coinage in the 16th century, and a centre of weaving from the 17th century. **Parish church** of St Stanisław 1726, by *Pompeo Ferrari*. Part of chancel 14th century, with Gothic vault, 1552–76, tower ca. 1580. Painted decoration and furniture 18th century. **Bernardine**

monastery (now Franciscan) founded 1456. Church 1639, by *Cristoforo Bonadura*. Tower added and church redecorated 1772. Monastic building 17th century, expanded 18th century. Arcaded gallery in front of church ca. 1730. **Protestant church** of Old Town, 1604, reconstructed after 1644 and after 1685. Neo-Romanesque **Town Hall** 1870, tower first half of 16th century. Burghers' **houses**, second half of 17th–18th century.

WYSOCICE   MAP 21 ✦

Parish church of St Nicholas, early 13th century. Portal and sculpture of Madonna contemporary. A well-preserved example of an ashlar Romanesque village church, the only later additons being a Gothic pulpit, ca. 1500, and a Baroque spire.

WYSOKA   MAP 9

Church of Lateran Canons 1729. Furniture contemporary.

WYSOKA CERKIEW   MAP 4 ✦✦

Parish church with pilgrimage complex, 1724. Tower ca. 1860. Furniture ca. 1724. Stairs with terraces and sculpture ca. 1736. Chapel of the Mount of Olives 1755. Fifteen small Rosary chapels ca. 1660.

WYSOKIE KOŁO   MAP 27 ✦

Dominican monastery and church, 1685. Painted decoration second quarter of 18th century.

WYSZKÓW   MAP 29

Parish church 1788. Neo-Classical furniture ca. 1790.

WYSZYNA   MAP 10 ✦✦

Interesting wooden **parish church**, sixteen-sided and centrally-supported, 1782. Ruin of Renaissance **castle** of Grodzicki family, second half of 16th century.

ŻABIN   MAP 4

Parish church, early 14th century.

ZĄBKOWICE ŚLĄSKIE (FRANKENSTEIN)   MAP 11 ✦✦

An early medieval settlement registered as a town in 1287, drawing its wealth from gold and silver mining. **Castle** of the dukes of Ziębice, originally 14th century, rebuilt as a Renaissance residence in 1532 by *Benedikt Ried*. **Parish church**, 14th–15th cents, much restored. **Dominican monastery** founded before 1302. Church 1669, tower 1714. Monastic building before 1687. Refectory ca. 1515. **Town walls** with towers, mid-14th century, superstructure first half of 16th century. Neo-Gothic **Town Hall** 1860s, by *A.Langer*.

ZABÓR (FÜRSTENEICH) MAP 4
Country house 1683, rebuilt in Rococo style 1745.

ZABORÓW MAP 18
Neo-Classical **parish church**, 1791. Vicarage 1840.

ŻAGAŃ (SAGAN) MAP 4
Capital of Piast duchy of same name, which later became the fief of the 30 years war general Albrecht von Wallenstien, who was made Prince of Sagan in 1628. The title passed through various families, including the Birons of Kurland, to Talleyrand, who sported Prince de Sagan among his titles from 1806.

Augustinian monastery founded 1284. Church of St Mary early 14th century, expanded 15th century. Vaulting 16th century. Renaissance arcaded courtyard in front of facade 1603. Furniture 18th century, altar ca. 1600, tomb of Henry V the 'Iron Duke' of Fłogów (d.1369), whose daughter Jadwiga married Kazimierz the Great, mid-14th century. Monastic building 1737.

Franciscan monastery founded 1294, later Jesuit College. Church of SS Peter and Paul 14th–15th centuries. Chancel after 1514, tower 1604. College building late 17th century, auditorium 1733. North wing second half of 18th century. Rebuilt in neo-Classical style after 1810.

Church of the Holy Ghost 1702. Furniture contemporary. Chapel of the Holy Sepulchre, early 17th century.

Country house of Lobkowitz, later Biron and Talleyrand families, 1674, by *Antonio della Porta*, incorporating remnants of Wallenstein palace, 1634. Interior redecorated 1792, by *Christian Valentin Schultze*, 1822, by *Gottlieb Schlegel*, and later. Neo-Classical orangery 1846, by *Leonhard Dorst von Schatzenberg*. Bridges over moat 1804, by *Johann Gottlieb Fellet*.

Town house, ca. 1800, by *Christian Valentin Schultze*.

Stalag VIII German **POW Camp**, with small **museum.** Nearby are two other camps for Allied airmen, Luft III Sagan and Luft IV Bellaria.

ZAGÓRZANY MAP 22
Neo-Gothic **country house** 1839, by *Franciszek Maria Lanci*, expanded 1928.

Castle of the dukes of Świdnica, later of Łagów family. Upper castle first half of 14th century, modified and expanded 1587 with addition of the foregate, the lower courtyards, the surrounding wall with rondelles, and the gatehouse. Some 19th-century romantic restorations.

Church of Knights Hospitallers of St John of Jerusalem founded 1166 by Henry, Prince of Sandomierz. Romanesque chancel from end of 12th century expanded in Gothic style 1353, also in 17th century, and 1901.

Parish church of St Giles 1739–68, with Rococo furniture. Attached to it is the older Lanckoroński chapel, 16th–17th centuries. **Reformed Franciscans' monastery** 1650. Wooden **Town Hall**, houses, granaries, shrines, and other vernacular buildings, 18th-19th century.

Part of a highland estate of Count Władysław Zamoyski, who donated it to the nation in 1919, this mountain resort became very

fashionable among Poland's artistic set from the 1880s onwards. They came to breathe the fresh air, to get away from social convention, to paint the scenery, to marvel at the music and folklore of the local highlanders (or have affairs with them).

Many picturesque turn-of the century villas, including the composer Karol Szymanowski's **Villa Atma**, and the **Villa Pod Jedlami**, 1897, designed in the vernacular style by *Stanisław Witkiewicz*, father of the writer and painter Stanisław Ignacy Witkiewicz (Witkacy).

Also **Tea House**, and the Jan Kasprowicz **museum**. Several other galleries and museums, including **Tatra Museum**.

Baroque wooden **church** of St Clement, 1851.

Neo-Gothic **church** 1876–96, by *Józef Pius Dziekoński*.

ZAKROCZYM MAP 18

Parish church,of the Exaltation of the Holy Cross, second half of 16th century.

ZAKRZEWO MAP 10

Wooden Carmelite **church**, 1745. Former convent building 1857.

ZALEWO MAP 15

Parish church, 1351. Tower 1407, rebuilt 19th century.

✦ ZAMARTE MAP 7

Bernardine monastery and church founded by Castellan Jan Grabowski, 1746. Stucco and painted decoration 1778, by Brother *Paschalis Wołos*.

✦✦✦ ZAMOŚĆ MAP 28

Ideal city founded from scratch in 1584 by Jan Zamoyski, Grand Hetman and Chancellor of Poland. After studies at the Sorbonne, the Collège de France and the University of Padua, of which he became Rector, and a political career which yielded the highest rank, he built up a vast fortune. By 1600 he owned 6,500 square kilometres of land in one block, and as much again in other parts of the country. It was as a capital and economic centre for this main block of land that Zamoyski intended Zamość. Being a passionate humanist, he was determined to create a city which would provide an 'ideal' environment and embody all the aspirations of the age. He chose the Mannerist architect *Bernardo Morando* of Padua (1540–1600), and collaborated with him actively on the layout of the town, the fortifications and most of the important buildings. Part of Zamoyski's programme was to create a reflection of the world, and he therefore encouraged the settlement of diverse elements. As a result the city had a very mixed population including Jews, Ruthenians, Armenians, Scotsmen, Italians and Magyars as well as Poles. After the first partition of Poland in 1772, the city itself, which was a formidable fortress, was expropriated by the Austrian government, which turned the palace into a barracks and neglected the city as a whole. The fortress was still modern enough to withstand a protracted siege by the Russians in 1813, when it was held for the Napoleonic Duchy of Warsaw. The famous revolutionary Rosa Luxemburg was born here in 1871. During the Second World War, the whole province was the subject of a major change of population, with the Germans removing all natives, leaving only young children with blond hair and blue eyes, who were given to incoming German colonists. The city was renamed 'Himmlerstadt' and intended to be a bastion of Germanness in the east.

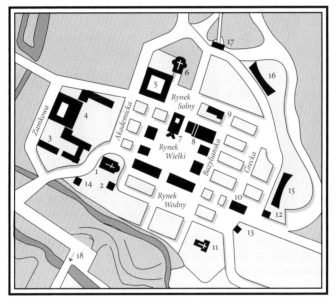

Collegiate church of St Thomas [1] (now cathedral of the Resurrection), founded by Jan Zamoyski, 1587, by *Bernardo Morando*. Stucco in Zamoyski chapel ca. 1634, by *Giovanni Battista Falconi*. Two chapels redecorated 1770, by *Jerzy de Kawe*. Italian font, mid-17th century. Bell-tower ca. 1825. Tomb slab of Jan Zamoyski 1610. Underneath, crypt containing coffins of three Zamoyski chancellors and other members of the family. This church was a prototype for a whole group of late Renaissance/Mannerist churches built over southern and eastern Poland, and is one of the first late Renassiance churches in the

country. "Infułatka" or deanery, 1620, housing small **museum [2]**, with vestments and sacral objects.

Palace of Jan Zamoyski **[4]** 1586, by *Morando*. Expanded with addition of galleries and wings, and two flanking buildings, 1751, by *Jan Andrzej Bem* and *Jerzy de Kawe*. Further altered after 1831.

Academy [5] 1648, by *Jan Jaroszewicz,* renovated 1761, by *Jan Andrzej Bem* and *Jerzy de Kawe*, and in neo-Classical style ca. 1825. This building housed the university, founded in 1594. **Theological Faculty Building** 1648, partly rebuilt ca. 1816.

Town Hall [7] begun 1591 by *Morando*, completed 1651, by *Jan Jaroszewicz* and *Jan Wolff*. Guardhouse with external stairs added 1770. Rear wings 1825, by *Louis Mallet*. Great **Market Square**, with houses 1590–1650 harmonized by arcaded passage and decorative parapet (much of which has been lost). No 23, with Mannerist vault decoration, 1591–9, by *Morando*. No 25, Morando's own house, begun 1599. City **Museum** [**8**], with exhibition of portraits of Zamoyski family and city notables, furniture, arms and armour, objects associated with the university, etc.

Synagogue [**9**] (now public library) with stucco decoration, first quarter of 17th century, expanded 18th century.

Franciscan **church** [**10**], now a cinema.

Orthodox (now Redemptorist) **church** [**11**], with Renaissance/Mannerist decoration, 1631, by *Jan Jaroszewicz(?)*.

Fortifications with bastions, on Italian system, 1587–1605, by *Morando*, completed 1619 by *Andrea del Aqua*, modernized 1694, by *Jan Michał Link*, outer earth ramparts added 1812, and further expanded 1831, by *Louis Mallet*, and later, up to 1866. New Lublin Gate 1822. North-eastern cavalier [**16**] 1835, by *Bernard Engbricht* and *Friedrich Rossman*. Eastern cavalier by same, 1830. Old Lwów Gate [**12**] 1599, by *Morando*, rebuilt 1821. New Lwów Gate [**13**], 1820, by *Jan Paweł Lelewel*. Szczebrzeszyn Gate [**14**] 1605, by *Błażej Gocman*, rebuilt 1770, 1825 in neo-Classical style, and second half of 19th century. Battery or rotunda [**18**]. Now a monument to the victims of German repression.

ZARĘBY KOŚCIELNE   MAP 25
Reformed Franciscans' monastery with Baroque Church, second half of 18th century.

ŻARNÓW   MAP 19
Romanesque **parish church** of St Nicholas, second half of 12th century, expanded by addition of chancel, 1510. Now constitutes transept of church erected 1903, by *Stefan Szyller*.

ŻARNOWIEC   MAP 8
Cistercian (from 1590 Benedictine) **convent**, founded 1220. Present church and monastery 14th-15th century.

ŻARY (SORAU)   MAP 3 ✦
An old settlement on the salt route. **Parish church** of St Mary, first quarter of 15th century. Tower superstructure second half of 16th century. Promnitz chapel 1672. Remodelled 1694. Furniture Baroque, late 17th century. Priest's house with Gothic gables, early 16th century, remodelled 1684 and 1733. **Franciscan monastery** founded 1274. Church of St Barbara, 14th–15th century, altered 1728. **Biberstein palace**, 14th–15th century, rebuilt in Renaissance style, with addition of arcaded galleries in courtyard, 1549. Stucco 16th century. Tower rebuilt in Baroque style ca. 1700. Buildings on south side ca. 1700. **Promnitz palace** (New Castle) 1705-26, by

J.F.Spanninger, Giulio Simonetti and others.Georg Philip Telemann was *Kapellemeister* here from 1704 to 1708.**Garden palace** (now hospital), completed 1723. **Town walls** 15th century. Bell-tower 1563.

✦ ZARZECZE   MAP 22

Neo-Classical Romantic **country house** of Morski family, 1819, by *Piotr Aigner*, stucco *Fryderyk Baumann*, expanded 1911. Park, with ranges and orangery, early 19th century.

ZATOR   MAP 21

Parish church 1393, rebuilt 1766 in Baroque style. Neo-Gothic **country house** 1836, by *Franciszek Maria Lanci*, based partly on walls of the castle of the Piast dukes, built after 1445.

✦ ZAWICHOST   MAP 27

Franciscan convent founded by Bolesław the Shy, in 1245 for his sister Salomea, after her husband's death in battle against the Tatars. Church ca. 1250, east wing of convent contemporary. Baroque **church** of St Mary ca. 1740, built on foundations of a Romanesque church.

ZBĄSZYN   MAP 4

Parish church 1757–96, by *Karl Martin Frantz(?)* Fortifications of **castle**, completed 1627. Gate tower partly reconstructed 1916.

✦ ZBORÓWEK   MAP 22

Wooden **parish church** 1459, expanded in brick 1908. Late Gothic triptychs and sculpture.

ZBYLITOWSKA GÓRA   MAP 22

Neo-Classical Romantic **manor house**, first half of 19th century.

✦ ZBYLUTÓW   MAP 6

Romanesque **parish church**, mid-13th century. Tower, sacristy and nave vault supported on central pillar, ca. 1492.

✦ ZBYSZYCE   MAP 22

Parish church, before 1447, with important furniture. Timber tower 18th century.

ZDUNY   MAP 11

Wooden Baroque **parish church** 1721, tower 1733. **Protestant**

church, Baroque, 1792, by *Johann Friedrich Hansen*. Baroque **Town Hall** 1684, expanded 19th century. Timber **houses** 18th century.

ZDUŃSKA WOLA   MAP 12
Birthplace of St Maksymilian Kolbe, martyred in Auschwitz. Neo-Classical **weavers' houses**, many wooden, second quarter of 19th century.

ZEBRZYDOWICE   MAP 21
Parish church of St Michael, 1602. Furniture contemporary. Renaissance Zebrzydowski family **manor house**, second half of 16th century. Expanded into hospital 1599, and 19th century.

ŻELAZKÓW   MAP 12 ✦
Radoliński family **manor house**, begun 1796, by *Franciszek Lessel*. Expanded by addition of curving colonnades, ranges, stables and ancillary building, first quarter of 19th century, by *Sylwester Szpilowski(?)*.

ŻELAZOWA WOLA   MAP 17 ✦
Birthplace of the composer Fryderyk Chopin. Outbuilding of vanished Skarbek family **country house**, before 1810, reconstructed as **Chopin Museum** in 1931. Everything about this place is phoney - when Chopin was born, the house had a beaten earth floor and none of the graceful ambiance it has now. See also BROCHÓW and SANNIKI

ŻELISZEW   MAP 25
Baroque **manor house** 1786, superstructure 19th century.

ŻEMBOCIN   MAP 21
Parish church, mid-13th century, expanded late 17th century.

ŻERKÓW   MAP 9 ✦
Parish church with ornate stucco work, 1718. Renaissance Roszkowski chapel 1600.

ZIĘBICE (MÜNSTERBERG)   MAP 11 ✦✦
Capital of a Piast duchy 1322–1428. **Parish church** of St Mary and St George 1275, chancel second half of 14th century, facade 1898. Two chapels 1423. Murals, tabernacle, triptychs and sculpture Gothic. Gabled parish hall 16th century. **Church of Knights Hospitallers of the Holy Cross** 1730. Neo-Classical Protestant **church** 1798, by *Karl Gottried Langhans*. **Town walls** late 13th-mid-14th century, super-

structure first half of 16th century.

✦ ZIELONA GÓRA (GRÜNBERG)   MAP 4
Parish church of St Jadwiga, mid-15th century. Chapels 16th century. Tower 1832. Timber **church** of Our Lady of Częstochowa (originally Protestant) 1748. Tower and facade neo-Classical, 1821–8. **Town Hall** 16th century, repeatedly rebuilt.

✦ ZIELONKI   MAP 21
Parish church of St Mary 1533, by *Jakub Żur* and *Kasper Simon*. Nave 1538, by *Jan Kapinos* and *Jan Bocheńczyk*, expanded 1899.

✦ ZŁOCZEW   MAP 12
Renaissance **parish church** 1619, by *Georg Hoffman*. **Bernardine church** of the Holy Cross, on a quatrifoil pattern, 1607.

ZŁOTORIA   MAP 10
Ruins of **castle**, originally 1370–77, rebuilt by king Władysław Jagiełło 1420 after his victory over the Teutonic Knights.

ZŁOTORYJA   MAP 6
A Medieval gold-ming settlement. **Parish church** 1241; nave first half of 14th century, eastern tower 1500, sacristy first half of 16th century. Renaissance pulpit 1583.

✦ ZŁOTÓW (FLATOW)   MAP 11
Parish church founded 1660 by Jędrzej Karol Grudzieński, Palatine of Poznań. **Protestant church** 1830, by *Karl Freidrich Schinkel*. **Country house** in the form of a castle, before 1850, also by *Schinkel*.

ZŁOTÓW   MAP 11
Baroque wooden **church**, originally Protestant, 1754.

ŻÓŁKIEWKA   MAP 27
Cradle of the Żółkiewski family. **Parish church**, ca. 1770. Decoration 1776, by *Gabriel Sławiński*.

✦ ŻÓRAWINA   MAP 11
Parish church, mid-14th century. Interior decoration 1602. Fortifications first half of 17th century, by *Valentin von Säbisch(?)*.

ŻORY   MAP 14
Parish church of St Philip and St James, late 13th-early 14th century, partly rebuilt early 16th century. Baroque chapels, late 17th century.

ŹRÓDŁA   MAP 11

Romanesque stone **church**, 1220s. Churchyard wall early 17th century.

ZUBRZYCA GÓRNA   MAP 21

Open-air folk building **museum**, with group of wooden buildings typical of Orawa and Żywiec regions from the 18th-19th centuries. Moniak farmstead in folk Baroque 1784, expanded 1813.

ŻUKOWICE (HERRNDORF)   MAP 4

Church, 15th century. Tower and mauzoleum 1587. Baroque **manor house** 1743, with remnants dating from 1586.

ŻUKOWO   MAP 8 ♦♦

Premonstratensian convent, founded 1209. Present church before 1375, altered 17th century. Sculpture Gothic, altars early 16th century. Fine 16th-century triptych from Antwerp. Surviving convent buildings 14th-17th centuries.

ŻUROMIN   MAP 17

Town founded by Chancellor Andrzej Zamoyski in 1765, on site of medieval settlement. **Jesuit college** (later Reformed Franciscans' monastery) church 1715–80.

ZWIERZYNIEC   MAP 27 ♦

Game park established by the Zamoyski family ca. 1600. Baroque **chapel** on the island, 1741. Overbuilt remnants of hunting palace.

ZWIERZYNIEC   MAP 13

Hunting lodge 1714, by *Christoph Tausch*(?) and *Michael Klein*. Stucco 1722.

ZWOLEŃ   MAP20 ♦

Parish church 1595. Kochanowski sepulchral chapel with epitaph of the poet Jan Kochanowski, 1610. Owadowski chapel 1620s.

ŻYROWA (BÜCHENHOH)   MAP 14

Gaszyński family **country house**, 1644, restored at turn of 19th century. **Parish church** ca. 1300, rebuilt in Baroque style first half of 18th century.

ŻYRZYN   MAP 27

Baroque wooden **manor house**, late 18th century.

ŻYTOWIECKO   MAP 11
Baroque **parish church**, 1777. Furniture contemporary.

ŻYWIEC   MAP 14
Parish church, first half of 15th century. Nave expanded 1583. Tower
with gallery 1585, by *Giovanni Ricci*, spire 1745. Renaissance
Komorowski chapel 1608. Bell-tower 1724. **Church** of the Holy
Cross. Chancel before 1428, nave 1690, tower 1910. Komorowski
family **castle** (Wielopolski from 1697 and Habsburg from 1838 to
1939) ca. 1500; expanded 1569 in Renaissance style, with addition of
arcaded courtyard. Some further alterations 1721 and third quarter
of 19th century. Farm buildings 1709. Chinese pavilion, second half
of 18th century. Open air **museum** of local vernacular wooden
architecture.

HISTORICAL GLOSSARY

Augustinians (Augustyni, Augustianie). Followers of the rule of St Augustine, including Augustinian Friars and Canons. The former were an eremitical order which evolved in the 13th century in Italy. As Martin Luther was an Augustinian, the order was brought into disrepute during the Reformation, but it has survived in several European countries. The Augustinian Canons arose from the Lateran Synod's (1509) pressure on groups of secular priests attached to cathedrals and collegiate churces to live according to some form of manstic rule. Some chose the rule of St Benedict, but many opted for that of St Augustine.

Arians (Arianie). see Polish Brethren.

Basilians (Bazylianie). Order of Orthodox monks based on the rule of St Basil (ca. 330-379).

Benedictines (Benedyktyni). Monastic order founded by St Benedict of Nursia (ca. 480—ca. 543) at Subiaco and later Monte Cassino on the rule named after him.

Bernardines (Bernardyni). Named after St Bernardino of Siena, an offshoot of the Franciscans who claimed to be closer to the rule of St Francis.

Bohemian Brethren (Bracia Czescy). see Polish Brethren.

Camaldolites (Kameduli). Religious order founded by St Romuald, a Benedictine monk who formed a colony of hermits near Ravenna in the tenth century. The order takes it name from his main colony at Camaldoli in the Appenines.

Canons Regular. Secular priests living together in communities often practised adapted versions of the rule of St Benedict or of St Augustine, the latter being known as Canons Regular or Augustinian Canons (see above).

Capuchins (Kapucyni). Off-shhot of the Franciscans, originating in 1520, when a group of friars of that order decided to return to a stricter form of observance and adopted the habit with pointed hood (capuche) that they believed St Francis had worn. They specialised in preaching and ministering to the poor.

Carmelites (Karmelici, Karmelitanki). Religious order founded by a Calabrian crusader knight, who established himself with a group of friends in a cave on Mount Carmel in the middle of the 12th century. Under threat from the Saracens, in 1240 they moved to Cyprus, and thence to Europe. Owing to the difficulties of pracitsing the eremitical life in Eruope, the order was transformed into one of mendicant friars. The rule was progressively relaxed until the nun Teresa from the Carmelite house at Avila founded a stricter observance in 1562. Owing to their return to the original foootwear of sandals, they became known as barefoot or discalced Carmelites.

Carthusians (Kartuzi). Monastic order founded by St Bruno and six companions at Chartreuse outside Grenoble in 1084. The Carthusian rule, written down in 1130, is one of great austerity and provides for an almost eremitical life.

Castellan (Kasztelan). Originally the king's lieutenant in a given area, later a titular office. Castellans had a seat in the Senate.

Cistercians (Cystersi). Strictly observant branch of the Benedictine order, established in 1098 by St Robert at Citeaux in Burgundy. In 1112 St Bernard came to Citeaux and inspired an expansion of the order through the creation of four great 'daughter' houses, at La Ferté, Pontigny, Clairvaux and Morimond, which, by the end of the century, had spawned over 500 communities.

Collegiate Church (Kolegiata). Church with a community (college) of lay priests - i.e. not members of an order

Commonwealth (Rzeczpospolita). The Polish Commonwealth was established by the Union of Lublin in 1569. It comprised the Kingdom of Poland, the Grand Duchy of Lithuania, Royal Prussia, the Palatinate of Livonia and the Duchy of Kurland.

Confederation (Konfederacja). An association of szlachta who came together either in a national emergency, or as a sign of protest, or as a provincial assembly. A confederation elected a marshal and acted as a parliamentary body. If it was a nationwide movement, it would form into two branches, one Polish and one Lithuanian. A confederation could also be declared within the Sejm, at which point all legislation was passed by majority vote.

Congress Kingdom (Królestwo Kongresowe, Kongresówka). The Kingdom of Poland created by the Congress of Vienna in 1815, with the Tsar of Russia as king. It lasted until 1830.

Discalced Carmelites (Karmelici Bosi). see Carmelites.

Dominicans (Dominikanie). Order of preaching friars founded by St Dominic at Toulouse in 1215, based on the rule of St Augustine.

Franciscans (Franciszkanie). Religious order founded by St Francis of Assisi in 1209. The friars travelled about preaching and earning their daily bread by working, but after the death of its founder, the order began to grow rich and to found permanent houses and churches.

Galicia (and Lodomeria). Name given by Austria to the provinces it acquired from Poland in the partitions. A pseudo-latinisation of the Duchies of Halicz and Włodzimierz.

Hanseatic League (Hansa). A trading organisation set up by the mercantile cities of the Baltic and the North Seas.

Hasidism. Jewish fundamentalist movement which started in eastern Poland in the 18th century.

Hetman. The highest military rank. The Grand Hetman and the Field Hetman of the Crown commanded the Polish army, the Grand Hetman and the Field Hetman of Lithuania the Lithuanian. The Grand Hetman of the Crown had overall command. The Hetmans did not have ministerial rank, but could attend the sessions of the Sejm at the king's side.

Hospitallers. Order of the Knights Hospitallers of St John of Jerusalem, founded in the Holy Land in the 11th century to care for sick pilgrims and defend the pilgrimage routes and shrines. They later fell back on Rhodes, and later still on Malta, becoming known as Knights of Malta in later centuries.

Hussites. Followers of Jan Hus, the Czech heretic who was burnt at the stake at the Council of Constance 1415.

Jesuits (Jezuici). Name commonly given to members of the Society of Jesus, a religious order founded in 1540 by St Ignatius Loyola. The order was abolished in Poland following the Papal brief of 1773 suppressing it, and its wealth was used to fund the Commission for National Education. The Society was restored by Papal bull in 1814.

Kashubians (Kaszubowie). A non-Slavic people that have survived in northern Poland, mostly on the coast.

King (Król). The King of Poland was also the Grand Duke of Lithuania, Duke of Prussia and Livonia, and overlord of Kurland. After 1572 he was elected for life by the whole szlachta of the Commonwealth.

Kuyavia (Kujawy). Province of central Poland.

Kurland, Duchy of. The rump of the state of the Knights of the Sword, which acceded to the Commonwealth in 1551 as a vassal duchy.

Lithuania, Grand Duchy of (Litwa, Wielkie Księstwo Litewskie). Comprised nine Palatinates, covering not only ethnic Lithuania, but also a large section of White Russia (Byelorussia, Belarus).

Livonia, Palatinate of. Originally like Kurland, it was incorporated directly into the Commonwealth.

Małopolska (Lesser Poland). The soputhern of the two core provinces of the Kingdom of Poland.

Marshal of the Sejm. The lower chamber of the Sejm elected two marshals, one for Poland, one for Lithuania, who presided alternately and were responsible for the conduct of proceedings.

Mazovia (Mazowsze). Large province including the land around and to the north of Warsaw, part of the Kingdom of Poland until 1138, when it was ruled autonomously by its own branch of the Piast dynasty. The last of the Mazovian Piasts died in 1526, and Mazovia rejoined the Kingdom of Poland.

Ministers. The Grand Marshal of the Crown and the Marshal of Lithuania were responsible for home affairs; The Grand Chancellor of the Crown and the Chancellor of Lithuania for foreign affairs, assisted by the Vice-Chancellor of the Crown and the Vice-Chancellor of Lithuania; the Grand Treasurer of the Crown and the Treasurer of Lithuania managed the state finances; the Crown Court Marshal and the Court Marshal of Lithuania managed the royal revenues.

Missionaries. The Pious Society of Missions, a religious congregation founded in Rome in 1835 by the Blessed Vincenzo Palloti. Devoted to spreading the word of God, the priests of the congregation are often called 'Pallotines' after their founder.

Oratorians (Oratorianie). Religious order founded by St Philip Neri of Florence in 1575 to spread the word of God by preaching and prayer.

Pacta Conventa. Conditions, drawn up by the Sejm convoked at the death of a king, under which the prospective monarch could rule. The king elect had to swear to honour these before he could be crowned. If he defaulted on them, his subjects could refuse him their loyalty.

Palatinate (Województwo). Administrative provincial unit.

Palatine (Wojewoda). originally the royal governor of a province, later largely honorific title that went with nomination to the Senate. Wojewodas were revived in the 20th century, and are nominated by the President.

Pallotines (Palotyni). see Missionaries.

Paulines (Paulini). Order of monks founded in Hungary in the13th century emulating the hermit St Paul of Thebes, and following the rule of St Augustine.

Piarists (Pijarzy). Popular name of a Catholic educational order, the 'Clerici Regulares Scholarum Piarum', founded in Rome by Joseph of Calasanza in 1617. The Piarists played a leading role in the reform of education in Poland in the 1740s.

Piast. First royal dynasty of Poland, whose main, royal, line died out with King Kazimierz the Great in 1370, but lingered on through his niece Queen Jadwiga, who died in 1399. Other branches of the family, ruling a selection of duchies in Silesia and Pomerania, survived for a couple more centuries. The last Piast ruler, George William of Legnica, died in 1675.

Poland, Kingdom of (sometimes referred to as 'the Crown', Korona). Comprised the provinces of Wielkopolska (Greater Poland), which consisted of twelve Palatinates; Małopolska (Lesser Poland), which consisted of eleven Palatinates; and Royal Prussia, which consisted of three Palatinates and the episcopal principality of Warmia.

Polish Brethren (Bracia Polscy). Originally a polonisation of the Bohemian Brethren, Protestants in the tradition of Jan Hus rather than Luther, who settled in Poland at the beginning of the sixteenth century. The Polish Brethren included a number of variants, and they were often also known as Arians (after Arius, who at the Council of Nicea in AD 235 voiced their two fundamental tenets - the human nature of Christ and the rejection of the Trinity), or as Socinians, after Fausto Sozzini, one of their chief lights. They believed in a gentle and rather literal enactment of the teachings of Christ, and they were expelled from Poland for refusing to bear arms during the Swedish invasion of 1655.

Poor Clares (Klaryski). Order of contemplative nuns founded by St Clare along the same lines as that of her friend St Francis.

Premonstratensians. Order of Canons founded in 1120 by St Norbert, a friend of St Bernard of Clairvaux. They follow a strict version of the Rule of St Augustine. Sometimes aslo known as Norbertines, they take their name from a place in France, Prémontré, where St Norbert established the first monastery.

Primate. The Archbishop of Gniezno, head of the Church in Poland, senior member of the Senate and, during an interregnum, supreme authority (*interrex*) in the Commonwealth.

Royal Prussia. The segment of the state of the Teutonic Knights that was incorporated into Poland in 1466 (the remainder became a vassal duchy of Poland in 1520, seceded in 1656, and became part of the kingdom of Prussia).

Senate. Upper chamber of the Sejm, consisting of 136 senators, including 17 bishops, 32 Palatines, 86 Castellans and one Starosta, all of them appointed by the king.

Sejm. National Parliament, meeting once a year for four weeks, with possible extensions. Once every three years it met not at Warsaw, but at Grodno in Lithuania. The lower chamber consisted of 178 deputies elected by the szlachta at local assemblies called Sejmiks. The upper (Senate) and lower chambers of the Sejm would sit separately for purposes of debate, and join together to legislate, under the supreme presidency of the king. The name was taken up by the modern parliament in 1919, and is used today.

Silesia (Śląsk). Area originally inhabited by the western Slav tribe of the Ślęzanie which became part of the Polish state under Bolesław the Brave (992-1025). In 1138, when the kingdom was divided up between Bolesław III's five sons, Silesia went to the eldest. It was subsequently divided up further between his children and grandchildren

Starosta. Incumbent of a starosty, originally the king's officer and magistrate in a given area, later an honorific title granted by the king.

Starosty (starostwo). An estate belonging to the Crown, granted in life tenure to a deserving citizen, with the understanding that he paid one-quarter of the estate's revenues into the Treasury.

Szlachta. The nobility, or rather the noble caste that made up some 7 per cent of the population and enjoyed full political rights and exemption from taxation in return for its alleged preparedness to fight for the country.

Templars. Order of Knights of the Temple in Jerusalem, founded in the 12th cent to defend the Holy Places from the Saracens, suppressed in 1312.

Teutonic Order (Krzyżacy). The Teutonic Order of the Hospital of St Mary in Jerusalem, founded in Acre in 1197 on the model of the Templars. After the fall of Acre they transferred their crusading activities to Hungary, but the Hungarian king soon grew wary of their territorial and political ambitions and expelled them. In 1226 Duke Konrad of Mazovia invited them to set up a commandery at Chełmno in order to help him combat the heathen Prussian tribes.

They conquered large areas of Prussian land, gaining a strong territorial base in the process. After the attack on the Templars, they transferred their headquarters to Prussia in 1309 and became, in effect, a state. They were defeated several times in war with Poland, and from 1466 were allowed to hold Prussia only as vassals to the Polish Crown. In 1520 the knights went over to Luther and the Order was secularised. The incumbent Grand Master, Albrecht of Hohenzollern, became Duke of Prussia and paid homage to the King of Poland. His successors seized every crisis in Poland to loosen the bond of vassalage and to tighten that with their cousins the Electors of Brandenburg. The two Hohenzollern inheritances eventually fused, and in 1701 the Elector of Brandenburg Frederick declared himself 'King in Prussia'.

Titles. The Polish commonwealth did not recognise titles of nobility on principle, but families of Lithuanian or Ruthene dynastic origin, such as the Czartoryski, Czetwertynski, Massalski, Oginski and Sanguszko were allowed to bear the title of prince. Somewhat inconsistently, the Sejm of 1658 bestowed the title of count on the Chodkiewicz family, the Sejm of 1764 that of prince on the brothers of Stanisław Augustus Poniatowski, that of 1768 one of prince on the Sapiehas, and that of 1773 on the Ponińskis. All other titles borne by Polish families were given either by the Holy Roman Empire, or by Austria, Russia, Prussia, the Holy See, etc.

Uniates (Unici). Sometimes also known as Greek Catholics. Christians of the Eastern Rite who accepted the supremacy of the Pope in return for being allowed to keep their own liturgy and practices, by the Union of Brześć in 1596.

Visitation, Nuns of the (Wizytki). Order founded by St Francis of Sales in 1610 at Annecy in Savoy. Their mission was to visit the poor and give them spiritual comfort, but this was soon found to be impracticable, and they turned into a contemplative order.

Warmia (Ermeland). Episcopal principality in Royal Prussia in which the bishop was temporal as well as spiritual ruler.

Wielkopolska (Greater Poland). One of the two core provinces of the Kingdom of Poland

POLISH KINGS AND PRINCES

THE PIAST DYNASTY

Mieszko I, 960-992
Bolesław the Brave, 992-1025
Mieszko II, 1025-1034
Kazimierz the Restorer, 1034-1058
Bolesław the Bold, 1058-1079
Władysław Herman, 1079-1102
Bolesław the Wrymouth, 1102-1138

Period of Fragmentation:

Władysław II the Exile, 1138-1146
Bolesław the Curly-headed, 1146-1173
Mieszko III the Old, 1173-1177
Kazimierz II the Just, 1177-1194
Mieszko III the Old, 1194-1202
Władysław Spindleshanks, 1202
Leszek the White, 1202-1210
Mieszko Tanglefoot, 1210-1211
Leszek the White, 1211-1227
Władysław Spindleshanks, 1228-1229
Konrad I of Mazovia, 1229-1232
Henry the Bearded, 1232-1238
Henry the Pious, 1238-1241
Konrad I of Mazovia, 1241-1243
Bolesław V the Chaste, 1243-1279
Leszek the Black, 1279-1288
Henry IV Probus, 1288-1290

Period of Reunification:

Przemysł II, 1295-1296
Vaclav II of Bohemia, 1300-1305
Vaclav III of Bohemia, 1305-1306
Władysław the Short, 1306-1333
Kazimierz III the Great, 1333-1370

THE ANGEVIN DYNASTY

Louis of Hungary, 1370-1382
Jadwiga (Hedwig) of Anjou, 1384-1399

THE JAGIELLON DYNASTY

Władysław II Jagiełło, 1386-1434
Władysław III of Varna, 1434-1444
Kazimierz IV the Jagiellon, 1447-1492
Jan I Olbracht, 1492-1501
Aleksander I, 1501-1506
Zygmunt I the Old, 1506-1548
Zygmunt II Augustus, 1548-1572

THE ELECTED KINGS

Henri de Valois, 1574-1575
Stephen Bathory, 1576-1586
Zygmunt III Vasa, 1587-1638
Władysław IV Vasa, 1632-1648
Jan II Kazimierz Vasa, 1648-1668
Michał Korybut Wiśniowiecki, 1669-1673
Jan III Sobieski, 1674-1696
Augustus II the Strong of Saxony, (house of Wettin), 1697-1706
Stanisław I Leszczyński, 1704-1709
Augustus II the Strong, 1709-1733
Stanisław I Leszczyński, 1733
Augustus III of Saxony (house of Wettin), 1733-1763
Stanisław II Augustus Poniatowski, 1764-1795

DUCHY OF WARSAW 1807-1814

Frederick Augustus of Saxony (house of Wettin), 1807-1814

KINGDOM OF POLAND 1815-1830

Alexander II (Alexander I of Russia), 1815-1825
Nicholas I (Nicholas I of Russia), 1825-1830.

ROYAL FAMILY TREES

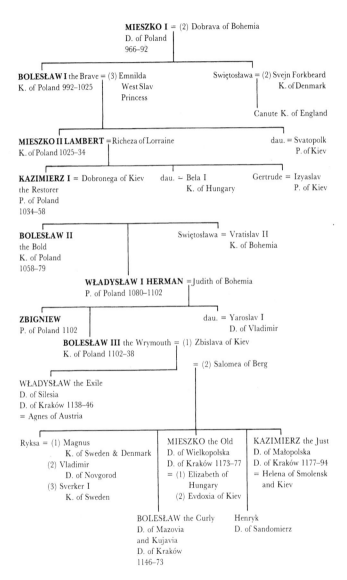

MIESZKO I = (2) Dobrava of Bohemia
D. of Poland
966–92

BOLESŁAW I the Brave = (3) Emnilda
K. of Poland 992–1025   West Slav
Princess

Świętosława = (2) Svejn Forkbeard
K. of Denmark

Canute K. of England

MIESZKO II LAMBERT = Richeza of Lorraine
K. of Poland 1025–34

dau. = Svatopolk
P. of Kiev

KAZIMIERZ I = Dobronega of Kiev
the Restorer
P. of Poland
1034–58

dau. = Bela I
K. of Hungary

Gertrude = Izyaslav
P. of Kiev

BOLESŁAW II
the Bold
K. of Poland
1058–79

Świętosława = Vratislav II
K. of Bohemia

WŁADYSŁAW I HERMAN = Judith of Bohemia
P. of Poland 1080–1102

ZBIGNIEW
P. of Poland 1102

dau. = Yaroslav I
D. of Vladimir

BOLESŁAW III the Wrymouth = (1) Zbislava of Kiev
K. of Poland 1102–38

= (2) Salomea of Berg

WŁADYSŁAW the Exile
D. of Silesia
D. of Kraków 1138–46
= Agnes of Austria

Ryksa = (1) Magnus
K. of Sweden & Denmark
(2) Vladimir
D. of Novgorod
(3) Sverker I
K. of Sweden

MIESZKO the Old
D. of Wielkopolska
D. of Kraków 1173–77
= (1) Elizabeth of
Hungary
(2) Evdoxia of Kiev

KAZIMIERZ the Just
D. of Małopolska
D. of Kraków 1177–94
= Helena of Smolensk
and Kiev

BOLESŁAW the Curly
D. of Mazovia
and Kujavia
D. of Kraków
1146–73

Henryk
D. of Sandomierz

1   *The early Piast kings. (Only the more important members of the dynasty are shown. Dates given are those of reigns. The family tree continues overleaf.*

297

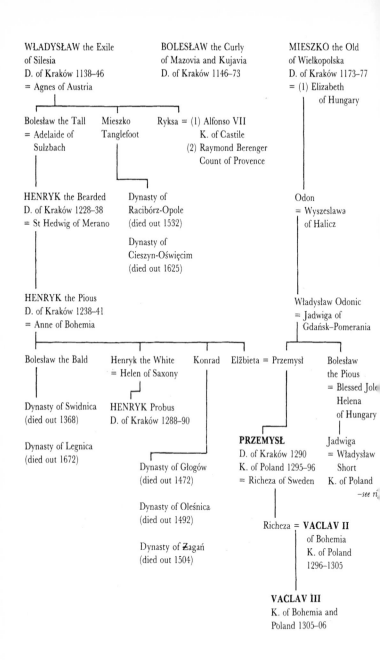

WŁADYSŁAW the Exile
of Silesia
D. of Kraków 1138–46
= Agnes of Austria

BOLESŁAW the Curly
of Mazovia and Kujavia
D. of Kraków 1146–73

MIESZKO the Old
of Wielkopolska
D. of Kraków 1173–77
= (1) Elizabeth
      of Hungary

Bolesław the Tall   Mieszko   Ryksa = (1) Alfonso VII
= Adelaide of   Tanglefoot   K. of Castile
  Sulzbach   (2) Raymond Berenger
                                               Count of Provence

HENRYK the Bearded   Dynasty of   Odon
D. of Kraków 1228–38 Racibórz-Opole   = Wyszeslawa
= St Hedwig of Merano (died out 1532)   of Halicz

                      Dynasty of
                      Cieszyn-Oświęcim
                      (died out 1625)

HENRYK the Pious   Władysław Odonic
D. of Kraków 1238–41   = Jadwiga of
= Anne of Bohemia   Gdańsk–Pomerania

Bolesław the Bald   Henryk the White   Konrad   Elżbieta = Przemysł   Bolesław
                    = Helen of Saxony   the Pious
                                                                      = Blessed Jole
Dynasty of Swidnica HENRYK Probus   Helena
(died out 1368)   D. of Kraków 1288–90   of Hungary

Dynasty of Legnica   PRZEMYSŁ   Jadwiga
(died out 1672)   D. of Kraków 1290   = Władysław
                    Dynasty of Głogów   K. of Poland 1295–96   Short
                    (died out 1472)   = Richeza of Sweden   K. of Poland
                                                                       –see ri
                    Dynasty of Oleśnica
                    (died out 1492)   Richeza = VACLAV II
                                                          of Bohemia
                    Dynasty of Żagań   K. of Poland
                    (died out 1504)   1296–1305

                                                VACLAV III
                                                K. of Bohemia and
                                                Poland 1305–06

2   The later Piasts.

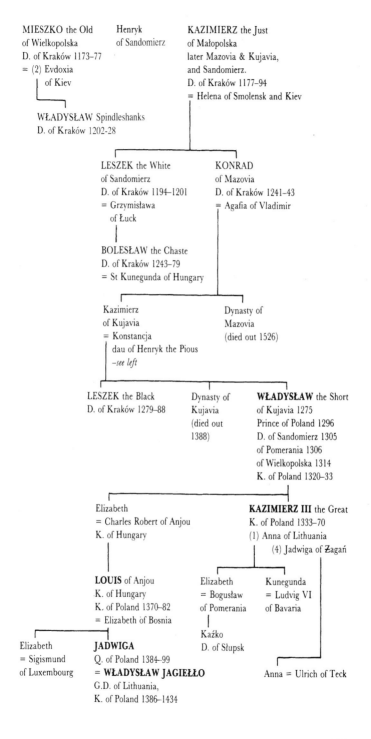

MIESZKO the Old
of Wielkopolska
D. of Kraków 1173–77
= (2) Evdoxia
⎿ of Kiev

WŁADYSŁAW Spindleshanks
D. of Kraków 1202-28

Henryk
of Sandomierz

KAZIMIERZ the Just
of Małopolska
later Mazovia & Kujavia,
and Sandomierz.
D. of Kraków 1177–94
= Helena of Smolensk and Kiev

LESZEK the White
of Sandomierz
D. of Kraków 1194–1201
= Grzymisława
of Łuck

BOLESŁAW the Chaste
D. of Kraków 1243–79
= St Kunegunda of Hungary

KONRAD
of Mazovia
D. of Kraków 1241–43
= Agafia of Vladimir

Kazimierz
of Kujavia
= Konstancja
dau of Henryk the Pious
–see left

Dynasty of
Mazovia
(died out 1526)

LESZEK the Black
D. of Kraków 1279–88

Dynasty of
Kujavia
(died out
1388)

WŁADYSŁAW the Short
of Kujavia 1275
Prince of Poland 1296
D. of Sandomierz 1305
of Pomerania 1306
of Wielkopolska 1314
K. of Poland 1320–33

Elizabeth
= Charles Robert of Anjou
K. of Hungary

KAZIMIERZ III the Great
K. of Poland 1333–70
(1) Anna of Lithuania
(4) Jadwiga of Żagań

LOUIS of Anjou
K. of Hungary
K. of Poland 1370–82
= Elizabeth of Bosnia

Elizabeth
= Bogusław
of Pomerania

Kaźko
D. of Słupsk

Kunegunda
= Ludvig VI
of Bavaria

Elizabeth
= Sigismund
of Luxembourg

JADWIGA
Q. of Poland 1384–99
= WŁADYSŁAW JAGIEŁŁO
G.D. of Lithuania,
K. of Poland 1386–1434

Anna = Ulrich of Teck

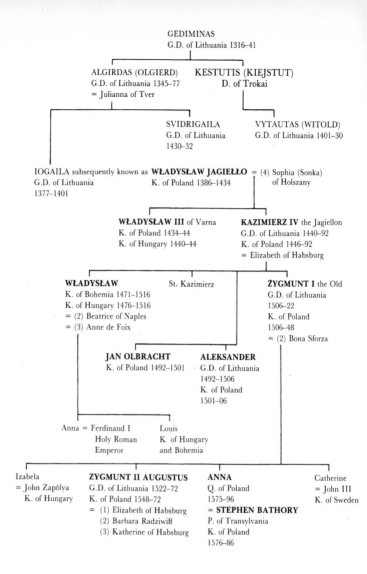

GEDIMINAS
G.D. of Lithuania 1316–41

ALGIRDAS (OLGIERD)
G.D. of Lithuania 1345–77
= Julianna of Tver

KESTUTIS (KIEJSTUT)
D. of Trokai

SVIDRIGAILA
G.D. of Lithuania
1430–32

VYTAUTAS (WITOLD)
G.D. of Lithuania 1401–30

IOGAILA subsequently known as **WŁADYSŁAW JAGIEŁŁO** = (4) Sophia (Sonka)
G.D. of Lithuania   K. of Poland 1386–1434   of Holszany
1377–1401

WŁADYSŁAW III of Varna
K. of Poland 1434–44
K. of Hungary 1440–44

KAZIMIERZ IV the Jagiellon
G.D. of Lithuania 1440–92
K. of Poland 1446–92
= Elizabeth of Habsburg

WŁADYSŁAW
K. of Bohemia 1471–1516
K. of Hungary 1476–1516
= (2) Beatrice of Naples
= (3) Anne de Foix

St. Kazimierz

ŻYGMUNT I the Old
G.D. of Lithuania
1506–22
K. of Poland
1506–48
= (2) Bona Sforza

JAN OLBRACHT
K. of Poland 1492–1501

ALEKSANDER
G.D. of Lithuania
1492–1506
K. of Poland
1501–06

Anna = Ferdinand I
Holy Roman
Emperor

Louis
K of Hungary
and Bohemia

Izabela
= John Zapòlya
K. of Hungary

ZYGMUNT II AUGUSTUS
G.D. of Lithuania 1522–72
K. of Poland 1548–72
= (1) Elizabeth of Habsburg
(2) Barbara Radziwiłł
(3) Katherine of Habsburg

ANNA
Q. of Poland
1575–96
= **STEPHEN BATHORY**
P. of Transylvania
K. of Poland
1576–86

Catherine
= John III
K. of Sweden

3   *The Jagiellon dynasty of Poland-Lithuania.*

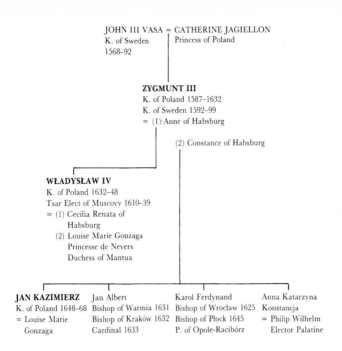

JOHN III VASA = CATHERINE JAGIELLON
K. of Sweden | Princess of Poland
1568–92

ZYGMUNT III
K. of Poland 1587–1632
K. of Sweden 1592–99
= (1) Anne of Habsburg

(2) Constance of Habsburg

WŁADYSŁAW IV
K. of Poland 1632–48
Tsar Elect of Muscovy 1610–39
= (1) Cecilia Renata of
     Habsburg
   (2) Louise Marie Gonzaga
     Princesse de Nevers
     Duchess of Mantua

JAN KAZIMIERZ	Jan Albert	Karol Ferdynand	Anna Katarzyna
K. of Poland 1648–68	Bishop of Warmia 1631	Bishop of Wrocław 1625	Konstancja
= Louise Marie	Bishop of Kraków 1632	Bishop of Płock 1645	= Philip Wilhelm
Gonzaga	Cardinal 1633	P. of Opole-Racibórz	Elector Palatine

4   *The Vasa Kings of Poland.*

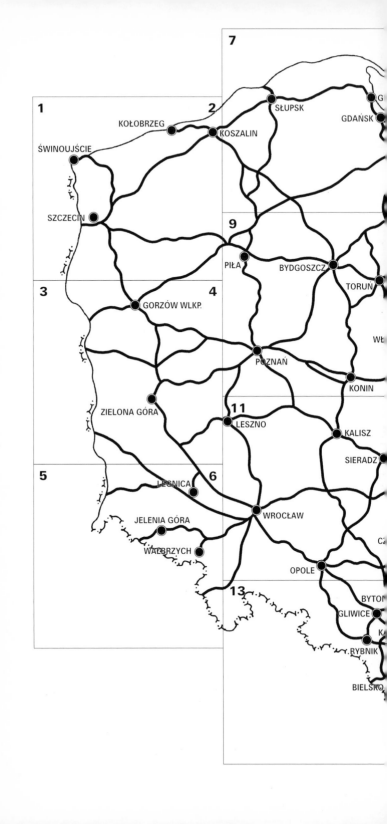

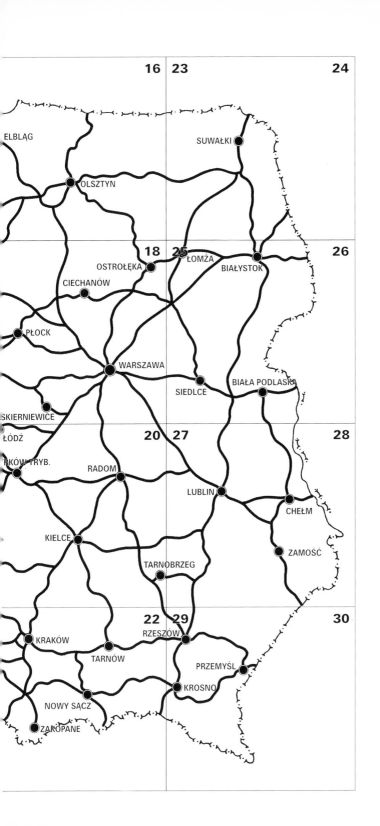

MORYŃ

Chwarszczany

GORZÓW W

KOSTRZYŃ

Słońsk

OŚNO

SŁUBICE

ZIE

Brody Biecz Tuchola Żarska

LUBSKO

ŻARY

Ż

ZGORZELEC

Trójca

Jerzmanki

Studniska

Radomierzyce

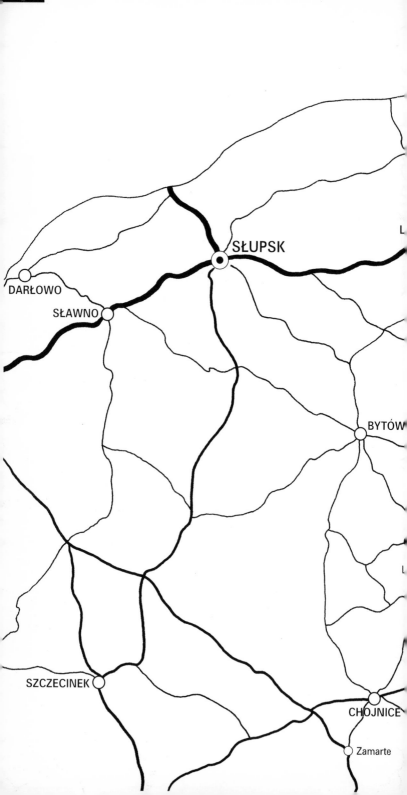

Żarnowiec

PUCK

WEJHEROWO

GDYNIA

OLIWA

GDAŃSK

KARTUZY

ŻUKOWO

Trutnowy

TCZEW

MALBORK

STAROGARD
GDAŃSKI

Mątowy Wlk.

SZTUM

PELPLIN

GNIEW

Piaseczno

KWIDZYN

Pieniążkowo

NOWE

Szynwald

BARTOSZYCE

Drogosze

Barciany

Łabędnik

Galiny

Sztynort

Stoczek

Kiwity

Reszel

KĘTRZYN

GIŻYCKO

Św. Lipka

Bezławki

Tłokowo

lesie

JEZIORANY

Szestno

MRĄGOWO

BARCZEWO

Pasym

SZCZYTNO

A

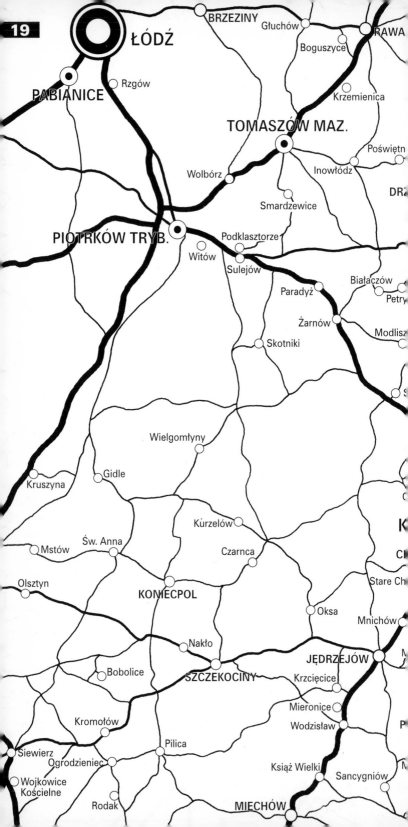

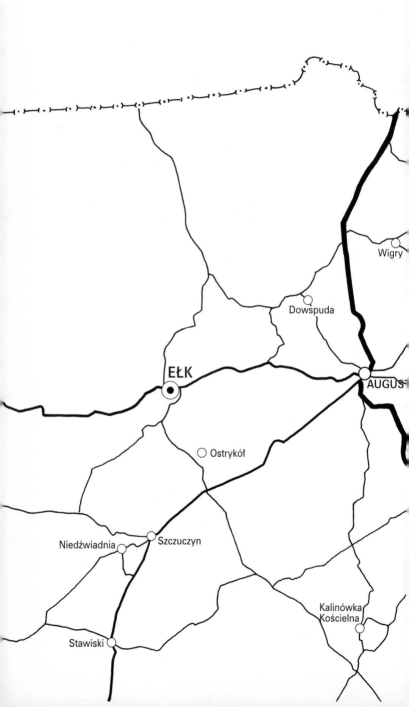

Wigry

Dowspuda

EŁK

AUGUS

Ostrykół

Niedźwiadnia

Szczuczyn

Kalinówka
Kościelna

Stawiski

SEJNY

Różany Stok

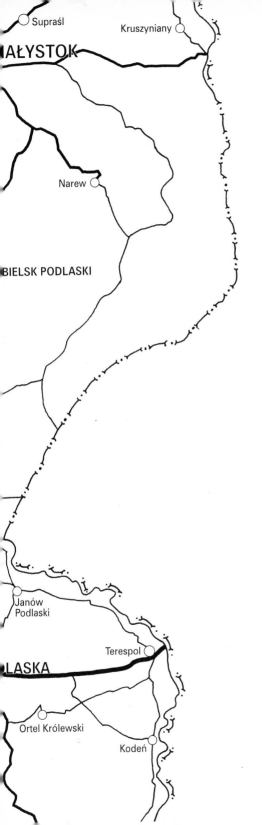

Supraśl

Kruszyniany

AŁYSTOK

Narew

BIELSK PODLASKI

Janów
Podlaski

Terespol

LASKA

Ortel Królewski

Kodeń

Radruż

ACZÓW